Con O'Neill

Last Gaelic Lord of Upper Clannaboy

The White Row Press

Con O'Neill

Last Gaelic Lord of Upper Clannaboy

The White Row Press

First published 2019 by
the White Row Press
159 Lower Braniel Road
Belfast BT5 7NN

Visit our website:
www.whiterow.net

Lisburn &
Castlereagh
City Council

The publishers would like to record their grateful thanks to
Lisburn & Castlereagh City Council for their sponsorship of this book

Front cover: Map of the north of Ireland c.1600, cartographer unknown,
Dartmouth Collection, National Maritime Museum, Greenwich

Back cover: Giraldus Cambrensis, Topographia,
National Library of Ireland, Dublin

ISBN 978 1 870132 51 0

Printed by W.G. Baird Ltd., Antrim
A catalogue record for this book is available from the British Library

Contents

Preface

My purpose in writing this book is to tell the story of the Clannaboy, and more particularly the story of Con O'Neill, Upper Clannaboy's enigmatic last chief. As well as informing and I hope entertaining my readers, I want to use the occasion of the four hundredth anniversary of Con's death in 1619 to help to restore this forgotten lord and his people to their rightful place at the heart of the history of eastern Ulster.

This has involved delving into the dark recesses of Irish history to discover the origins of the Clannaboy. The book then traces their extraordinary rise to prominence, and their dominance of life in eastern Ulster in the mid-sixteenth century, when they were at the zenith of their powers. Finally, we focus on the events in the latter part of that century and the beginning of the 17th century which led to their undoing, and resulted in the mass migration of lowland Scots into Upper Clannaboy, a migration which paved the way for the plantation of the whole of Ulster.

Much has been written about the O'Neills of Tyrone, and indeed the O'Neills of Lower Clannaboy, in County Antrim. Much less is known about the O'Neills of Upper Clannaboy in County Down, and in particular the line of Con O'Neill of Castlereagh. Furthermore, the historical record is often contradictory and misleading. Unravelling the tangled web that is the dynasty of the O'Neills of Upper Clannaboy has been a major challenge, to put it mildly. Here, I would like to take my hat off to the historians and genealogists for whom this is 'bread and butter' and apologise in advance for any errors I have made; hopefully they are few in number and insignificant in their impact!

Con lived through change on a scale that is quite unimaginable to us today. He saw the death throes of the Gaelic way of life and the birth of the Ulster-Scots tradition that has largely forged the demographic footprint of northern County Down today. How many of the residents of East Belfast, much of South Belfast and Lisburn, Bangor, Holywood, Newtownards, Dundonald, Comber, Carryduff, Saintfield, Donaghadee and Portavogie know that they are living on the lands that Con once ruled?

I would contend that in Northern Ireland we have been granted a unique opportunity to celebrate two wonderful cultures, Ulster Scots and Gaelic Irish. Of course, it would be naive to suggest that the Scots and Irish cultures do not have contentious and conflicting elements, however this should not preclude my enjoyment of my brother's culture, nor his enjoyment or acceptance of mine. Irish culture should not be a cold house for unionists, nor should the expression of Ulster Scots' culture blow an icy breeze across the shoulders of nationalists. Not an easy circle to square I accept, nevertheless, we must cradle the thistle and the shamrock in the same palm if we are to build the shared future for which we all yearn.

I am neither an historian nor an author by trade; rather I am one of those dangerous people; an enthusiast, who hopes to ignite fires of interest and inquiry, as together we examine the rich tapestry that is our shared history. We cannot choose the histories that shaped Northern Ireland, but we can seek to understand them, and in so doing, learn something more of who we are and how we came to be.

My special thanks to my editor Peter Carr, who (mostly!) kept me on the straight and narrow, and whose numerous suggestions and amendments have greatly enhanced the text; Dr. Gordon McCoy, a fellow Con aficionado, for his moral support and readiness to share; Noel Brown for setting and laying out the book; Lindsay Hodges for proofreading it; Alice Roper and Lorna Stitt for reading my script and encouraging me to keep going; 'Boys on Tour', for not reading the manuscript, and Molly, my pug, who faithfully sat at my feet through the long hours of studying and writing.

Roy H. Greer.

This book is dedicated to my wonderful daughter Lauren, and my late grandfather, Hugh Gourley of Larne, County Antrim: docker, all-weather swimmer, cyclist, dulse and whelk gatherer, raconteur, role model, inspiration and Christian man.

Last Tanist of the Yellow-haired Clan

No, there's little known about him round the hills of Castlereagh,
And the grass has hid his grey old home
This manys a day:
But they tell me out in Holywood they sometimes see the man,
Late afoot and sorrowing
For the yellow-haired clan.

Richard Hayward

1
Mythical beginnings

The brooding hulk of Castle Reagh (Caisleán Riabhach) once cast a long shadow across the Castlereagh plateau, which commands the southern flood plain of the River Lagan.[1] Probably built in the late fifteenth or early sixteenth century, this once imposing tower house delineated the end point in the remarkable journey of the Clannaboy O'Neills from their heartland in north-eastern Tyrone and the upper reaches of Lough Neagh, into Antrim and Down.[2]

Vanished greatness. Buttercups and vetch grow in the field where Caisleán Riabhach (Castle Reagh) once stood. Over the years the castle has given its name to, amongst other things, a 19th century statesman, a range of hills, a council, and two baronies.

The twelfth century Book of Leinster provides invaluable information on the early history of the O'Neills. (Trinity College, Dublin)

Standing at least four storeys tall, Castle Reagh announced the overthrow of the Anglo-Norman order in east Ulster and the re-establishment of Gaelic authority. It also proclaimed the power of the Clannaboy O'Neills and declared that their presence would be enduring, their overlordship no mere flash in the pan.[3]

For two hundred and fifty years, the Clannaboy O'Neills would control a huge territory north and south of the River Lagan, a patrimony to rival that of the Great O'Neill in Tyrone. Although related to the Tyrone O'Neills, the Clannaboy, literally the Clann Aodha Buidhe, or the Clan of Yellow Hugh, were an independent people, inaugurating their chief on a stone chair atop the *tulach tionóil*, or hill of gathering at Castlereagh. However, today there is no trace of their castle; its ancient stones are lost, and the story of its builders is forgotten.

Unravelling Con's knotted genealogy

Much has been written of the genealogies of the O'Neills of Tyrone. Much less has been recorded about the O'Neills of Upper Clannaboy in County Down, and Con O'Neill of Castlereagh. There are records of dates, names, births, marriages, crownings, battles, slayings and accounts of innumerable struggles. Unfortunately, however, the records are often confused and contradictory, which has meant that establishing the genealogy of the Upper Clannaboy O'Neills has proven to be a quite mind-boggling task. There are many Cons, Aodhs, Brians and Nialls. Names with variant spellings, in Gaelic forms, Anglicized forms, Scottish forms, mis-transcribed forms, misinformed forms, phonetic forms and misspellings are all there, lying in wait to trip up the unsuspecting researcher.

The clansfolk had their own, very earthy way of cutting through the confusion. They would call their chief by a nickname which highlighted some distinguishing feature. These give us Shane the Proud, Brian the Freckled, Niall of the Black Knee, Hugh of the Fetters, Red Hugh, Con the Lame, Brian the Bright Star, Murtagh the Long-head, and last but not least, Hugh the Lazy-arsed Boy.

One nickname, however, stands out, Aodh Buidhe or Yellow Hugh, the great progenitor of the Clann Aodha Buidhe or Clannaboy O'Neills. Eight hundred years after his death, Yellow Hugh, distinguished by his golden locks, has given his name (albeit in its anglicised form, Clandeboye) to a hotel, country estate, golf club, school, yoghurt, forest, church, festival, a football ground, and numerous roads and tree-lined avenues. How many modern Bangorians know that Clandeboye takes its name from a flaxen-haired, thirteenth-century chief from County Tyrone?

Niall of the Nine Hostages and the origins of the O'Neills

The royal line of the O'Neills, the most famous and highly revered of Ireland's clans, predates that of most of the royal families of Europe, having its roots in the mists of pagan Ireland. The Books of Leinster and Ballymote

describe how the O'Neills are descended from Niall of the Nine Hostages, who ruled as High King of Ireland from 379-405.

As Roman power waned, the legions withdrew from Britain, leaving it virtually defenceless. Sensing an opportunity, Niall invaded Scotland and then marched south into England. During this campaign, Niall adopted a tactic much favoured in ancient Greece and Rome. In each region he conquered, he compelled the ruling families to surrender up a son or daughter as a surety that they would not rebel against him. In return for their submissions, Niall permitted each ruler to retain his kingdom, demanding only a simple tribute in the form of cattle or crops in return, a tactic he had used in Ireland to bring rival chieftains under his authority.[4]

Niall became one of the most powerful lords in the British Isles. He ruled as High King across Ireland's five provinces (including Meath), large swathes of Scotland, Wales, the north of England and Brittany, creating an Irish empire that extended across nine kingdoms, hence Niall of the Nine Hostages.[5] Imperial Ireland and Irish colonialism – now that is a thought to be conjure with!

Niall's death is the stuff of legend; reputedly killed by a lightning bolt on a Scottish mountain or by an arrow, shot low across a Scottish valley. Whatever the truth, his death resulted in Ireland being divided between his twelve sons, four of whom settled in Ulster.[6]

Around the year 430, Niall's youngest sons Conaill and Eoghan marched north. Conaill settled in the far north-west, in what became Tyrconnell, or Donegal. Eoghan occupied the area known as Aileach at the foot of the Inishowen Peninsula, before eventually settling in Tir Eoghain, the land of Eoghan. For many centuries, these two great O'Neill families alternated the High Kingship of Ireland, ruling from the Hill of Tara.

Their archaeological footprint can be seen in the numerous raths, cashels, crannogs, souterrains and ecclesiastical sites and monuments that still dot north-western Ulster.

The Grainan of Aileach in Inishowen. Before the impressive stone fort was built, Aileach was reputedly home to Eoghan, son of Niall of the Nine Hostages. (Discover Ireland)

Ulster at the time of St. Patrick. Two of the sons of Niall of the Nine Hostages (in blue) made their homes in the north west.

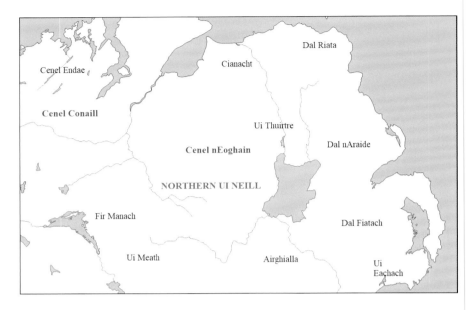

Niall of the Black Knee

Five hundred years later, Niall Glandubh (Niall of the Black Knee), a descendant of Eoghan, reigned as High King.[7] His territory extended over the modern counties of Tyrone, Londonderry and north Armagh.[8] With encouragement from the Primate of Armagh, he tried to expel the Vikings from Ireland and repeatedly marched against them. In 919, he was mortally wounded in an attack on Sigtryg, the self-styled Viking King of Dublin. It is a small, incidental detail, but in a poem commemorating his death, Niall's wife Gormlaith writes of his fair hair:

Viking longships from a tenth century martyrology. In 919, Niall Glandubh died trying to expel the Vikings from Ireland. (Morgan Library, New York).

Niall's grandson, Domnall Ardmacha, paid the Vikings back in kind, attacking them using currachs on Lough Ennell. (Giraldus Cambrensis, Topographia)

Lift off the bright-hair'd Niall Glandubh;
Monk, remove thy foot[9]

a striking, perhaps talismanic feature that would also distinguish his illustrious descendant, Aodh Buidhe (Yellow Hugh), the founder of the Clannaboy.

The descendants of Niall Glandubh are collectively known as the O'Neill, or the descendants of Niall.[10] Genetic research has suggested that twenty per cent of males in the north-west of Ireland, and one in twelve on the island as a whole, are directly descended from the O'Neill gene pool.[11]

Niall Glandubh's grandson, Domnall Ardmacha (of Armagh) who ruled from 956-980, was first to take the surname O'Neill, meaning 'of Niall'. He is described in the Annals as a patron of learning and a man of faith, who donated 'the full of St. Patrick's Bell of silver' to the Archbishop of Armagh, which was quite a windfall for the Archdiocese.

Like his grandfather, Domnall was also a fierce warrior chief, who took the fight to the Viking invaders, carrying small boats, or currachs, overland to raid their lakeland settlements on the islands of Lough Ennell, before ultimately defeating them in Meath. Unfortunately, Domnall's grandsons would develop a deep rivalry that would plague the House of Tyrone. One of their descendants, Lochlainn, formed the Mac Lochlainn clan, who for the next two hundred years would vie with their O'Neill brethren for the right to rule in Tyrone.

In uniting the Red Hand with the Salmon of Knowledge in their coat of arms, the Clannaboy present themselves as determined and wise.

The Red Hand in the coat of arms of Lisburn and Castlereagh City Council acknowledges the region's associations with the Clannaboy O'Neills.

The Red Hand of the O'Neills

For centuries the emblem of the O'Neills has been the Red Hand, the origins of which are obscure. The most celebrated mythical tale associated with the emblem describes how two Milesian princes, Éireamhón and Eber, took part in a 'winner takes all' boat race for control of Ulster. Forget the Oxford and Cambridge race and the America's Cup, this was *the* blue-ribbon event!

With the fastest boats chosen and the best oarsmen recruited, the princes set sail for Ulster. As the coastline loomed into view, Eber's boat had a clear lead, and Éireamhón's cause appeared lost. That was until, in the sort of heroic gesture that would also typify his descendants, Éireamhón drew his sword and with a single blow, severed his hand.

With pain racing through his body, Éireamhón picked up the severed hand and launched it towards the beach. Time stood still as the lifeless hand arched in a blood-splattered rainbow towards the beach, landing with a dull thud. Suddenly, the silence was broken, as a jubilant chorus rang out from the trailing boat. Through this grotesque act of self-mutilation, Éireamhón had won Ulster. In time, his severed hand would be immortalised as *Láimhe Deirge Uladh*, or the Red Hand of Ulster, and become a potent symbol of his descendants, the O'Neills.

However this is not the only colourful explanation of the origins of the Red Hand. Others include the claim that it is based on the Dextra Dei, an ancient Christian symbol for the hand of God, and that it comes from the biblical story of Zerah. It has also been said to derive from a bloodied sword hand pictured on the battle standard presented to Éireamhón following his defeat of the Tuatha Dé Danann, and to have its origins in a red handprint left on a rock after a battle between two mythical giants.[12]

Scholarly debate continues as to its early use by the O'Neills. Katherine Simms traced its first literary appearance to a fifteenth century praise poem addressed to Art McHugh, chief of the Magennis clan of South Down. In it, the poet describes the Magennis Clan and their predecessors, the Ulaidh, as, *laochraidh na láimhe deirge*, or warriors of the red hand, meaning 'the shedders of blood', who had 'repeatedly slaughtered the men of the rest of Ireland' without making recompense.[13]

According to Brehon Law, after a murder, restitution had to be made by the perpetrator to the victim's family. A man who did not deliver this restitution was said to be *fear na láimhe deirge*, or a man with blood on his hands.

It has been suggested that the O'Neills appropriated the emblem when Kings of Ulster, to signify that they would ruthlessly suppress opposition. However, the term is also found in the nickname of Cathal O'Connor, King of Connaught (1153-1224), who was known as 'Cathal the red-handed'. His epitaph makes clear that he was a worthy bearer of this insalubrious title being:

a man calculated to strike fear and dread more than any Irish man of his day… who burned the greatest number of homesteads and took the greatest number of prey.[14]

The first recorded use of the hand by the Tyrone O'Neills appears in the seal of Aodh Reamhar O'Neill (d.1364), which depicted a right hand with two dragons and the Latin legend, SUODONIS ONEILLE REGIS HYBERNICORUM ULTONIE, or 'Hugh O'Neill, King of the Irish of Ulster'.[15] We also know that the symbol was used by the Clannaboy O'Neills, as 'a seal discovered near Magherafelt is attributed to Murtagh Ruadh O'Neill… ruler of Clandeboye from 1444-68.'[16]

Ironically, the Red Hand of the O'Neills is always depicted as a right hand, which is usually taken to be the sword hand. This can be seen in 'the bloody hand' on the silver signet ring belonging to Turlough Luineach O'Neill, the sixteenth century chief of Tyrone.[17]

However, when James I founded the Order of Baronets of Ulster in 1611, the left hand (sinister) was chosen. Yet the emblem of the Province of Ulster is the 'dexter' or right hand, an anomaly which inspired the following skittish verse:

The Red Hand of Ulster's a paradox quite,
To Baronets 'tis said to belong:
If they use the left hand, they're sure to be right,
And to use the right hand would be wrong.
For the Province, a different custom applies,
And just the reverse is the rule:
If you use the right hand you'll be right, safe and wise,
If you use the left hand you're a fool.[18]

Today, the Red Hand survives in the Ulster Banner (the flag of Northern Ireland), as the symbol of the province of Ulster, as emblem of the Ulster rugby team, and on the badge of Tyrone Gaelic Athletic Association. It is also part of the coat of arms of Lisburn and Castlereagh City Council, a reminder that the borough is heir to lands once ruled by the Clannaboy O'Neills.[19]

The seal of Aodh Reamhar, bought at auction for 75 guineas in 1853. (Ulster Journal of Archaeology).

The Red Hand dexter appears on this sixteenth century, silver signet ring made for Turlough Luineach. (Ulster Journal of Archaeology)

2
The foundation of the Clann Aodha Buidhe
1167-1318

This chapter charts the thirteenth-century origins of the Clann Aodha Buidhe and their early struggles for survival.

1167 was a pivotal year in O'Neill history. The Annals tell us that in that year Rory O'Connor, High King of Ireland, partitioned north-western Ulster between two rival chieftains. He granted most of County Tyrone to the O'Neills, and the Inishowen Peninsula and County Londonderry to the Mac Lochlainns. An exchange of hostages cemented the agreement between the three Kings.

The arrival of the Anglo-Normans

Two years later, in 1169, the Earl of Pembroke, Richard Fitzgilbert de Clare, better known as Strongbow, and a force of four hundred men arrived in Ireland to help Dermot MacMurrough reclaim the throne of Leinster.

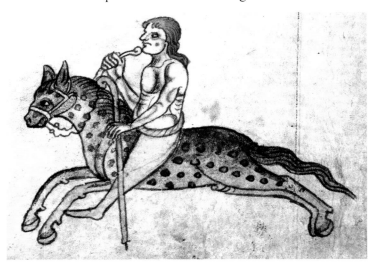

Irish warrior riding bareback. (Giraldus Cambrensis, Topographia, National Library of Ireland, Dublin)

Strongbow not only achieved this, but also married Dermot's daughter, Aoife. In 1171, he succeeded his father-in-law, to become the first non-native King of Ireland.

Two points should be considered at this defining moment in Ireland's relationship with England. Firstly, the Anglo-Normans came by invitation, the King of Leinster having prevailed upon Strongbow to intervene. Secondly, Ireland's invaders would have been deeply insulted by the idea that they were English. They were Anglo-Normans, a people with their own distinctive culture and heritage, who now gave Ireland the treatment they had meted out to England just a hundred years before.

The Anglo-Normans soon extended their reach northwards. In 1177, John de Courcy, accompanied by twenty-two handpicked knights and three hundred foot soldiers, set out from Dublin on a 'freelance' mission to take eastern Ulster.

De Courcy targeted the Hill of Down,[1] seat of Rory MacDunlevy, King of Ulster (Ulidia).[2] Taken unawares by this lightning strike, Rory was forced to flee. Although he would return with a massive force, he was unable to oust de Courcy, who established Down (soon renamed Downpatrick) as his capital and base for further conquest. His power would soon extend along the eastern seaboard from Warrenpoint through Carrickfergus to Coleraine and Inishowen.

To secure his new territory, John de Courcy built numerous mottes – small earthen fortifications protected by a wooden palisade and perhaps a watchtower – superb examples of which can still be seen in Donaghadee and Dundonald. Some forty were erected in County Down and a further seventy in County Antrim, and they mark out the extent of de Courcy's fiefdom.

De Courcy's lands now bordered those of the O'Neills, and he would prove a formidable adversary, intervening on the side of the O'Neill's

Dermot MacMurrough, King of Leinster, who invited the Anglo-Normans to Ireland. (Giraldus Cambrensis, Expugnatio Hibernica)

Clogh motte and bailey, County Antrim, c.1220, by Philip Armstrong. (Mid & East Antrim Borough Council)

John de Courcy's coat of arms, displaying the three birds which prophesied a knight would invade Ulster.

Murtagh, 'The Mac Loughlainn', King of Tyrone, deposed by Aodh Macáem. (University of Pittsburgh)

rivals, and raiding Tir Eoghain in 1200 and 1204. The Welsh chronicler, Geraldus, described him as:

of huge size, tall and powerfully built with bony and muscular limbs, wonderfully active and daring, full of courage and bold…[3]

De Courcy ruled Ulster for over twenty-five years until his expulsion by Hugh de Lacy in 1205.

Hugh the Lazy-arsed Youth

Rory O'Connor's settlement of the north-west proved far from peaceful, with continual antagonism and intermittent warfare between the Mac Lochlainns and the O'Neills. Indeed, it was this rivalry that would ultimately lead to the birth of the Clann Aodha Buidhe under the leadership of Aodh Buidhe O'Neill, 'Fair-haired or Yellow Hugh', who ruled in Tir Eoghain from 1260-83. His predecessors also ruled in Tir Eoghain, making Aodh Buidhe's royal credentials second to none.

Aodh Buidhe was the great-grandson of Aodh Macáem Tóinlesc O'Neill or Hugh the Lazy-arsed Youth, King of Tyrone from 1167-77. His bizarre nickname was no derisory term, but one earned with pride. As a youth, Aodh Macáem had refused to stand in the presence of Murtagh, 'the Mac Lochlainn', King of Tyrone and High King of Ireland. Aodh Macáem did not stand because he refused to defer to the man who had killed his father. Fortunately, Aodh's grandfather diffused the standoff and spirited the feisty youth away.

The orphaned Aodh Macáem was fostered in the territory of Airgialla, and after the death of the Mac Lochlainn in 1166, the King of Airgialla supported Aodh's claim to the kingship of Tyrone. After almost two centuries of exclusion and subservience to their Mac Lochlainn kin, the O'Neill's had returned, centre stage in Tir Eoghain under the leadership of Aodh Macáem – defiance and determination were qualities that existed in abundance in Aodh Buidhe's ancestral DNA.

Aodh Macáem was a powerful king who could muster an army of upwards of three thousand men. The defiance that had characterised his youth re-emerged again in the winter of 1171 when he refused to submit to King Henry II at his court in Dublin. Ironically, Aodh Macáem was killed near Armagh just prior to de Courcy's invasion in a revenge attack by Malachy, the Mac Lochlainn's son – long ran the Mac Lochlainn fox!

Aodh Macáem's death was followed by a period of chaos and uncertainty in which 'the churches of Tír Eoghain, from the mountains south, were left desolate, in consequence of war and internecine commotion, famine and distress'.[4] This turmoil, which may have assisted de Courcy's conquest of eastern Ulster, continued until the maturity of Aodh Macáem's son, Aodh Meith O'Neill, some nineteen years later.

Aodh Macáem had four sons. Two of them would bring a new and bloody rivalry to Tyrone – Niall Ruadh, whose descendants would become the Earls of Tyrone, and Aodh Meith, whose descendants would become princes in Clannaboy. In time Niall Ruadh's descendants would come to be known as the senior sept of the O'Neills and Aodh Meith's the junior. The two septs would become bitter and often deadly rivals.

Aodh Meith

In 1196, Aodh Meith (Hugh of Omeath) succeeded to the kingship of Tyrone. He would rule until his death in 1230.

Aodh Meith would prove a powerful leader, withstanding the threat posed from within his own family and externally from the Mac Lochlainns and de Courcy. Indeed, in 1199 he took the fight to the Anglo-Normans, leading five ships in a seaborne attack on Olderfleet Castle at Larne. Eighteen Normans were killed, the villages of Larne and Kilwaughter were burned to the ground, and de Courcy's proposed invasion of Tyrone was halted. To be able to mastermind such a seaborne strike from his inland kingdom in the Sperrins speaks volumes about Aodh Meith's military ingenuity and power. He could not attack via the River Bann as Coleraine was an Anglo-Norman town, so in all likelihood the expedition was launched from Lough Foyle or Lough Swilly – quite a naval feat!

The remains of Olderfleet Castle, which Aodh Meith's troops stormed in a daring attack in 1199.

De Burgh Coat of Arms. The de Burghs, one of the most powerful Anglo-Norman dynasties, defeated Aodh Meith in 1201.

That same year, Aodh Meith defeated the combined forces of Tyrconnell and Fermanagh to secure his south-western border, and married Beanmidhe, daughter of the King of Fermanagh. For good measure, he roundly defeated de Courcy in battle outside Donaghmore.[5] Aodh Meith now held sway north and south of the Sperrins.

Buoyed by his military successes, Aodh Meith continued to harass the Anglo-Normans. However, in 1201, he suffered a significant defeat at the hands of William de Burgh in Connaught, resulting in a temporary loss of control in Tyrone.

In 1205, de Courcy was ousted, and Ulster became more fully integrated within the Anglo-Norman state as an earldom under Hugh de Lacy. In this period of transition, Aodh Meith proved himself an able politician, successfully negotiating terms with the new earl. Aodh's alliance with de Lacy strengthened the hand of the junior sept and led the Normans to acknowledge him as the supreme Gaelic leader in Ulster.

In the summer of 1210, when Hugh de Lacy rebelled and was besieged at Carrickfergus by King John, Aodh Meith and a massive force came to his aid. The King prevailed, but the defeated Aodh Meith refused to provide him with hostages, and instead thumbed his nose at him, absconding with a plunder of horses, sheep, cattle and provisions.[6] However good an idea this seemed at the time, it did not work out, and the humbled Aodh Meith was made to pay the King a fine of three hundred cattle for taking part in the revolt, and a further three hundred and twenty-one for the privilege of continuing to call himself King of Tyrone.[7] With de Lacy in exile, the earldom went into a period of 'direct rule', being administered by royal officials and a justiciar.

When de Lacy returned in 1222, Aodh Meith rallied to his cause and accompanied him in successful assaults on Coleraine Castle and the new territories of the Scots. His support helped de Lacy win back the earldom in 1227.[8]

Throughout Aodh Meith's rule he found himself in conflict with the Kings of Fermanagh and Tyrconnell, the Galloway Scots and the Anglo-Norman barons. However, unlike his predecessors, Aodh lived to die of natural causes. The Annals of Connaught eulogise his accomplishments, proclaiming him:

defender against the Galls (foreigners)… a prince eligible de jure for the kingship of Ireland… who never gave pledge or hostage or tribute… who wrought slaughterings and great routs on the Galls… who was the support of any Gaels who were in banishment or homeless… the most generous and excellent of all the men of Ireland who ever lived.

Small wonder his descendants, the Clann Aodha Buidhe, would become such a force to be reckoned with.

The feud between the O'Neills and Mac Lochlainns was brutal and frequently bloody. Note the axes. Giraldus wrote that the Irish carry axes as other peoples carry staffs. (Giraldus Cambrensis, Topographia)

Domnall Óg

Immediately following Aodh Meith's death, the Mac Lochlainns briefly challenged for control in Tyrone but were defeated by Aodh Meith's son, Domnall Óg (Domnall the Younger). He acquired the dual titles King of Cenel Eoghain (straddling the modern counties Londonderry and Tyrone) and King of Ulster.

In an attempt to break the cycle of feuding between the two warring dynasties Domnall Óg married Cicely Mac Lochlainn, daughter of his sworn enemy. Their marriage is of the greatest significance to our story as it produced Aodh Buidhe, the founder of the Clann Aodha Buidhe. However, notwithstanding marital ties, hostilities were soon resumed and in 1234 Domnall Óg was deposed and killed by his rival Domnall Mac Lochlainn.

Brian of the Battle of Down

The Mac Lochlainns now consolidated their control in Tyrone. However, in 1238 Hugh de Lacy deposed Domnall Mac Lochlainn in favour of Brian, the son of Niall Ruadh, head of the senior O'Neill sept. Then, at the decisive Battle of Cameirge in 1241, he killed Domnall Mac Lochlainn and ten of his immediate family.[9] Brian was hailed King of Ulster. His victory all but extinguished the Mac Lochlainn dynasty and ushered in a period of O'Neill supremacy in Tir Eoghain and Ulster that would endure for the next three hundred and fifty years.

The seal of Brian of the Battle of Down, who smashed the stranglehold of the Mac Lochlainns and ruled as High King of Ulster.

Whilst the O'Neills and Mac Lochlainns feuded, the Anglo-Norman earldom flourished. Towns grew up at Carrickfergus, Antrim, Newtownards and Downpatrick. Friaries and abbeys were founded at, amongst other places, Greyabbey, Blackabbey and Carrickfergus. Stone castles were built at Dundrum, Olderfleet, Ardglass, Greencastle, Coleraine, Dunluce and Carrickfergus.

However, following Hugh de Lacy's death in 1242, the earldom was run by officials of the crown. The absence of a powerful, resident earl created new opportunities for Brian. In 1253, he levelled the justiciar's castle at Moy Cova (Iveagh), having submitted to him the previous year. Then, he audaciously crossed the Upper Bann, looting and burning the earldom's unprotected towns and castles along the plain of Down.[10] This act, which in de Courcy's time would have triggered ferocious retribution, won Brian only glory. In 1258, recognising his strength, the Council of Irish Princes at Belleek proclaimed him High King of Ireland. The senior line of the O'Neills was now in full control.

Emboldened by his success, Brian formed a Great Irish Confederacy to expel the Anglo-Normans from Ulster, and attacked the heart of the earldom. In 1260 his forces met those of the Lord Justice, Stephen de Longespée at Downpatrick. Brian's army was decimated, and he and many Gaelic nobles died. Local legend places his death at the junction of Scotch Street and Irish Street. Ironically, the vast majority of the foot soldiers in the Anglo-Norman army on that fateful day were Irish mercenaries, making it likely that the last High King of Ireland died at the hands of a fellow Gael.

Brian's severed head was sent to King Henry III. He was posthumously revered as Brian Cathan an Duin, or Brian of the Battle of Down.

Aodh Buidhe, founder of the Clann Aodha Buidhe
The next three kings of Tir nEogain were descendants of Aodh Meith, who had come to an arrangement with the new earls of Ulster, Walter de Burgh or Burke (d.1271), created earl in 1266, and his son Richard de Burgh[11]

Brian Cathan an Duin was succeeded by his second cousin, Aodh Buidhe, meaning Fair or Yellow Hugh.[12] Born around 1230, Aodh was the son of Domnall Óg and Cicily Mac Lochlainn and was known as Aodh Buidhe because of his distinctive fair hair.

Back in 1259, encouraged by the Lord of Tyrconnell, Aodh Buidhe had begun to plot against his uncle, Brian O'Neill. However, he kept his powder dry and even stood with Brian at the Battle of Down. Now, somewhat fortuitously, Brian's death allowed the ambitious young pretender to succeed him as King in Tir Eoghain. However, Aodh Buidhe's authority was hotly disputed, and within the year he was deposed and banished when his own brother, Niall Culanach, was promoted to the kingship. Undeterred, Aodh continued to press his claim, unseating his brother in the following year.

In 1263, Aodh Buidhe revisited Brian Cathan an Duin's ambition to take the earldom and sent an emissary to Magnus, King of Norway, offering him the throne of Ireland if he would assist in the task. However, with his offer rejected, the ever-resilient Aodh changed tact and literally jumped into bed with the Anglo-Normans, marrying Eleanor de Nangle, a cousin of Walter de Burgh, Earl of Ulster. This marriage restored peaceful relations between the earldom and Tyrone, and enabled Aodh Buidhe to retain the kingship.

For modern readers too, it has a huge symbolic significance. For it means that, in its foundation and at its highest level, the Clann Aodha Buidhe was born in the mingling of noble Gaelic and Anglo-Norman blood. Such inter-communal marriages were not confined to the aristocracy. In many instances, across the social spectrum, Gael and Gall were kith and kin.[13]

King Magnus VI Haakonsson of Norway who declined the High Kingship of Ireland. (Stavanger Cathedral)

'The fair Prince of Tyrone'
Walter de Burgh died in 1271 and was succeeded by his son, Richard, widely known as the Red Earl. Contentions now arose within and between both the earldom and Tyrone. In 1273, Aodh Buidhe, accompanied by the O'Kanes and renegade de Mandevilles attacked Carrickfergus, only to be repelled by Hugh de Bisset, assisted by none other than Aodh Buidhe's brother, Niall Culanach! Niall was a formidable adversary, who continued to press his claim to Tyrone. During the raid, five houses, three mills and two thousand crannocks of wheat were destroyed.

Undaunted in defeat, Aodh Buidhe attacked William Fitz Warin, the Seneschal of Ulster, slaughtering two hundred of his troops in the process. Then in 1281, assisted by Thomas de Mandeville, he inflicted a crushing defeat on his one-time allies the O'Donnells at the Battle of Desertcreat, near Dungannon – the same O'Donnells who had supported his initial claim to rule in Tir Eoghain. Ulster politics, it would seem, were ever thus, a bear pit of duplicity and intrigue!

Aodh Buidhe would reign in Tir Eoghain for a combined total of twenty-one years, until his death at the hands of the men of Oriel (Monaghan) and Fermanagh in 1283. He was accorded a noble homily in the Annals of the Four Masters:

Hugh O'Neill, the fair Prince of Tyrone, the head of the generosity and valour of the Irish, the most distinguished man in the North for gifts and for wealth, the most dreaded and victorious of his House, and a worthy Heir to the Throne of Ireland, was killed by Bernard MacMahon.

The prestige attaching to Aodh Buidhe's name was such, that after his death, bathing in his reflected glory, his descendants would call themselves the Clann Aodha Buidhe or Clannaboy, the Clan of Yellow Hugh.

Domnall the comeback king
Over the next sixty years, control of Tyrone would continue to be fiercely contested by the senior and junior O'Neill septs.[14]

Aodh Buidhe was succeeded by his cousin Domnall from the senior sept, the son of Brian Battle of Down. Like Aodh Buidhe, Domnall had a difficult inaugural year. He was detested by the Red Earl, and his right to rule was challenged by Aodh Buidhe's brother, Niall Culanach, who hadn't gone away. Eventually, in 1286, the pressure told and Domnall was deposed by the Red Earl in favour of Niall Culanach of the Clann Aodha Buidhe.

Niall Culanach ruled until 1290, when Domnall returned to Tir Eoghain at the head of a huge army which included many gallowglasses, and ousted him for a second time. Domnall would spend one more year in power, during which time he killed Niall Culanach. There was no more insecure job in Tir Eoghain than being that kingdom's leader.[15]

However, in 1291, aided once more by the Red Earl, the revolving door of Tir Eoghain again opened to Aodh Buidhe's eldest son, Brian Buidhe, who deposed Domnall and became chief. In a possible attempt to unite the warring septs, Brian Buidhe styled himself, 'Prince of Tyrone and Clannaboy'. However, there was no possibility of unity. The rivalries ran too deep. Domnall killed Brian Buidhe near Glenavy and reclaimed Tir Eoghain. Determined not to be unseated again, he consolidated his strength by transferring his headquarters from Tullahogue to Dungannon, where he erected a castle and established his capital. Domnall would rule for thirty years, 'and so ended the rivalry of his line.'[16]

Tonsured but unshaven medieval scribe. The Annals of Ireland, which tell us so much about the O'Neills, were penned by scribes and copyists such as this. (Giraldus Cambrensis, Topographia)

The ambition of the Clann Aodha Buidhe

Domnall's triumph humbled the junior sept of the O'Neills and brought its decades of contending for supremacy in Tir Eoghain to a temporary close. However, the Clann Aodha Buidhe remained restless and powerful and would seek other ways of expressing their dynastic ambition.

By the beginning of the fourteenth century, the Clann Aodha Buidhe was settled in Killetraghe in the western reaches of the barony of Lochinisholen.[17] In 1312, to strengthen the hand of the junior sept, the Red Earl granted Glenconkeyne to Brian Buidhe's son Henry.

The Clann Aodha Buidhe's territory lay west of the Bann, in south Londonderry, at the north-west extremity of Lough Neagh. Nestling at the foot of Slieve Gallion and Carntogher, and enclosed by the Ballinderry and Moyola Rivers, it included the dense, impenetrable forest of Glenconkeyne. Today it corresponds to an area including the towns of Magherafelt, Bellaghy, Castledawson, Clady, Desertmartin, Draperstown, Inisrush, Kilrea, Knockloughrim, Maghera, Swatragh, Tamlaght, the Loup, Tobermore and Upperlands.

As the strength of the senior branch increased, the Clann Aodha Buidhe began to look eastward towards the increasingly faction-riven earldom. The Earldom of Ulster was in the grip of a crisis, which would shortly be compounded by a major, hostile intervention from across the sea. This crisis would in time create the political void into which the Clann Aodh Buidhe would pour.

Edward I, a close ally of Domnall O'Neill, who fought for Edward in Scotland. (Dulwich Picture Gallery)

Edward Bruce invades Ireland

King Domnall had assisted Edward I, the so-called Hammer of the Scots, in his early campaigns in Scotland. However, when his successor Edward II made a similar call for support, Domnall chose instead to align himself with Robert the Bruce in his struggle to restore the Scottish monarchy, a struggle which led to victory at Bannockburn.[18]

In 1315, Domnall further antagonised the Plantagenet King and Red Earl by renouncing his claim to the High Kingship of Ireland and inviting Robert the Bruce's brother Edward to accept the throne in his place, an act that would have horrendous consequences. Edward duly accepted and landed a flotilla of three hundred ships and six-thousand men at Olderfleet (Larne). The Red Earl marched against him but was roundly defeated at the bloody Battle of Connor. Edward Bruce ran rampant. Within a few short months he had:

sacked and razed… Belfast, Greencastle, Kells, Belturbet, Castletown, Newtown… and rooted out the noble families of the Audlies, Talbots, Tuchets, Chamberlaines, Maundevilles and the Savages out of the Ards.[19]

In May 1316, Edward Bruce was proclaimed High King of Ireland at Carrickfergus by Domnall O'Neill, Chief of Tyrone, accompanied by twelve Gaelic lords, Robert de Bisset and the Antrim Scots. The Bruce boys were – for now – Kings in Scotland and in Ireland.

Edward Bruce's short, destructive reign as High King was ended at Faughart Hill. (Fergus Cannan)

Edward's reign was short-lived, and in 1318, on Faughart Hill outside Dundalk, the heavily outnumbered Scots were defeated at the hands of Sir John Birmingham. That day, Bruce lost his Irish kingdom and his Scottish head. His body was quartered, and his limbs were sent to the four corners of Ireland as a warning against insurrection. His decapitated head was salted and sent as a trophy of war to Edward II.[20]

Following its defeat at Faughart, the Scottish army retreated into Ulster, where they, 'consumed and wasted whatsoever they had left before unspoiled… Thus was all that goodly country utterly wasted.'[21] The devastation of warfare, 'was followed by famine, and famine was followed by disease.' Unsurprisingly, the Annals record that Bruce's death was met with rejoicing in Ireland.[22]

3
Crossing the Bann
1318-1482

A wind of change

Following the English victory at Faughart, Richard de Burgh recovered the earldom, but its ravaging by the Scots left his position greatly weakened. Domnall O'Neill, who had triggered an appalling catalogue of death and destruction by inviting Bruce to Ireland, now found his authority challenged by both Richard and the *derbfine* of Aodh Buidhe.

Richard acted decisively, expelling Domnall, killing his *tánaiste* and installing Henry Buidhe, grandson of Aodh Buidhe, as king in Tir Eoghain.[1] However, the weakened state of the earldom allowed Domnall to survive the crisis and regain partial control, albeit of a diminished kingdom. He ruled until his death in 1325, 'at his island castle on Loch Laoghaire'.[2] Domnall's death allowed the Clann Aodha Buidhe to regain total control in Tir Eoghain.

In 1326, the earldom also changed hands. The Red Earl died and was succeeded by his grandson, William de Burgh, known as 'the Brown Earl,' who when he reached maturity became powerful enough to impose joint stewardship of Tir Eoghain upon the junior and senior septs:

Henri Ua Neill and Domnall's son Aed Remar, who were jointly responsible for paying rent for the kingship of Tir nEogain and supporting a quota of the earl's mercenary soldiers billeted on their territory.[3]

In 1333, the balance of power shifted again, when the young earl was murdered at Le Ford (Belfast) by Robert de Mandeville, in revenge for the murder of the Lord of Connaught. This Judas blow delivered a mortal wound to Anglo-Norman power in eastern Ulster. The earldom now imploded upon itself, as Norman blade fell on Norman bone.

Panicked by his murder, the Brown Earl's widow Countess Matilda fled to England with their young daughter Elizabeth, who would later marry Edward II's son, Lionel, Duke of Clarence. Neither Lionel nor his son-in-law, Edmund Mortimer, had any inclination to live in war-torn Ulster. They served instead as absentee earls, leaving the earldom hanging by a thread.

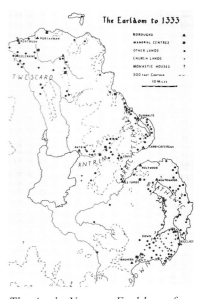

The Anglo-Norman Earldom of Ulster to 1333.

This gave the Scots and Gaels a chance to re-assert their power, and few were better placed to do so than the Clann Aodha Buidhe.

The eastward exodus

Henry Buidhe proved a powerful king of Tir Eoghain, and was hailed as one of the *Principales Hiberniae,* or leading men of Ireland. Some gave him the title King of Ulster. Such was his significance that, in 1335, he was summoned to assist Edward III in his war with Scotland.

In 1338, relations between the rival septs in Tyrone were put on a new footing when the Clann Aodha Buidhe signed a treaty severing their links with the senior branch of the Tyrone O'Neills. However, the defining moment in this ancient rivalry came in 1344, when the King's justiciar, Sir Ralph d'Ufford, deposed Henry Buidhe in favour of Aodh Reamhar (Domnall's son) and expelled him to Scotland. The senior sept had established an iron grip on the kingship. Henry had ruled in Tir Eoghain for nineteen years and although he returned from exile in 1345, the days when the Clann Aodha Buidhe would vie for authority had ended.[4]

Aodh Reamhar's usurption ultimately led to the full-scale exodus of the Clann Aodha Buidhe from Tyrone and Londonderry into Trian Congaill and the earldom, where they already had a foothold, having crossed the Bann to annex territory around Toome and Masserene in the wake of the Bruce invasion. As the earldom became less able to defend itself, the encroachment became a full-scale invasion which would in time transform the fortunes of the junior sept.

Both 'push' and 'pull' factors produced this easterly movement – however, the balance between the two is uncertain. As are the precise stages in the clan's advance, which are known to us only indirectly, as the clan is recorded as occupying territories that once lay outside its borders.

However, the basics are clear. As their native Tyrone increasingly became a cold house for the Clann Aodha Buidhe, opportunity opened in Antrim and Down. Anglo-Norman power in Ulster had been irreparably weakened by the Bruce invasion and the assassination of the Brown Earl. The Clann Aodha Buidhe secured new territories in this war-torn region, causing a 'new chieftaincy of O'Neill of Clann Aodha Buidhe' to be born in the smouldering ashes of the earldom.[5] Henry Buidhe, the last of the junior sept to rule in Tir Eoghain, would be the first to rule this newly constituted principality.

The irresistible rise of the Clann Aodha Buidhe

Over the following decades, the Clann Aodh Buidhe continued to expand into Antrim, and from there across the Lagan into Down, subjugating and displacing Anglo-Norman families such as the Whites, Jordans, Chamberlains, Copelands, Martels and Ridals, some of whom withdrew into Lecale and the Lower Ards. Even Robert Savage, executor of the Brown Earl's Estate, retreated from the Six-Milewater to Portaferry and

From Killultraghe and Glenconkeyne the Clann Aodha Buidhe swept across the Lower Bann into eastern Ulster. (Archive of the Duke of Northumberland, Alnwick Castle)

Ardkeen. By now many of these families had lost much of their distinctive cultural identity, gaelicising themselves to the point at which they became indistinguishable from native lords.[6]

Not that this could have saved them. The Clann Aodha Buidhe showed no more mercy towards the indigenous Gaels than they did to Anglo-Normans. They subjugated the MacDunlevys, the O'Lynns of Toome, and the O'Heircs of Lower Masserene. They expelled the M'Kearneys and M'Gees from Tyrone into the Ards and Portavogie respectively, and resettled the O'Gilmores in Holywood, Newtown and Bangor.[7] These seizures turned the tide of Irish history – here was a native clan taking territory from the Anglo-Normans. However, this will have been of little consolation to the incumbent Gaelic families who were also driven from their homelands.

Anglo-Norman influence in Antrim and Down was reduced to a skirt along the eastern seaboard, from Dundrum Bay to Belfast, and a second arc from Antrim through Carrickfergus and on to Larne. A third, more disparate area of settlement existed in the north-east, around Coleraine.[8]

The Bubonic Plague struck in July 1348, but may not have profoundly affected the Clannaboy. Its impact was felt most acutely in the Anglo-Norman settlements. (Royal Museums of Fine Arts, Brussels)

These positions were viable because of their sea links with Dublin and Britain, offering the Anglo-Normans beachheads from which to advance, or channels of escape, should the latter be required.

Brian Buide II and further expansion

When Henry Buidhe died in 1347, he was succeeded by his son, Brian Buidhe. This was a testing time in Ulster, with the Black Death wreaking havoc, particularly in the province's towns. Undaunted and perhaps only marginally impacted, Brian extended the borders of Clannaboy, until by 1350:

The extensive territory of the Clann Aodha Buidhe constituted what is now south County Antrim, north and east County Down and south-east County Londonderry[9]

establishing the Clann Aodha Buidhe as 'one of the most successful *uirrithe*, or under kings' in Ulster.[10]

Under the military leadership of its *tánaiste*, Brian Buidhe's son Aodh Flann (Red Hugh), the clan consolidated its influence.

According to the Annals, in 1354 Aodh Flann repelled a full-scale invasion of Clannaboy by its arch-enemy, Aodh Reamhar. Then, in 1359, on the eastern shore of Lough Neagh, he killed Murtagh O'Flynn of Moylinny, heir of the territory of Hy-Tuirtre, subsuming O'Flynn's territory into Clannaboy and expelling the O'Flynns to Inishargy and Kircubbin in the Ards. In effect, 'The expansion of the Clann Aodha Buidhe O'Neills… extinguished the old Gaelic dynasties of Central Ulidia.'[11]

Lord of the Baronies of Castlereagh and Lower Ards?

Brian Buidhe died in 1369 and was succeeded by his brother, Murtagh Ceannfada, meaning the long-headed – a reference to his shrewdness rather than the shape of his cranium!

Murtagh died in 1395 and was buried in the ecclesiastical capital of Armagh, an indication of his importance. At the time of his death Murtagh was described as, 'Lord of the Baronies of Castlereagh and Lower Ards… (and) the towns of Carrickfergus, Belfast, and Lisnegarry'.[12] This may be true, but that is not certain. The Clannaboy had influence in Carrickfergus, the seat of royal power in Ulster, but they did not rule it or occupy its castle. The reference to Lisnegarry, now Lisburn, is also intriguing. If correct, it means that there was a settlement here more than two hundred years before the generally accepted date of Lisburn's foundation, a settlement of sufficient standing to be grouped with Carrickfergus and Belfast. Murtagh's domain included the Baronies of Toome, Antrim, Belfast, Masserene and Lochinisholen. He was succeeded by his son, Brian Ballach.

The humbling of the Clann Aodha Buidhe

Like his father before him, Brian had his own nickname, ballach, meaning freckled. An educated and cultured man, Brian Ballach was also a capable military commander who consolidated control of Trian Congaill, and in the early 1400s expelled the O'Mulcreevys from the Lagan Valley and Castlereagh to Groomsport on the Ards Peninsula.

He also enjoyed success against the English and the King of Tyrone. Indeed, it appeared that under his leadership, the Clannaboy might once more usurp the senior O'Neill line when, in 1420, he helped expel 'The O'Neill' from Tir Eoghain. One year later he took Owen O'Neill of Tyrone prisoner, fearing that he was about to form an alliance with the English. Owen's wife had to pay an enormous ransom of 'cows, horses and other gifts' to secure his freedom.[13]

Upon his release, Owen set about exacting revenge, and at the head of a 'great confederation (of) the chiefs of the entire province', entered Clannaboy, retook his ransom and forced a suitably humbled Brian to provide him with hostages. The Clann Aodha Buidhe had been slapped back into its junior place. But even in defeat they could take comfort from the fact that it had taken a pan-Ulster alliance to beat them.

Throughout the 1400s, the balance of power in eastern Ulster swung back and forth. Loyalty shifted like dry sand on a windswept beach. In 1424, the pendulum swung again. Thousands of English troops under the command of James Butler poured into Ulster enabling the Crown to inflict significant defeats upon the Gaelic clans.

In 1426, Brian Ballach died an inglorious death at the hands of 'the peasantry of Carrick'.[14] Carrickfergus would pay dearly for this outrage. The Clannaboy exacted an annual fine or *Eric* of £40 from the town. Known as 'Breyne Balafs Erick', this continued to be paid until 1581. The Annals remember him as:

the most distinguished man of his time for hospitality, goodness, and learning, and the knowledge of many sciences.

The Kings of Tyrone 1176-1397, showing rulers from the junior (orange) and the senior septs (blue). The junior sept would become the Clannaboy.

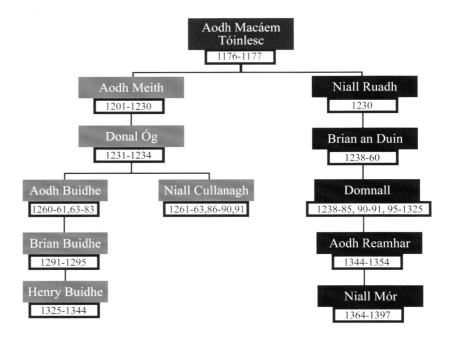

Aodh Buidhe II and the plantation reversed

Unrest now swept through Clannaboy as rival claimants vied for supremacy. Eventually however, after many vicissitudes, the young Aodh Buidhe succeeded his father as 'Prince of Clannaboy'.[15]

Aodh Buidhe understood the power of diplomacy and used it adroitly to outmanoeuvre his rivals and supplicate his enemies. He became a much-respected leader. In 1442, the Primate of Armagh called on him to adjudicate in 'a dispute respecting the right to the rectory' of Breda, suggesting that the Clannaboy had authority in the Barony of Castlereagh.[16]

However, Aodh Buidhe did not completely shun the strong-arm tactics of his predecessors. In 1442, he inflicted a devastating defeat on the MacQuillans of the Route and Henry O'Neill of Tyrone. In defeat, Henry was forced to give up his son as a hostage. Then in 1443, we find him reinforcing his supremacy in Clannaboy by compelling his older brother, Murtagh Ruadh, to give up a share of the spoils he had taken after a raid on a neighbouring territory. Notwithstanding his reputation for hospitality and diplomacy, Aodh Buidhe was every inch a warrior king and met his death on the battlefield in Iveagh, from 'the cast of a javelin'.[17] He 'continued in the agonies of death for twenty-four days' before finally expiring in May 1444, one year short of his fortieth birthday.[18]

The Annals record that Aodh Buidhe, 'planted more of the lands of the English, in despite of them, than any other man of his day,'[19] a belated acknowledgement by Gaelic Ireland that the Clann Aodha Buidhe had effected a plantation in reverse.

The battles of Dufferin Wood and Ardglass

Aodh Buidhe was succeeded by his elder brother, Murtagh Ruadh (Murtagh the Red). Almost immediately, his position and indeed the whole security of Clannaboy came under threat from Tyrone. Owen O'Neill, leader of Tyrone, assembled a second great coalition to 'plunder and destroy the Clann-Hugh-Boy.'[20] The odds were overwhelmingly stacked against Murtagh Ruadh, but cometh the hour, cometh the man, and this was his hour.

Murtagh Ruadh assembled his forces in the dense woods of the Dufferin, on the western shores of Strangford Lough. The Annals record how he ordered his men to cut a narrow passage through the woods 'in the direction which they conceived the enemy would approach them.' The trap was now set by which the Clannaboy spider would catch the Tyrone fly. Sure enough, when Owen led his troops along this newly cut passage the men of Clann Aodha Buidhe attacked the rear-guard of his force. Owen was forced to plead for terms and surrender nineteen hostages, before returning to Tyrone 'in disgrace'.

Victories like this allowed the Clann Aodha Buidhe to consolidate their control of much of Antrim and Down, and through this they amassed great wealth. However, they did not have it all their own way. The Anglo-Normans continued to maintain a presence, and the earldom had not been entirely abandoned by the Crown. In 1449, for example, Henry VI required the inhabitants of Ulster to pay £40 annually for five years towards the walling of Newtownards, 'the inhabitance of vllester shall paye yearly… towards the muradg of the newton', suggesting that, whatever the situation

The Dufferin, an area of dense, broadleaved forest (highlighted in purple) on the western shore of Strangford Lough.

on the ground, Anglo-Norman control of the town had not been entirely ceded.[21]

In 1453, Murtagh Ruadh was heavily defeated by Janico Savage, the Seneschal of Ulster, at the Anglo-Norman port of Ardglass.[22] Unknown to Murtagh, the seneschal's forces had been unexpectedly swollen by English troops and sailors who had been provisioning in Ardglass after pursuing pirates who had made an audacious raid on Dublin, kidnapping the city's archbishop. These soldiers and sailors made all the difference. Five hundred and twenty sons of Clannaboy reputedly died that day.[23] The defeat called the leadership of Murtagh Ruadh into question and the clan looked to the sons of Aodh Buidhe for its next chief.

The dark-eyed Conn

Aodh Buidhe's son Conn (Constantine) was viewed as the clan's rising star. He had proven himself in battle, defeating the English of Lecale on Cave Hill in 1468. There he had captured his uncle, the Lord of Clannaboy, Murtagh Ruadh, and killed Angus MacDonnell, heir to the Glens, along with Robert Savage of Lecale, in a regular Who's Who of carnage. This victory paved the way for his succession in 1471.

Conn maintained castles at Edendubhcarrig, Belfast and Castlereagh. He married Mary McDonnell, daughter of the Lord of Kintyre, in order to maintain a peaceable border with the Scots of the Glens.

Sketrick Castle. Attacked several times by the Clannaboy as they sought to impose their will on the Dufferin.

Ulster c.1482, showing the Clannaboy's dominance of eastern Ulster.

His tenure was characterized by constant warfare and horrific acts of terror. He was continually at odds with the MacQuillans of Dufferin, attacking their castle at Sketrick Island on several occasions. In 1472, he fought against the MacQuillans of the Route, killing their chief, Cormac. At times he fought with the Tyrone O'Neills, at times he fought agin' them. One thing was constant: Conn fought.

In 1476, Henry O'Neill of Tyrone invaded Clannaboy and destroyed Conn's castle at Belfast. However, the Clann Aodha Buidhe rallied, and his attack was repulsed. Then, when the Anglo-Norman earldom attempted a resurgence, in a particularly brutal encounter in Lecale, Conn captured, blinded and emasculated Patrick Savage, the Seneschal of Ulster.[24]

However, Conn was not just a soldier, he was also a munificent supporter of the arts. When he died in 1482, he was described in the Annals as the 'general patron of the literati of Ireland', which should not surprise us, given the cultured nature of the House of Clannaboy. His poets reciprocated, writing:

Hail prince of Erin – Honour's noblest son,
A thousand welcomes greet the dark-eyed Conn!

The Clann Aodha Buidhe triumphant
During the fifteenth century the Clann Aodha Buidhe became masters of eastern Ulster. Amongst its lordships, Clannaboy was now third after the

Tyrone O'Neills and the O'Donnells of the north-west in terms of land mass and political influence. The Clannaboy had retained their foothold in Tyrone and south Londonderry (lands they would later lose) and added a huge territory east of the Bann which extended:

from Carrickfergus Bay and the River Lagan westward to Lough Neagh, and contained… the baronies of Belfast, Massarene, Antrim, and Upper Toome, in the County of Antrim… in the County of Down… Claneboy comprised the baronies of Ards, Castlerea, Kinelarty, and Lecale, and extended… from the Bay of Dundrum to the Bay of Carrickfergus or Belfast Lough.[25]

To understand their territory's extent, consider the modern towns that fall within its jurisdiction: Moira, Dromore, Hillsborough, Saintfield, Ballynahinch, Belfast, Comber, Holywood, Bangor, Newtownards, Donaghadee, Portavogie, Crossgar, Lisburn, Glenavy, Crumlin, Antrim, Ballyclare, Ballymena, Portglenone, Kells, Connor, Templepatrick, Cullybackey, Clady, Randalstown, Toome, Maghera, Magherafelt, Desertmartin, Draperstown, Tobermore, Cookstown, Tamlacht, Moneymore and Newtownabbey.

One thousand years after Niall of the Nine Hostages, the Clann Aodha Buidhe had emerged as a people in their own right. Forged in the crucible of conflict, the Clann Aodha Buidhe had bested the Anglo-Norman earldom, and survived countless clashes with their Tyrone brethren, the English and the Scots. Warfare was part of the ebb and flow of life. Peace was a transient, fleeting commodity. The Clannaboy would rule by the sword until the Gaelic world collapsed in 1603.

4
The great lordship of Clannaboy
1482-1555

The lordship of Clannaboy was made up of a jigsaw of *sleughts* or component clans, each of which had its own territory. All gave allegiance to their overlord and were required to provide him with an annual tribute, to offer him military service, and to allow him to billet his men and horses on their land. The heads of these septs and their families made up Clannaboy's gentry, and the high-born hostages used to guarantee political deals and treaties usually came from their ranks.

Upper Clannaboy's principal *sleughts* included the Sleught Neills of Drumbo, Saintfield, Killaney and parts of Kilmore, Knockbreda, Blaris, Lambeg and Drumbeg; the McGillechreves de le Gallagh (Knockbreda, Galwally and Forestside); the Mulchrieves[1] de le Tawne (from Knockbreda and Ballymacarret southwards); the Sleught Henrickies (Tribe of Henry the Blind) settled in Magherascouse (Ballygowan), Barnymaghery, Killinchy,

The territories of the Sleught of Upper Clannaboy and the Ards, who owed their allegiance voluntarily or otherwise to the O'Neills. (After J.R.H. Greeves)

Kilmood and part of Kilmore; the Sleught Kellies (originally from Drumbo) who settled in parts of Comber and Tullynakill; the Sleught Hubricks (Tribe of Freckled Hugh) settled in north-eastern Comber, south-western Newtownards and south-eastern Dundonald, dwelling mainly 'between Scrabo and the town of Comber'.[2]

The Sleught Bryan Boy inhabited four townlands in Holywood Parish and the townland of Ballymoney or Craigavad. There were also the Sleught Durnings (Dornans) and Sleught Owen MacQuin dwelling in Holywood and Dundonald and the adjacent parts of the parish of Newtownards, the Sleught McCarteglane, and in the Great Ards the Sleught Mortagh M'Edmond, the McGillmurres, the Sleught Brian O'Neile, the Turtars of Inishargy, and the M'Kearneys and M'Gees of Portavogie.[3]

Edendubhcarrig, now Shane's Castle near Antrim, built in 1345 by the Clannaboy, and burned in 1490 during the fight for the succession. (Alba Marie Photography)

Niall Mór and the golden age

Following Conn's death in 1482, outright control of Clannaboy (Upper and Lower) was disputed by his sons and near relatives (the *derbfine*), with everything eventually falling to his son Niall. The Annals record that the early years of Niall's reign were economically difficult, with soaring livestock prices and a scarcity of salt. To make matters worse, not everyone was happy with Niall's election, and in 1490 his cousin Felim burned and ravaged Niall's castle at Edendubhcarrig near Antrim on the banks of Lough Neagh. The transfer of power was often achieved through violent rivalry, thought necessary for the health of the clan as it ensured the success of the strongest candidate.

However, with support from the English garrison at Carrickfergus, the tide turned in Niall's favour and his troublesome cousin Felim was dispatched near Rasharkin. Niall became undisputed Lord of Clannaboy and would come to be hailed as Niall Mór, or Niall the Great, and rule Clannaboy and Trian Congaill until his death in 1512.[4] Marriage to

Franciscan brothers, such as might have been seen in Niall Mór's friary in Carrickfergus. (John Paul Getty Museum)

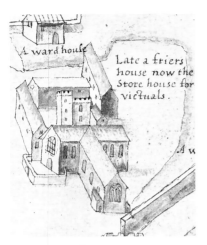

Late sixteenth century representation of Niall Mór's friary at Carrickfergus. (British Library, London)

Beanmídhe MacMahon, daughter of the King of Tyrconnell, further consolidated his position, allowing Niall to style himself the 'Royal Heir of Ulster', a declaration that the Clannaboy had usurped the Tyrone O'Neills as the north's leading power.

However, Niall Mór was not content with titles. In 1503 he led a great army across the Bann to subdue Tir Eoghain. However, his attack was repelled and he was captured by the English, who demanded sixteen hostages (all of them members of leading Clannaboy families) to secure his release. Freed from jail, Niall Mór mustered his troops and stormed the walled town of Carrickfergus, released his hostages and imprisoned the town's mayor.

Niall Mór was a deeply religious man and in 1497 founded the Friary of the Friars Minor de Observantia in Carrickfergus.[5] The decision to site it in Ulster's 'capital' provides another indicator of Clannaboy's influence and ambition. Niall Mór also endowed the Church of St. Columbkille at Knock with valuable privileges and lands (lands that now lie around the dual carriageway). Like his predecessors, Niall Mór kept a sophisticated court and is noted in the Annals as a lover of history, poetry, music, and the sciences – all in all, something of a renaissance man. Upon his death in 1512, he was interred in his friary in Carrickfergus. His twenty-seven-year reign marked the Clannaboy's ascent to the pinnacle of its power.

Turmoil in Clannaboy
Niall Mór had six sons; Aodh Dubh O'Neill (Hugh the Dark), Brian Ballach (the Freckled), Phelim Bacach (the Lame), Domnall, Murtagh, and Niall Óg (Niall the Younger), who is most significant to our story. Over the next hundred years, four of these sons and their descendants would repeatedly vie for control of Clannaboy.

Around this time the English Record Commissioners published *The State of Ireland and a Plan for its Reformation*, proposing to 'exyle, banyshe and expulse' the Clannaboy O'Neills from their mighty kingdom, which stretched from Portavogie to the Bann.[6] The Clannaboy were to be replaced by settlers from England, Wales and Cornwall and:

assigned and suffered to have their habitation and dwelling in the great forest Keyultagh (Killultagh), and the Pheux (Fews), which habitations and places they hath and dwelleth often before, now by compulsion.[7]

The Clannaboy O'Neills had joined the Tyrone O'Neills, and Scots of the Glynnes, as major challenges to English authority in Ulster.

Three of Niall Mór's sons, Aodh Dubh, Brian Ballach and Niall Óg are variously recorded as having been Lords of Clannaboy, either in part or in its entirety. Some genealogies also attribute the chiefdom to Phelim Bacach.[8] We know that Phelim's son, Brian McPhelim, would become chief.

Unfortunately for the brothers, their exalted positions made them targets and each met a violent death. Aodh Dubh's luck ran out in October 1524, when he was killed by rival O'Neills and Fitzgeralds, who ambushed him on his return from a raid on a neighbouring territory. Brian Ballach was killed in sinister circumstances in 1529, tricked by Cormac MacQuillan 'who went out of Carrickfergus in company and friendship with him', and then murdered him in cold blood.

Niall Mór's youngest son, Niall Óg, then gained control of a part of Lower Clannaboy (Antrim) and all of Upper Clannaboy (Down), ruling from his 'half stronghold, half residence' of Castlereagh. Significantly, this is the first time that Castlereagh is recorded as the seat of power of Clannaboy. However, despite having successfully repelled an invasion by the 1st Earl of Tyrone, Niall Óg was killed in 1537, by 'the shot of a ball' from a Scottish musket.[9] Niall Óg is described as the 'Lord of Trian Congail' and 'last chief of all Clannaboy'.[10]

Clannaboy divided

The killing of Niall Óg inflicted a 'triple whammy' on the Clannaboy. Not only had the clan been defeated, but their champion had been killed as was his *tánaiste*, who was also 'slain by the Scots'. In the ensuing crisis, Clannaboy was 'partitioned between two contenders', Niall Óg's son Brian

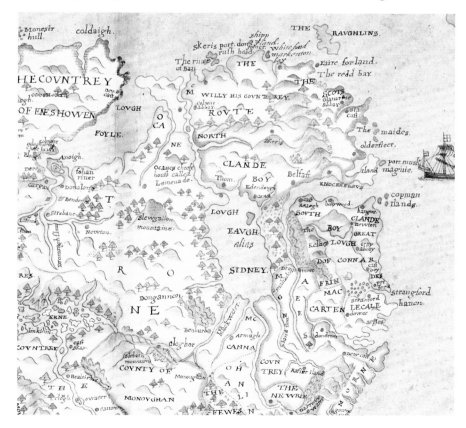

Late sixteenth century map showing the division of Upper and Lower Clannaboy. (National Maritime Museum, Greenwich)

Brian Faghartagh was fostered in Kinelarty by the MacCartans, one of whose homes was a crannog on Loughinisland.

Faghartagh, who ruled in Upper Clannaboy, and one of Niall's nephews, probably Murtagh, the son of Brian Ballach.[11] Clannaboy was becoming two distinct domains, divided (mostly) by the meandering River Lagan. The kingdom to the north of the Lagan was designated Lower Clannaboy, and the kingdom to the south of the Lagan became Upper Clannaboy; names that seem back to front until we remember that the geopolitical reference point was the capital city, Dublin.

Although at this stage there was no sense that Clannaboy's partition would be permanent, its rivals and the government are likely to have welcomed the division as it diluted Clannaboy's strength, and would enable its opponents to play one territory against the other.

Clannaboy's 'brilliant star', Brian Faghartagh

Brian Faghartagh was the eldest of Niall Óg's sons. He was named Faghartagh as he was 'fostered in MacCartan's country of *Cinel-Faghartaigh* or Kinelarty.'[12] Fostering was common, particularly among high-born families, so Brian was raised in accordance with the customs of his time. The records identify him as Brian, Bernard, Bryan, Ferto, Ferty, Faghartach, Fagartach, Fegharty and Fertagh; which doesn't make his story any easier to follow.

Brian Faghartagh is a significant figure in our story, being father to Niall McBrian, the father of our protagonist Con O'Neill of Castlereagh. Reeves also describes Brian Faghartagh as the earliest known occupant of Castlereagh, although this is open to dispute.

Brian controlled significant portions of both Upper and Lower Clannaboy. He was a charismatic figure, and is referred to in the Annals as 'that brilliant star of the tribe'.[13] He was also wealthy, owning an extensive herd of cattle, partly accumulated through cattle-raiding. Brian also negotiated an annual tribute of £20 sterling from the English families in Lecale in return for land rights and his protection, indicating that his authority extended beyond Clannaboy's borders.[14]

A seemingly innocuous quarrel between Brian Faghartagh and the Earl of Tyrone over the detention of Phelom McShane for the theft of 'a great number of kine and draft horses' may have contributed to his premature death. Brian claimed that the Earl had no jurisdiction over Phelom 'as he is not of the country of Tyrone, or under the rule of the said Earl'. The Lord Deputy agreed and had Phelom released into the hands of Sir Donald Magennesse to await trial. The Lord Deputy's adjudication stated:

Brian Fertagh is totally exempted from the rule of the said Earl, it is further ordered that the same Brian and his successors, and all others of Claneboy, shall be exonerated against the said Earl and his heirs, from all rents, bonnaughts, tributes, services, and personal obediences, and pay all dues to the King.[15]

This shows that, according to law, Clannaboy and Tyrone had equal standing and that neither was a vassal kingdom of the other. Clannaboy's claim to independence had been vindicated.

But Brian Faghartagh did not get long to enjoy his victory. In 1548, just eleven years after his inauguration, he was 'assassinated by Shane O'Neill, Prince of Tyrone'.[16] His obituary describes him as:

a prosperous and warlike man, and a man distinguished for benevolence and hospitality and the resplendent luminary of his tribe.[17]

Loughinisland Church, where Brian Faghartagh would have worshipped as a child.

Shane O'Neill, who murdered Brian Faghartagh.

Edward VI by William Scrots. After beating the King's forces near Belfast, Hugh MacNeill submitted to King Edward and so avoided retribution. (Private collection)

Shane's motives are unknown. Perhaps Shane viewed the formidable Brian Faghartach as a rival for the leadership of Gaelic Ulster. Perhaps it was revenge for his abduction as a child from the home of his foster parents by the men of Clannaboy. Perhaps it was an attempt by Tyrone to reassert its authority over the Clannaboy. Whatever his motives, through this bloody act the Tyrone O'Neills had clawed their way back to the top – for now.

Hugh MacNeill

Brian was succeeded by his younger brother Hugh MacNeill. Again, Hugh MacNeill was not the outright ruler of Clannaboy, as Murtagh remained in charge of significant territory north of the Lagan, although he was weak and 'and unable to miantayne the same'. Hugh MacNeill, on the other hand, was a strong leader, supported in his claim to the lordship by his cousins, the sons of Phelim Bacach. In 1553, the Lord Chancellor, Sir Thomas Cusack wrote that:

The same Hugh hath two castles, one called Bealefarst... the other, called Castlerioughie is fower miles from Bealefarst, and standeth uppone the playne in the midst of the woodes of the Dufferin.[18]

We are beginning to see a clear division between the two Clannaboys with the ford of Belfast providing the hinge between the two regions.[19]

Around this time, 'a hosting (was) made by the Lord Justice... against the son of Niall Óg (Hugh MacNeill) and the Scots'. The men of Clannaboy took to the field near Belfast, defeating the intruders and slaying Patrick Savage, 'with forty or sixty others'.[20] Although victorious, Hugh MacNeill now found himself in a vulnerable position, as retaliation might follow with greater force. His way out was to submit to Edward VI and gain a royal pardon.[21]

Hugh proved himself an able negotiator. He petitioned for and received back his castle of 'Belferside' and the monasteries of Clannaboy. This included 'the monastery of the friars of Knockfergus' which housed 'the sepulchres of his ancestors', the resting place of the royal line of Clannaboy. In return, he agreed to 'forfeit his captaincy and all his lands, goods, flocks, and farms if ever he should depart from his faith or obedience'.

This peace accord of 1552 reveals the critical importance of Clannaboy to the balance of power in Ulster, and Hugh's ready access to the ear of the King. English control in Ulster was then tenuous, with Lord Deputy Crofts unable to assert any meaningful authority. Perhaps this is why, despite Henry VIII's dissolution policy, Hugh regained control of the monasteries. However, the clause concerning the forfeiture of his lands was most telling and would become the legal noose from which the authorities in changed times would hang Hugh MacNeill's descendants out to dry.

Map of 1646, modelled on Speed's map, showing 'The Nether Clan de Boy' in County Antrim, and the territories of some of the leading Clannaboy septs in County Down. (Jansson in Novum Atlas of Britain)

Once more the Earl of Tyrone invaded Clannaboy, but with the assistance of the Scots was routed and three hundred of his men slain. Clannaboy had avenged Brian Faghartagh's murder and reasserted its primacy in Ulster. But it did not last. In 1555, Hugh MacNeill met the same fate as his father, being shot dead by the McDonnells of the Glens – the same Scots who one year previously had fought with him to quell the expansionism of Tyrone. Ulster politics was ever thus: a fickle and dangerous game played out on endlessly shifting sands! Hugh MacNeill received an impressive obituary:

Hugh, the son of Niall Óge, son of Niall, son of Con, son of Hugh Boy, son of Brian Ballagh O'Neill, Lord of Clannaboy, an influential, bountiful, generous, and truly hospitable man, a prince over chieftains, a mighty lord in defending, a man who had not yielded submission or obedience to any of the Irish, who had never given

Clannaboy's soldiery? Durer's famous depiction of Irish warriors in 1521 shows a nobleman flanked by unshod kerne, along with a chainmailed gallowglass. (Musée des Beaux Arts, Paris)

pledges or hostages for his territory,[22] and who had received hostages himself, a man who had given many defeats to the English and Irish in the defence of his territory against them, was killed by the Scots, with the shot of a ball.[23]

Clannaboy's continuing but perilous ascendancy would now depend on the smoothness of the succession.

5
Sir Brian McPhelim and the shock of plantation 1555-74

After Hugh MacNeill's death, dissention was rife in Clannaboy as its leading men jockeyed for power. This gave Lord Deputy Sussex the opportunity to reassert the earlier division of the territory. Upper Clannaboy in County Down was granted to Hugh's brother, Con McNeill Óg, third son of Niall Óg and brother of Brian Faghartagh. Lower Clannaboy in County Antrim was granted to their cousin, Hugh McPhelim, son of Phelim Bacach.

    Con Óg and Hugh McPhelim despised this imposition and protested vehemently against it. When they threatened insurrection, both were seized

Carrickfergus c.1560, by Philip Armstrong. Though an 'English' town, Carrickfergus's character was influenced by the Clannaboy, whose royal family were buried in the impressive friary buildings (r). (Mid and East Antrim Council).

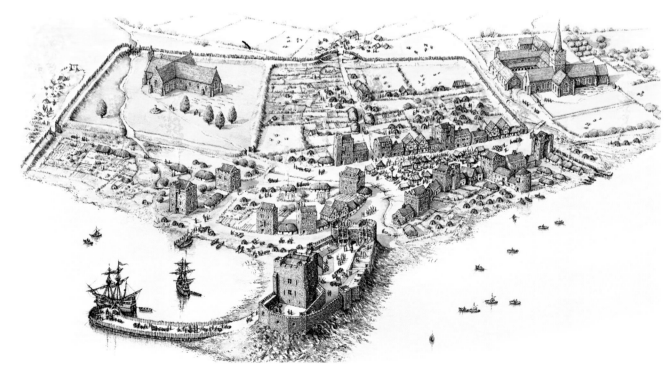

and thrown into prison, whereon Brian McPhelim stepped forward to claim lordship of both Clannaboys – Lower from his older brother Hugh McPhelim, and Upper from his cousin, Con McNeill Óg. Clannaboy was reunited again.

Brian McPhelim of Castle Reagh

In the mid-1560s the English took firm control of Carrickfergus under Captain William Piers. Piers was a formidable physical specimen, described as, 'a tall burly man, with a big, brown beard.' A shrewd operator, he established cordial relationships with the Clannaboy O'Neills and their northern neighbours the McDonnells in a strategy to undermine Shane O'Neill, now 'The O'Neill,' who by 1566 was belligerently asserting Tyrone's leadership of Ulster.

To counter this cosy alliance, Shane established a powerbase at Edendubhcarrig, a source of great discontentment to Brian McPhelim, the new Lord of the Clannaboys. Shane saw himself as having every right to do this as he viewed Clannaboy, 'as one of his *urriaght* (vassal) territories.'[1]

But Brian McPhelim will have bristled at Tyrone's pretensions. He saw Shane the Proud's claim of lordship over Clannaboy as an anachronism, which no longer reflected reality. Shane's murder of the effervescent Brian Faghartach also remained a piercing thorn in Clannaboy's collective memory.

With his position secured and powerful allies in tow, Brian McPhelim began to work against the mighty Shane O'Neill. He formed an alliance with Sussex, placing one hundred foot soldiers and thirty horsemen at his disposal. He brought his father-in-law, Bryan Caragh McCormock and Hugh McMoretagh into the English fold. Such was the high esteem in which he was held that when he fell ill in the winter of 1566, Piers wrote, 'God be pleased (Brian McPhelim) is recovered.'[2]

Shane was stopped. But not by Brian McPhelim. In June 1567, he was

Shane O'Neill's murder was notorious enough to feature on Speed's map of 1599, thirty years after his death. Was Brian McPhelim involved in his murder? (Private collection)

butchered in a frenzied attack by the McDonnells. Lurking in the shadows was the Machiavellian Captain Piers, who had brokered a deal with the Scots to ensure Shane's bloody end.

Arise Sir Brian

Shane's death did not improve relations between Clannaboy and the Tyrone O'Neills. On the contrary, Clannaboy drew closer to the Crown. In September 1567, Brian McPhelim received a knighthood, and a payment of £626 from the Lord Deputy, Sir Henry Sidney. In return he promised:

- To help build a bridge at the ford of Belfast
- To provide one night's sustenance and safe passage for any of the Queen's soldiers travelling through Clannaboy
- To clear passes through the forest of Kilwarlin
- To provide wood to fuel the brickworks at Carrickfergus
- Not to burn any ships docked at Belfast
- To provide victuals for the English garrison there[3]

This suited Brian McPhelim, who was still haunted by a well-founded fear of Tyrone and the sense that Clannaboy's security lay in closer ties with the government. But it also advanced English interests. Forest clearance would aid the movement of Crown forces. Troops could now cross Clannaboy freely and be fed from the local larder. Commerce would continue unhindered at the port of Belfast, across the new bridge and along clearways cut through the forests. And the manufacture of bricks would facilitate the building of new English-style manors and settlements. Brian had signed up for the Anglicisation of Clannaboy.

Brian then offered his lands to the Crown and received them back under terms. This was in accordance with English policy of 'Surrender and Regrant', established in the reign of Henry VIII, by which Gaelic chiefs gave up their lands to the Crown, recognised the legitimacy of its rule in Ireland, and as a result had their lands returned to them for an annual rent. By this English doctrine, the lands of each clan were viewed as being:

vested soley in the chief, so that on his forfeiture and fall, the whole "interest being drawn to him," was transferred as a matter of course to the Crown.[4]

The Crown believed that Surrender and Regrant would achieve an amicable pacification of Ulster. They thought it:

must breed quietness, obedience and profit. Love to their children will make them fearful to disobey the laws and desirous to build houses, purchase land and grow wealthy.[5]

Confidential government papers of the time describe Brian in glowing terms as, 'a true subject' and ally of the Queen in rebellious Ulster. He resolutely refused to unite with Shane's successor, Turlough Luineach O'Neill against the Crown, despite constant threats and inducements. In March 1569, Captain Piers helped Brian to repel an attack by Turlough Luineach near Castle Reagh.[6] In English eyes, Sir Brian McPhelim had become a model Irish chief.

Cattle and cowboys

As Lord of Upper Clannaboy Sir Brian McPhelim was a very wealthy man, owning '30,000 beeves or 60,000 horns', herded by, 'wandering *creaghts*, living Arab fashion, among the beautiful glens and plains of Clannaboy.'[7] His drovers were the equivalent of wild-west cowboys, using their powerful horses to control their herds. Their lives were bound up with their cattle, which were a source of meat, milk, butter, blood, cheese, leather, warmth in winter, and a living currency with which to trade.

These drovers lived in huts called *boleys*, constructed of turf walls, branches and rushes. A makeshift corral protected the herd from the wolves that roamed the hills. Many a wolf's side was thrust through by a drover's spear, with the pelt providing a warm cloak for the winter.

The herds traversed Clannaboy seeking grazing. With no fences to mark boundaries, bloody disputes were frequent. Herds could stray onto neighbouring lands, and clans would often engage in cattle rustling.

Whilst cattle were the measure of a chief's wealth, the horse was a statement of his standing. The leading families of Clannaboy would all have travelled by horse, and Brian would have been a skilled rider, surveying his herd, collecting tribute, hunting wild boar, even raiding astride his steed.

We should not, however, assume that tillage had been forsaken. According to one account there were 'more ploughs going in Clannaboy than there had been for one hundred years'. Labourers tilled the land using a stocky horse known as the 'garran', and a short wooden plough attached to the horse's tail. This let the horse pause if the plough struck a rock, thus avoiding damage to the blade. Gerard Mercantor's map of 1595 depicts *pascafdry ennomies* or fish traps in Strangford Lough, showing that fishing was also a part of local life.

Life was pastoral but far from idyllic. Failed harvests, hard winters, hunger, disease and the frequent threat of violence meant the lives of many

Cattle were the mainstay of the Clannaboy economy, and the measure of its ruler's wealth. Woodcut by John Derricke, 1581 (Mansell Collection)

'A store house of graine'. This c.1570 map depicts Sir Brian's grain store near Castle Reagh (bottom left), clear evidence of cultivation in Clannaboy. (ex Benn, History of the Town of Belfast)

were a struggle for survival. And the political storm clouds were gathering. Brian's strategy of cooperation was about to fall apart.

Plantation replaces cooperation

At this time ideas of 'plantation' were in very much in vogue. Even the Queen got caught up in these, and in a bewildering turnaround granted lands in Clannaboy to two English adventurers, Captains Browne and Borrowe. They showed no regard for Brian McPhelim stating:

It is most necessary to have Castle Rewghe out of his hands, and so to put him over the water into Clandeboy (Antrim)…

Misrepresenting Upper Clannaboy's septs as, 'Wood Kerne and Outlaws that inhabited the forests,' they proposed clearing Clannaboy of the sleughts which owed allegiance to Sir Brian, including:

the Slott Neilles, the MacNeill Óges... Slut Henrickies... MacBrian Carto... Patrick M'Neill O'Kelly, M'Morito ne Kelly, Gildough McDonagh O'Kelly and Neil M'Patrick O'Kelly.[8]

Arguing that Brian only held Castle Reagh as a result of his annexation of Upper Clannaboy following the imprisonment of Con Óg, and had no lawful entitlement to it, Barrowe acted decisively and took the castle with just fourteen men. Whether or not Brian was resident is unknown. If he was he presumably retreated to the safety of his castle in Belfast.

Browne then invaded the Ards, building a tower house costing 'fowre hundreth marks and upwards' at the fording point at Mahee Island on Strangford Lough.[9] However, Browne was unable to hold either stronghold. Brian soon regained control – and a new tower house to boot!

The 'Coronation Portrait' of Queen Elizabeth, who capriciously signed away Sir Brian's land. (National Portrait Gallery, London)

The seven year land grab

Undeterred by this fiasco, Elizabeth's Principal Secretary of State, Sir Thomas Smith, 'one of England's leading intellectuals', now boldly entered the frame. He argued that Ulster should be planted on the grounds that: [10]

- It had been deemed forfeit to the Crown following Shane O'Neill's revolt
- The whole of Ulster 'lieth waste'
- It would 'repress' the 'wicked barbarous and uncivil Scots and Wild Irish, such as were late in rebellion'
- It would be 'a benefit to Her Majesty... to have the same peopled with good and obedient subjects'
- Colonisation would 'bring the rude and barbarous nation of the wild Irish to more civility of manner'
- It would prevent Spain or France from using Ireland for the invasion of England[11]

Smith publically asked for the Queen's permission to plant Clannaboy and the Ards, and privately whispered against Sir Brian at court, claiming that he could not be trusted.

As soon as he learned of Smith's petition, Brian wrote to the Queen, affirming his loyalty and pleading to be left in peace. Far from being a rebel, he reminded the Queen that he had suffered at rebel hands, having, 'been both banished (from) the country by the rebels and driven to great misery.'[12]

Brian also recounts how Elizabeth had acknowledged his service with a gift, conveyed to him by Captain William Piers – possibly in payment for some hand Brian may have had in the murder of Shane O'Neill. However, money talked and Sir Brian's plea fell on deaf ears. Smith was granted Letters Patent for the Ards and Upper Clannaboy for the sum of £10,000. But his grant was time-limited. He would forfeit all rights to the territory if his plantation was not completed by March 1579, a detail that would render all future Smith claims on Clannaboy null and void.

Clannaboy Holdings Ltd.

Smith did not believe in 'softly softly.' When the Scots had caused problems along the border with England, he had advocated sending in 'the Queen's peacemakers' (i.e. cannon!). He was also a life-long risk-taker and entrepreneur, having invested heavily in an unsuccessful venture to extract precious metals from iron ore. Smith would do whatever it took to make his plantation work.

His grant included most of North Down and the Ards, and ran from Belfast Castle and the lower reaches of the Lagan to the Abbey of Massarene, Mowbary's Castle and Castle Toome, an area of approximately four hundred and eighty square miles. This was deemed sufficient to settle

1200 men. To break even, Smith needed to attract one hundred colonists, every additional settler would represent a profit.

Smith thought there were many young English gentlemen who would jump at the chance to establish estates in Ulster, especially if Clannaboy could be presented as a land of opportunity. To this end, he engaged in a slick marketing campaign, publishing a broadsheet, a map of the area and a sixty-three-page promotional brochure 'on the Peopling of the Ards' aimed at enticing gentlefolk to come to:

a lande that floweth with milke and hony, a fertile soil… There is timber, stone, plaister and slate commodious for building everywhere abundant, a countery full of springs, rievers and lakes… full of excellent fish and foule, no part of the countery distant above viii miles from a most plentiful sea…'[13]

Thomas Smith's map of the Ards from his promotional brochure of 1572. (British Library)

The coming of the redcoats
The new settlers would assume the role of 'soldier-farmers'[14] after the style of Roman colonisation, and travel armed with 'pike, or halberd or caliver… staffe… dagges'. They were also to be clearly identifiable, wearing a 'livery cloke of red colour, or carnation, with black facing' – a choice of garment that seems to have been almost designed to present Smith's enemies with a target.

Smith claimed that he was repatriating lands that were once part of the Anglo-Norman earldom.[15] He sought to further legitimise his land grab through the Act of Attainder, which followed the rebellion of Shane O'Neill. By this, Shane's lands and those of his under-kings, actual or nominal, namely Tyrone, Clannaboy, Iveagh, the Glynns and the Route, were forfeited to the Crown. The Gaelic lords would be expelled and the peasantry retained as a cheap and ready labour force. Smith was convinced that the 'churle of Ireland', had had enough of being 'eaten out with *cesse, coyne,* and *liverie*', and would gladly come 'to live under us, and to farm our ground', a statement that would return to haunt him.

The four forts
Phase one of his project was to establish a base at 'Newcastle in the Ardes'; chosen for its proximity to Savage's castle at Portaferry, and because it had a quay that would allow access to the sea. It is marked on Boazio's Map (1599) as the 'townland called Newcastle' three miles east of Portaferry, and lies just north of the picturesque village of Kearney.[16]

From Newcastle, Smith would advance north and 'build three forts across North Down, thus securing the Peninsula.'[17] Smith describes them as 'garrisons placed in a straight neck of land, by which it was joined to the rest of the island.'[18] They were to be positioned close to the settlements of Comber, Dundonald and Holywood, effectively annexing the peninsula behind a military curtain. These represented a provocative military build-up, directly facing the O'Neill stronghold of Castle Reagh.

Brian McPhelim's signature.
(Ulster Journal of Archaeology)

Smith scoffed at the failures of previous plantations, and claimed that his venture was fail-safe. Only when he cautioned that the dispossessed Irish could, 'lay wait to intrap and murther the Maister himself, sometime setting fire on his reekes or townes', did Smith's plans deal in reality.[19]

Sir Brian betrayed

It was now clear that the agreement Sir Brian had struck with the Crown was worthless. That Elizabeth had reneged on their legally binding covenant shocked and bewildered him. Now, betrayed by the Queen and with his bridges burned with the Gaelic and Scottish Lords, the Lord of Clannaboy stood alone, trapped between a rock and a hard place! In March 1572, in a desperate last attempt to halt Smith, Sir Brian again wrote to the Queen assuring her of his loyalty:

I have ever since my youth continued... immovable from my loyal duty to my said Sovereign Lady... I will undoubtedly persevere in the same during my life.

He informed Elizabeth of 'certain books spread in print' that claim she had given Smith lands that had 'been possessed by (his) ancestors above fourteen descents', a lineage of biblical proportions, through which Sir Brian traced his title back to Aodh Buidhe.[20] The Queen, her Deputy, and Smith all wrote reassuring Sir Brian that his lands were not threatened. However, Smith's arrival in Strangford Lough would soon prove the emptiness of these replies.

Not an inch!

In 1572, England was preoccupied with the threatened annihilation of the Protestant Huguenots in France. Sir Thomas Smith was summarily dispatched to the French court to argue their case, leaving his son, Thomas Junior, to claim the Ards on his behalf.

Smith Junior assembled an expeditionary force of eight hundred would-be settlers at Liverpool dock. His enterprise was vehemently opposed by the Lord Deputy, Sir William Fitzgerald, and Turlough Luineach, who demanded that 'Mr Smith may not be permitted to inhabit the lands of Sir Brian McPhelim'. Captain Piers warned that Clannaboy was already 'in an uproar at Mr Smith coming over to plant' and that it was likely to rebel if his venture proceeded.[21] The Lord Deputy further advised that the grant 'will

Thomas Smith Junior, who was given a task that was beyond him, and perhaps beyond anyone. (National Portrait Gallery, London)

Newtown Priory was set ablaze by Sir Brian and restored by Hugh Montgomery in the early 1600s.

bring the Irish into a knot to rebel.'[22] Smith's departure was delayed. But only by several months.

In July 1572, having obtained final approval, Thomas Smith sent a conciliatory letter to Sir Brian outlining his plans for settlement and requesting that Brian treat him as a good neighbour. Sir Brian's reply was uncompromising. Just as he was burning Smith's letter, he said, he would burn any ground on which Smith set foot.

Baulking at these alarming rumours, Smith's settlers voted with their feet. His expeditionary force dwindled to just one hundred men, a 'ludicrously small number for such an enterprise.'[23] This should have given Thomas Smith pause for thought. He must have known his father's plan was reckless. The younger Smiths knew the country, indeed Thomas' brother John, a Dublin apothecary, had attempted to poison Shane O'Neill using contaminated wine, a fact that will not have endeared him to Turlough Luineach.[24] No wonder the expedition was seen as a provocation.

Finally, on August 30th 1572, Smith sailed for the 'promised land,' disembarking at Strangford. He was met by Henry Savage and accompanied to Newcastle, having strict instructions not to enter Savage's lands in the Little Ards. Savage's cooperation gave the expedition an important fillip. Another came from Niall McBrian Faghartagh, a relative of Sir Brian and an influential inhabitant in the Ards, who initially sided with Smith to advance his designs upon Upper Clannaboy's lordship.[25]

Clannaboy erupts

In September, Smith travelled to Carrickfergus, where he attempted to negotiate terms with Sir Brian. Sir Brian refused to meet the self-styled 'Colonel of Ards', and upped the ante by kidnapping a Lieutenant Thomas Moore and holding him to ransom. The Lord Deputy responded by threatening to release Con Óg from prison, a prospect that filled Sir Brian with such dread that Moore was immediately released.

Harassed on the peninsula, Smith retreated to Ringhaddy Island on the edge of the Dufferin Wood, where he regrouped before re-crossing the Lough to establish his fort at Newcastle.

His return stirred up a veritable hornet's nest. Sir Brian 'with all his force' marched into the Ards where he 'took all the prey, and set fire upon some towns'.[26] He destroyed any building that might offer Smith shelter. The monasteries at Comber, Movilla, Newtownards Priory, Blackabbey, Nendrum, Greyabbey, Bangor Abbey and Holywood Priory were all burnt to deny Smith haven:

Holywood Priory, burnt by Sir Brian McPhelim to deny Thomas Smith's men shelter.

O'Neill burned the Ardes from Belfast to Ardkeen (where the Savages had their castle) and all the villages between. Nowhere were there more than three houses left standing together.

In addition, 'the Tounne of Carrickfergus', symbol of English power in Ulster, 'was for the most parte destroyed by fier' and Brian threatened its abbey and storehouses.[27] A hundred troops were dispatched from Newry to protect the pier. Sir Brian also targeted Henry Savage for assassination, halting only when his youngest daughter Brighid was captured, leading Brian to sue for her safe return.

The Tyrone-Clannaboy alliance
As the crisis deepened, Captain Nicholas Malbie warned that Sir Brian planned to rendezvous with Turlough Luineach at Dundrum, from whence he would attack Kinelarty, before riding into the Ards to expel Smith. Sir Brian's strategy to date had been to compel Smith to leave. Now, if Malbie is to be believed, he appeared ready to take Smith on.

This was probably unnecessary, for Sir Brian's strategy was working. Young Smith was assailed on all sides. His demanding father was impatient at his lack of success. He had lost the respect of his men and been 'illhandled' by ten of his own soldiers. Niall McBrian Faghartagh 'and all his *creaghts*' had returned their allegiance to Sir Brian. Smith's encampment in the Little Ards was barely tolerated, and his presence in the Great Ards was anathema to almost the whole of Clannaboy. His position had become untenable.

Essex's great expedition
However, English eyes remained fixed on Clannaboy. With Smith's plantation failing, Elizabeth granted Lower Clannaboy and the Route (virtually all of County Antrim) to Walter Devereux, 1st Earl of Essex.

Eager to please his Queen, Essex gallantly offered to subdue and colonize Lower Clannaboy and to 'expel the Scots Islesmen' from the North Coast.[28] Brian must have felt the noose tighten around his neck – both Clannaboys were now in danger.[29]

In September 1573, Essex sailed from Liverpool to Carrickfergus, accompanied by a body of earls, knights and gentlemen and a force of twelve hundred men. His trump card was Turlough Luineach, the Chief of Tyrone, with whom he had entered a treaty in 1572. Turlough had promised to assist Essex in facing down all opposition to the Crown in Ulster.

Initially, Brian accepted Essex as 'Governor of Ulster', supplying his troops with cattle and assuring him of his fidelity. However, on realising his true intent, he took back his cattle and followed Turlough Luineach into open revolt.

Essex established garrisons at Belfast and Holywood, but depleted by 'Captain Travel, Captain Sickness, Captain Cold and Captain Hunger', and continually harassed by the Irish of Clannaboy his forces were unable to mount any attack.[30] Essex had underestimated both the tenacity of his adversaries and the size of the task he had embarked upon.

Walter Devereux, 1st Earl of Essex. Defeated Sir Brian at Ballymacarrett in 1573, and subsequently had him executed for treason. (National Portrait Gallery, London)

The death of Thomas Smith

On October 20th 1573, Essex finally engaged Sir Brian McPhelim in battle at Massereene. Brian was defeated. During the affray forty *kerne* were slain and four hundred of Sir Brian's cattle were taken. Ironically, that very same day Thomas Smith was shot dead near Mountstewart by one of his Irish retainers, his corpse allegedly being boiled in a vat by Con Mackmeleog[31] and then thrown to hounds.[32] A second equally gory account has Smith taken prisoner by *kerne* and thrown to their hunting dogs which tore him to pieces.

We also know from Smith's correspondence that he feared his Irish labourers, most of whom, as men of Clannaboy, would have been loyal to Sir Brian. Almost inevitably, this led to the suspicion that his assassination had been ordered by Niall McBrian Faghartagh or indeed Sir Brian himself.[33]

A bloody October

Smith's men retreated to Comber where they were besieged by Sir Brian's forces. Alerted to their dire circumstances, Hugh O'Neill of Tyrone and the English garrison came to the aid of Smith's beleaguered men. However, they were halted at the Ford of Belfast by a force loyal to Brian. It appeared that the relief force would be overwhelmed, until Essex arrived, accompanied by three hundred foot and one hundred horse.

Sir Brian's men evaporated into woodlands surrounding Belfast. Essex then proceeded to Comber, which he found in flames, having been raised to the ground by Smith's men as they made their escape into the 'Little Ards... conducted there by Ferdoragh Savage.'[34] Ferdoragh granted them sanctuary, and land to build a tower house, now known as Quintin Castle.

The Battle of Ballymacarrett

With Smith's men ensconced in the Little Ards, Essex returned to the Ford of Belfast where his way was once more impeded by Sir Brian's men.[35] This time, however, there would be no melting away. In October 1573, on the soft sands and in the forests that fringed the ford, the forces of Sir Brian and Essex met in combat. After two hours of heavy fighting Essex prevailed. Sir Brian was forced to retreat. One hundred Clannaboy warriors lost their lives, and that night, in their camp, the English heard the keening, 'for the loss of them that were dead'.[36]

The defeat at Ballymacarrett put Sir Brian on the back foot. He resisted Essex throughout the winter of 1573, but by the spring of 1574 realised that he had little alternative but to sue for peace.

In May 1574, Sir Brian wrote to the Queen from Belfast, advising that he had made a treaty with Essex. The 'Treaty of Kells' won Brian a pardon and allowed him to remain as the Queen's *fermor* in Clannaboy in return for an annual rent of 1500 cattle, a number he promised to increase as his lordship prospered.

The Queen responded positively to his letter, confirming that Essex had full authority to act on her behalf. Sir Brian also agreed to join with Essex against Turlough Luineach, and to refurbish Belfast Castle, which Essex secretly confided that he intended to confiscate for the Queen.[37]

Treachery at Belfast Castle

No sooner had the wax seal hardened on the Treaty than George Smith arrived in the Ards to claim his brother's patent. Sir Brian snapped. Throwing caution to the wind he seized the Carrickfergus garrison's cattle and attempted to starve Essex into abandoning the town. Essex's troops were already sick and starving, with fifteen to twenty dying every day. Brian's tactics worked. Essex withdrew to Newry, but concluded that peaceful coexistence with 'his truculent neighbour' was impossible, writing:

I have no occasion to trust the Irish… My first actions showed nothing but leniency… my next shall show more severity... [38]

Sir Brian was labelled a traitor and a £200 bounty was placed on his head. Determined to unseat him, Essex asked the Lord Deputy to release two high profile prisoners into his custody, namely Sir Brian's older brother, Hugh McPhelim, and his notorious cousin, Con Óg. They would be used, 'for the confusion of Brian, who hath usurped upon them both'.[39]

However, Essex's enemy Lord Deputy Fitzwilliam played havoc with his scheme by setting Con Óg free. Sir Brian now had a triple headache to contend with. Firstly, Essex planned to kill him; secondly, his older brother Hugh remained in Essex's custody; but worst of all, Con Óg, arguably Upper Clannaboy's legitimate ruler, was on the loose and seeking revenge.

Essex turned Fitzwilliam's mischief-making to his advantage, offering to restore Con Óg to his lands on condition that he killed Sir Brian. His offer was readily accepted. Con Óg and two hundred men hid within Carrickfergus, waiting to ambush Sir Brian on his return.

The feast soon turned to treachery. Woodcut by John Derricke. (Mansell Collection)

Sir John Norreys, who led the slaughter of the Clannaboy at Belfast Castle. (National Trust)

But Sir Brian did not come. A new plan was needed. A parley was arranged between Sir Brian and Essex in Belfast Castle. Would Essex and Sir Brian be reconciled? The two entourages gathered and, 'passed three nights and days together pleasantly and cheerfully, all good friends.' Then:

when they were eating and drinking and making merry the treacherous Essex struck, seizing Bryan, his wife and his brother and putting Brian's men unsparingly to the sword – in Bryan's own presence.[40]

Led by Sir John Norreys, who had served with Coligny's Huguenots, Essex's henchmen slaughtered over a hundred of Sir Brian's followers, without regard for age or gender. How long and how loud were the screams of the O'Neills that night in Belfast Castle? How deep ran their blood on its wooden boards and muddy streets? It is hard to overstate the night's horror.

Sir Brian, his wife and Rory Óg were taken to Dublin, where they were tried, found guilty of treason and hung, drawn and quartered. 'Such,' writes Richey, 'was the end of their feast.'

Not guilty M'lord!

Essex was unrepentant, even exultant in the wake of the slaughter. He rebutted all accusations of impropriety, claiming Sir Brian had no legal entitlement to Clannaboy, which properly belonged to Con Óg. Furthermore, Brian had burned numerous monasteries, along with the garrison town of Carrickfergus, from which he had stolen cattle and reduced the garrison to starvation. He had killed Henry Savage Esq., beheaded English soldiers, and been implicated in the murders of Messers Moore and Smith Junior.

Essex maintained he had acted upon intelligence that Sir Brian was 'joined in full confederacy' with Turlough Luineach and 'about to rebel', intending to rendezvous with Turlough at Dundrum Castle. He claimed that Brian's rebellion had been encouraged by rumours 'that the King of Spain was to send speedy aid to the Irish.'

'I gave order that evening to lay hold on him within the castle of Belfyrst in where he lay', he wrote, acknowledging that Sir Brian had been arrested while he slept.[41] He further stated that Sir Brian's men, who were 'lodged in the Towne', offered 'some resistance' and that one hundred and fifteen had been slain. To add insult to injury, Essex confiscated 'three thousand head of cattle besides certain stud mares' from the Ards. Essex then presented six of Sir Brian's best horses to the Lord Deputy to buy his acquiescence.

Was Essex right? Was Sir Brian about to rebel? This question was, indirectly, settled in court. Not content with butchering Sir Brian and his wife, Essex attempted to root out Sir Brian's few, loyal English friends, and accused his confidante Captain Piers of passing military intelligence to Sir Brian. Piers was arraigned. The court passed its own judgement on Essex's claims. It returned a 'Not guilty' verdict.

6
The return of Con Óg
1575-89

Clannaboy divided

Emboldened after Brian McPhelim's execution, Essex re-divided Clannaboy. Under the 'Dromore Agreement' of July 1575, Niall McBrian Faghartagh, son of Brian Faghartagh, became Lord of Upper Clannaboy in County Down. Sir Brian McPhelim's eldest son Shane McBrian was granted three-quarters of Lower Clannaboy in County Antrim, centred on Belfast, while his cousin, Neil received one quarter, centred on Edendubhcarrig. The unpredictable Con Óg and Brian's brother Hugh appear to have been sidelined.

Niall McBrian Faghartagh submitted to the authority of the Queen, promised to be loyal, and was declared Lord of Upper Clannaboy, for the annual rent of one hundred cows.[1] The treaty was copper-fastened by Niall giving up three members of the prominent O'Gilmore family as hostages – being a son in a junior sept could be a precarious position![2] Through this agreement the Crown regained a measure of control in Clannaboy.

Lord of Upper Clannaboy? This sympathetic portrayal of an Irish lord and his attendants, 1581, is by John Derricke, who accompanied Sir Henry Sidney on his campaigns in Ireland. (Mansell Collection).

Sir Henry Sidney, the new Lord Deputy, who knighted Sir Brian McPhelim in 1567, and had the temerity to rename Lough Neagh, Lough Sidney. It didn't stick. (National Portrait Gallery, London)

Significantly, Essex made no protest when Niall McBrian Faghartagh drove the second Smith colony from the Ards.

What state was Upper Clannaboy in when Niall McBrian inherited it? The hugely diminished rent suggests that the years of warfare had taken their toll. The Lord Deputy, Sir Henry Sydney, described Clannaboy as 'all waste and desolate'.[3] In the same year, Essex wrote of Niall McBrian Faghartagh that:

(his) people were few, his cattle less, his husbandmen were starved, dead or run out of the country.'[4]

However, we should be cautious about these sweeping assessments. Military estimates show that in 1575 the Great Ards were settled and prosperous enough to offer the Crown a force of sixty horsemen and three hundred footmen, if called upon to do so.[5] The Sleught Kellies of Comber and Tullynakill could muster one hundred and twenty 'kerne and shott', a second indicator of a relatively healthy economy and population. These probably more telling assessments suggest that Upper Clannaboy's economy and social structure remained fundamentally sound.

Niall McBrian's territory

The Dromore Agreement defined the extent of Niall McBrian's realm. His territory of Upper Clannaboy was bounded by Killultagh to the west, Kilwarlin to the south-west, Kinelarty to the south and the Ards to the south-east. However, within a very short period, Niall had extended his borders to include territory in the Dufferin.

However, in sixteenth century Ulster, political treaties were fragile, contingent matters, instantly disposable should the political wind change. Niall McBrian acted in this spirit when he attacked Essex's successor, Sir Henry Sidney at Carrickfergus. However, given the threat posed by the Scots, Tyrone, and his Lower Clannaboy kin, Niall McBrian's ambivalence towards his agreement with Essex was short-lived and he soon returned to the English fold.

Consanguinity and remarriage

Niall McBrian married his second cousin, Katherine McPhelim, the daughter of Sir Brian McPhelim, and former wife of Hugh O'Neill, then Baron Dungannon. Katherine's first marriage had been annulled on grounds of consanguinity – being of the same blood – strange grounds, given how frequently blood relatives married in Gaelic Ulster.

This matrimonial triangle is replete with irony. First, Niall McBrian's marriage to Katherine also represented a case of consanguinity – one that passed without remark. Secondly Hugh O'Neill's divorce from Katherine was sanctioned by the same church hierarchy that just a few years earlier had so resolutely refused to grant a divorce to Henry VIII. Consider the far-reaching consequences of that debacle! Yet here is Gaelic Ulster's most iconic leader engaging in shenanigans similar to those of England's most notorious King.

Paradoxically, Katherine's brother, Shane McBrian, Lord of Lower Clannaboy, would soon become one of Niall McBrian's fiercest adversaries. Katherine, whom little is known about, would give birth to our protagonist, Con O'Neill.

The return of Con Óg

Con Óg's release from jail by the Lord Deputy posed huge problems for Niall McBrian. Con Óg was chief by tanistry and the ancient order of things. Niall McBrian was chief by the patronage of Essex, a legally perfect but altogether inferior claim.[6]

Con Óg's return to 'Civvy Street' bore all the hallmarks of a mafia don reclaiming his turf following a lengthy prison term. Con Óg saw himself as the rightful Lord of Upper Clannaboy, a view that in his heart of hearts, Niall McBrian probably shared. However, he could not in any circumstances admit this, and a bloody feud with his uncle seemed almost inevitable. Somehow, however, a power-sharing accommodation was found, whereby Con Óg ruled from Castlereagh as lord, with Niall McBrian accepting the subordinate yet significant role of Captain of the Ards.

The Lord Deputy, Sir Henry Sidney, reflected the new arrangement in his 1575 description of the Great Ards as:

almost an Island, a champion and fertile land, and now possessed by Sir Con M'Neill oig Onele, who hath planted there Neil M'Brian Ferto, with sondrey of his owne sirname. But the anncient dwellers there are the Ogilmers a rich and stronge sept of people alwaies followers of the Neils of Clandeboye.[7]

Con Óg had a fearsome reputation as a 'warlike chieftain', and was 'dreaded by the English' garrisoned at Carrickfergus, whose cattle he frequently plundered. According to Carew, his lengthy catalogue of crimes included slaying the Mayor, stealing four hundred cattle, killing the constable along with twenty-four townsfolk, kidnapping Mayor Wallis, and extracting a huge ransom for his release.

Con Óg lived up to his violent reputation in 1579 when he attacked Lecale at Turlough Luineach's behest. Later that year Turlough betrayed him, informing the government of his plot 'to massacre all the English in Lecale, Dufferin and the Ards in one day' – Con Óg did not do things by halves![8] As a consequence, Con Óg was outlawed with a bounty placed on his head. He and his loyal followers spent a year in hiding in the forests of Down, until 'he was taken by (Niall) Brian Feartagh, the rival claimant to his estates, and handed over to Captain Piers at Carrickfergus.'[9] However, this does not quite ring true, and the 'capture' may have been a means of bringing Con Óg in from the cold without causing him to lose face. Con Óg served another short prison stretch, then took control of Upper Clannaboy for the third time.

Con Óg reformed

The Con Óg who returned to power was an altogether mellower figure than the Con Óg of old. He worked within the Dromore Agreement, accepting its formerly unacceptable premise that it was:

thought good to divide the greater government into smaller, that none should be so strong[10]

Though Upper Clannaboy included lands at Lisburn and Lambeg, the River Lagan remained for the most part the border between the Clannaboys, with

Dunluce Castle. Con Óg's son Hugh was killed shortly after an attack on the castle. His death opened the way for Con O'Neill to become tánaiste. (Ireland Highlights)

the English garrison at Belfast Castle policing the peace. Tensions remained in Lower Clannaboy. In Upper Clannaboy, however, things became more settled with Con Óg appearing to conform, and even attending Parliament in Dublin in 1585, 'as representative of the O'Neills of Clannaboy.'[11]

Con Óg's new-found peaceability did not prevent the young bloods of Upper Clannaboy from proving themselves in battle. In 1586, his son, Hugh, joined Alexander McDonnell of the Isles in attacks on Dunluce Castle and the garrison at Coleraine. There followed a pitched battle at Newtown Cunningham in County Donegal, during which Hugh was killed.[12] This fact is easily overlooked but has great significance for our story. It is highly likely that Hugh was Con Óg's *tánaiste* or heir, and that his sudden death allowed an eleven-year-old native of Castle Reagh, Niall McBrian's son, Con O'Neill, to take his place.

In March 1586, Con Óg formally surrendered Upper Clannaboy to Elizabeth. A year later, with its 'metes and bounds' established, it was re-granted to him for his 'faithful services and allegiance'. In return for an annual payment of two hundred and fifty oxen (to be made at Newry), and his agreement to provide sixty foot soldiers, twelve horsemen, and supplies for forty days' service to the Crown, if needed, Con Óg obtained a royal patent for Castle Reagh and 'all the lands from Belfast to Portaferry', to be 'held in *capite* by Knight's service.'[13] To cap it all, Con Óg became Sir Con McNeill Óg.

Con O'Neill, lord in waiting

Buoyed by his division of Clannaboy, Lord Deputy Perrot now partitioned the province of Ulster into nine counties, after the fashion of English shires. These counties will be familiar to the modern reader with the exception of Coleraine, now Derry or Londonderry. However, 'the law was never executed in these new counties by any sheriffs or justices of assize', meaning Gaelic lords still held sway over most of the territory.[14]

Down, a complex, problematic county, was divided into eight territories: Upper Clannaboy, Kilwarlin, the Dufferin, Kinelarty (McCartan's Country), the Great Ards, Iveagh (Magennis's Country), Lecale and Mourne. The Great Ards was included in the territory of Con Óg, along with Upper Clannaboy, Kilwarlin and parts of the forest of Killultagh.

Increasingly, Con Óg conducted himself as an ally of the Crown and in 1588, he accompanied the loyal Irish chiefs to Dublin to bid farewell to Perrot. Having secured the territory of Upper Clannaboy, he died at Castlereagh on the 7th April 1589, leaving no heir.

Sidney's successor Sir John Perrot, who created the nine counties of Ulster, and won the respect of the legendary Con Óg. (National Portrait Gallery, London)

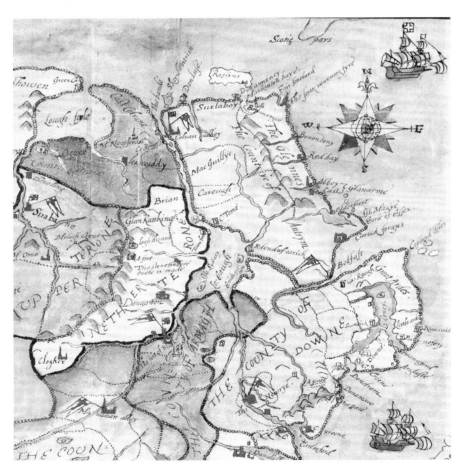

Jobson's c.1598 map of Ulster of shows Perrot's new counties, including 'Upper' and 'Nether Terone'. (Trinity College, Dublin)

7
The inauguration of Con O'Neill
1589

A royal lineage

After Con Óg's death, power passed to his *tánaiste* and great-nephew, Con McNiall McBrian Faghartagh O'Neill. Con was the chosen one, the fittest and most able candidate for leadership. However, at just fourteen years old, he was unready to take the reins of power, so his father Niall McBrian, Captain of the Ards, took on this role and ruled as 'regent' until 1601.[1] As Con matured he will have become increasingly involved in the clan's affairs, effectively serving a twelve year apprenticeship intended to prepare him for leadership and perhaps greatness.

Con McNiall McBrian Faghartagh O'Neill, or more simply Con O'Neill, was born around 1575 into a noble, indeed quasi-royal family. His triple-barrelled name aligned him with leading figures on the Clannaboy family tree, not least the legendary Brian Faghartagh, Lord of all Clannaboy, cruelly assassinated by Shane O'Neill. As such, they were not so much names as titles, which asserted his fitness for lordship and strengthened his claim to loyalty from the clan.

Every inch the aristocrat, Con could trace his lineage back three hundred and forty years to Aodh Buidhe I, father of the House of Clannaboy:

Aodh Buidhe I	(1260-83)	Tyrone
Brian Buidhe	(1291-95)	Tyrone
Henry Buidhe	(1325-47)	Tyrone & Clannaboy
Murtagh Ceannfhada	(1383-95)	Clannaboy
Brian Ballach	(1395-1425)	Clannaboy
Aodh Buidhe II	(1425-44)	Clannaboy
Conn	(1468-82)	Clannaboy
Niall Mór	(1485-1512)	Clannaboy
Niall Óg	(1529-37)	Upper Clannaboy
Brian Faghartagh	(1537-48)	Upper Clannaboy
Niall McBrian	(1589-1601)	Upper Clannaboy
Con	(1601-19)	Upper Clannaboy

As Con approached the inauguration mound the pipes will have played. Uilleann piper, by Albrecht Durer. (Musee des Beaux Arts, Paris)

Con's lineage was also distinguished on his maternal side. His mother, Katherine, was a daughter of Sir Brian McPhelim, and had been previously married to Hugh O'Neill, Lord of Tyrone.[2] It is incredible to think that, in Hugh O'Neill and Niall McBrian, Katherine had married two of the most powerful men in Ulster. More intriguing still is the fact that she bore children to both men, making Con a half-brother to her children by the mighty Earl of Tyrone.[3]

Dynastically aligned with distinguished past chiefs through both parents, Con had an impeccable claim to Upper Clannaboy's lordship.

Con's youth and education

Aside from the fact that Con had four brothers, 'Felymy Duff, Bryan Galtogh… Hugh Murtagh, and Tuathal (Toole)', and so presumably plenty of playmates, little is known of Con's childhood or youthful character.[4]

It is probable that he was educated at the school his brothers attended at Carrickfergus, among the nobility and gentry of Clannaboy. There he would have received a classical education, learning calligraphy (beautifully expressed in his signature), Latin, religion, philosophy and history. In this garrison town, he will probably also have acquired a good working knowledge of English.[5]

Con is also likely to have been fostered, but it is not known where and with whom.[6] There he would have learned the skills required of a chief, such as training in horsemanship and soldiering.

At home in Castle Reagh he will have been steeped in stories about the valiant exploits of his clan. The chief *ollamhs* of Clannaboy will have acquainted him with the intricacies of Brehon Law and the mechanisms of *coyne* and livery, tribute and *bonnaught* (the quartering of troops). He will have travelled the length and breadth of his kingdom at his father's side, learning the intricate politics of clan management, and observing his people as they drove cattle and planted the land. He will have met and got to know Upper Clannaboy's gentry, and been entertained in the houses of English captains and his aristocratic Gaelic neighbours. He will have learned the clan's customs and idiosyncrasies, a formal and informal education intended to prepare him for rule.

The election of Con

It is not known when Con was elected *tánaiste,* or successor to Con Óg. However, the process by which he was chosen is well understood. As we have seen, succession did not inevitably pass from father to son, rather an heir was elected during the lifetime of the chief from among his *derbfine,* or true kin, extending to four generations.[7]

Chosen by a grand council of the clan comprising its nobility, vassal chieftains, *ollamhs* and clergy and ratified by its freemen, the *tánaiste* was deemed the 'most worthy' among his eligible kin by:

virtue of shape and race and knowledge, through wisdom, rank and liberality and honesty, by virtue of hereditary right and eloquence, by strength of fighting and an army…[8]

Con went through this exacting process, and was found the best and strongest candidate.

Following Con Óg's death, the elders of the clan are likely to have acted quickly to ensure his succession, and to have moved relatively swiftly to his inauguration.

Imagining Con's inauguration

There are no accounts of Con's inauguration as chief in 1589, however from the work of Elizabeth Fitzpatrick and others we can imagine what would have taken place.[9]

On the day of Con's inauguration, excitement will have filled the air and a general hubbub of anticipation echoed through the castle. As Con was made ready, the chief men of Clannaboy will have assembled, flanked by gallowglasses, their banners unfurled. Priests in procession sent plumes of incense into the morning sky. Uilleann pipes droned in time to ancient drumbeats as, nervous and excited and with his father by his side, the fourteen year old Con appeared in the doorway of Castle Reagh and took in the awesome scene.

In 1595, six years after Con's inauguration, Hugh O'Neill was inaugurated at Tullahogue, surrounded by his vassal lords, gallowglasses and ollamhs. (National Maritime Museum, London)

Dressed in a simple tunic and followed by his principal vassals, Con will have made the short walk to the mound of anointing, where he would be hailed chief after the ancient rites of the Clann Aodha Buidhe.

A path will have opened amidst the assembled throng, made up of the religious elite, Con's *derbfine,* and the heads of Upper Clannaboy's various septs. Con's 'court' and advisors will also have been in attendance – his chief counsellor, his treasurer, the keeper of his hostages, his Brehon lawyer, poets, bards of literature and history, his chief builder and his physician, the captains of the wood kerne, his steward and house keeper, his procurator, charged with the procurement of arms and victuals, the keeper of his horses, the keeper of his hounds, his keeper of cattle, his butler and his minstrels, among others.

Then, like his ancestors before him, Con will have climbed the sacred mound to be inaugurated on Clannaboy's historic stone throne.

The ceremony was steeped in ritual. Similar ceremonies had taken place for centuries on the hilltops of Ireland. Sir Henry Sidney mentions an attempted inauguration on this very coronation mound in 1568, when an attempt was made to use the prestige attaching to the mound to sabotage Sir Brian McPhelim:

A large band of Scotts intending, as was said, to create a new Lord of Clanna-boye not farre from Knockfergus, went under that pretence to enter a wood near Castell Reagh[10]

The anointing
Upper Clannaboy's leading clerics will have performed the ceremony's religious rites, including the ritual bathing or washing and anointing of Con's head with holy oil. Then, amid his nobles, warriors, bards and *ollamhs*, Con will have set aside his sword and taken:

an oath to preserve all the ancient former customs of the country inviolable, and to deliver up the succession peaceably to his *tánaiste* (successor); and then hath a wand delivered to him by one whose proper office that is, after which, descending from the stone, he turneth himself round thrice forward and thrice backward.[11]

This thrice-turning, or *deiseal,* symbolised the chief reviewing his territory and his subjects; in essence, claiming lordship over all he surveyed.

An O'Gilmore, being his chief vassal, will have stepped forward to put a mantle on his shoulders, then passed a wand of hazel over his head and placed it in his hand. This symbolised the transfer of power. He will then have taken off his shoe and passed it over Con's head in a symbolic gesture of loyalty.

Next came the *ollamh's* public recitation of the illustrious genealogy of the young prince, before his chief vassal proclaimed him, 'Con McNeill McBrian Faghartagh O'Neill, Lord of Upper Clannaboy' to the resounding cheers of the assembly, which repeated its new chief's name and title. This public affirmation of the chief's name and title was a vital element of the

The overgrown coronation mound of the O'Neills of Upper Clannaboy.

ritual, and is known as the *gairm anma* or *ord an anma*, the proclamation or the ritual of the name.[12]

With this rousing acclamation ringing in his ears, Con will have risen to his feet. Almost instantly, a deferential hush will have descended, as the noble assembly slowly backed away, bowing and kneeling before him. Con then held aloft in his right hand the *slat an tiarna*, the hazelwood rod of lordship, authority and correction.[13]

With the ceremonial concluded, the assembly offered Con its fealty by giving him gifts, often in the form of cattle. Con would have reciprocated by giving his horse to his chief vassal, an act denoting their mutual trust and Con's acceptance of the honour he had received.

Castlereagh's *tulach tionóil*

Con's coronation had all the attributes of ancient permanence. It followed rituals steeped in hundreds of years of tradition. Few attending will have imagined that this would be the last coronation on Castle Reagh's *tulach tionóil*, or hill of gathering.

Within a few short years the use of *tulach tionóil* would all but disappear, to the satisfaction of the English authorities, who feared them as symbols of Gaelic independence. Fear Flatha O Gnimh, the *ollamh* of Lower Clannaboy railed against the deconsecration of these sacred mounds, writing derisively of, *cruacha ar ardaibh aonaigheadh*, or corn stacks on the hills of assembly.[14] He correctly saw the 'agriculturalisation' of hills of assembly and the destruction of their associated stone chairs as a metaphor for the annihilation of Gaelic society.

Probably raised at the same time as the building of Castle Reagh, the *tulach tionóil* is the only element of the complex of structures that once stood on the hill of Castlereagh to survive. It can be seen today as an overgrown mound in the planting at the junction of the Ballygowan and Manse Roads.

Let the feasting begin

With the solemnities completed, the assembly would have returned to Castle Reagh, where a sumptuous *banais righe* or wedding feast would have been served to mark the new chief's marriage to his tribal territory.[15] This was a day for celebrating Clannaboy's rich traditions and past glories, but it was also a time for looking forward. Orations, poetry, music and dancing would have been the order of the day. Songs and praise poems would have been recited by minstrels and poets to mark the auspicious occasion.

Every available bounty of the kingdom would have been served to Con and his guests, each territory in his kingdom being proud to provide a part of the feast. No doubt he enjoyed much of the produce listed by Robert Payne in his account of Ireland's great abundance:

fresh sammon... herrings... makerels... sea breams... hens... egges... pigge... reede deare... beefe... mutton... wild swannes, cranes, phesantes, partriges,

Early seventeenth century wine bottles, fit for Con's table. (Alva MacGowan)

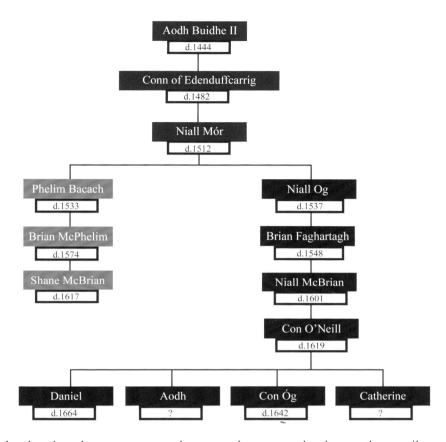

The patrilineal lineage of Con McNiall McBrian Faghartagh O'Neill, last Lord of Upper Clannaboy.

heathcocks, plouers, greene and gray, curlewes, woodcockes, rayles, quailes… oysters, muskels, cockels and samphiere…[16]

Then with the menfolk suitably plied with *aqua vitae* and Spanish wine, and earthen jars lying strewn around the tables, the invincible strength that rises from the euphoria of brotherhood may have stirred the Clann Aodha Buidhe to complete the final act, the *creach*, or cattle raid upon a neighbouring territory. This action proclaimed the strength of the tribe and its new leader. Creachs were not simply pageants, they were often bloody assaults, accompanied by burning, looting and the taking of hostages. Whether one took place that day, is also, alas, unknown.

8
The bloody inter-regnum
1589-1601

The O'Neill, Hugh O'Neill, Earl of Tyrone, the most powerful lord in Ireland. Pressured Niall McBrian into joining his campaign. (National Museums Northern Ireland)

Cartwheels and somersaults

The Ulster of Con's youth was a seething, volatile cauldron of sedition, revolt and intrigue. It is not surprising that Upper Clannaboy's elders asked his father, Niall McBrian, to take charge until Con came to maturity.

The State Papers confirm Niall McBrian's leadership, recording that 'instead of a yearly rent,' he 'keepeth some fifty soldiers' for the use of the Crown. They describe 'divers septs and nations,' such as the Sleught Neills and Sleught Kellies under his authority, who 'challenge to be petty lords, and would expect to be freeholders'. They also note that Niall McBrian is under pressure from within and without, and 'greatly desireth to surrender and to take a new estate of fee simple from Her Majesty, paying yearly rent and other services.'[1]

Reports by the Solicitor-General, Sir Roger Wilbraham, suggest that Niall McBrian ruled with an iron fist – understandable perhaps given the restlessness of the Sleught Neills and Kellies:

Niall McBrian Fertagh, Captain of the Ardes; and McCartan possess their several countries by tanistry and seek no letters patent so long as they may ravin at their pleasure upon the tenants; in no place in this country are the tenants permitted to depart from their lords but at the lord's pleasure… [2]

Pressure builds

Niall McBrian would now lead Upper Clannaboy into a dangerous game of political manoeuvring and intrigue, pitting his wits and military might against Hugh O'Neill in Tyrone, Shane McBrian in Lower Clannaboy, Sorley Boy McDonnell of the Glynnes, and the English garrisons in Carrickfergus and Lecale. He would prove himself a master of chicanery in this topsy-turvy world, alternating between loyalty to Tyrone and the Crown, all the while showing himself to be a tenacious leader and a shrewd reader of the political temperature of the day.

But he could not keep his borders inviolate. In March 1592, Upper Clannaboy was attacked from the north by Sorley Boy McDonnell, who stole, 'two hundred cows beside *garrans* (horses) and other spoil'.[3] In June 1593, Niall McBrian's son Felymy Duff was killed when Owen McHugh and an army of five hundred besieged Comber.[4] Upper Clannaboy was squeezed on all sides. Niall McBrian was under intense pressure.

Would-be English plantations posed another nagging threat. The most developed of these proposals was that of the Lord Chancellor, Sir Robert Weston, who saw County Down as 'a very good fruitful land', but under-farmed and lying 'waste and desolate' for want of 'freeholders'. He wanted to turn Ireland's tribal lands into English-style estates, with tenants paying rent to English-style landlords, who in turn would pay duty to the Crown.[5] Fortunately for Niall McBrian, Weston's plans came to nothing.

Niall McBrian's annus horribilis

In 1594, Hugh O'Neill, formerly Baron Dungannon and now Earl of Tyrone, went to war on the Crown. Nine years of bloody conflict followed, conflict that would change the face of Ulster. Initially, Niall McBrian wanted nothing to do with the rebellion, but Tyrone was determined to enlist Upper Clannaboy's support. In March, he unleashed his hound, Brian MacArt, into the region with two large companies of men. In a show of strength and brutality, MacArt killed local chieftain, Cormac McBrian and 'established himself in Killultagh'. He then proceeded into Lecale, where he 'destroyed seven or eight townlands', including Killyleagh and Ranahaddy, and 'in the most cruel manner, burned men, women and children in the houses.'[6]

In April, Brian MacArt joined forces with the restless Sleught Neills of Upper Clannaboy and Shane McBrian of Lower Clannaboy to attack

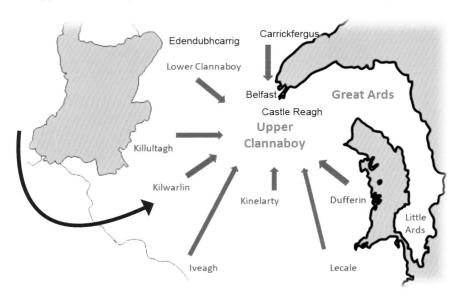

1594, Niall McBrian's annus horribilis. Upper Clannaboy was surrounded by potential enemies and unsettled within. The blue arrow shows Brian MacArt's advance.

Robert Devereux, 2nd Earl of Essex. His father had made Niall McBrian leader and he was as keen as O'Neill to enlist Niall McBrian's support. (National Portrait Gallery)

the English in the heart of Niall McBrian's territory at Castlereagh. Tyrone was making it clear to all Ulster that he would show no mercy to those who opposed or would not stand with him.

1594 was a particularly difficult year for Niall McBrian. He spent most of it walking on eggshells. However, its tribulations proved his mettle. On the 4th June, as Tyrone's rebellion gained momentum, Niall McBrian wrote in worried tone to the Lord Deputy that:

The Earl of Tyrone threatens to take his country and make Owen McHugh… Lord of it, except the writer becomes Tyrone's own man and forsake his Prince.

Niall McBrian wanted to remain loyal to Elizabeth, however Tyrone was intent on cajoling him and other Gaelic families into insurrection.[7] Indeed, whenever Rory Magennis, Captain of Kilwarlin, was about to surrender to the Crown in return for state protection and a patent for his lands, he was, 'utterly expelled out of his country and havoc made of all he had, by Bryan MacArt'.[8]

Killultagh, Lecale and Kilwarlin had already been targeted. Upper Clannaboy would be next. In August, MacArt visited Niall McBrian, compelling him to give a 'buying to the Earl of 3 horses and 60 cows.'[9] In other words, MacArt demanded he part pay for the upkeep of Tyrone's army of occupation.[10]

There was more intimidation to come. Shane McBrian now besieged Niall McBrian's stronghold at Castle Reagh: he was no longer safe in his own home. And in an equally sinister development, a murderous threat was issued against his sons. As a result, the boys were hastily removed from school in Carrickfergus and placed under the protection of Sir Henry Bagnall in Newry.

In November, Tyrone's threat was realised when Brian MacArt, Shane McBrian and Owen McHugh dispossessed Niall McBrian and established Owen McHugh as the pseudo-Lord of Upper Clannaboy. A lesser man would have crumbled, yet with the support of the septs who remained loyal, Niall McBrian managed to re-establish his authority.

In the face of all this turmoil, Carew confirms that Niall McBrian 'long stood for Her Majesty' and Bagnall describes him admiringly as:

the only great man of the neighbourhood who did not 'fly out' with the Earl.[11]

Niall McBrian was considered a loyal ally of the Queen.[12] However, like all loyalties, this was contingent. Niall McBrian was a pragmatist, whose only loyalties were to Upper Clannaboy and himself.

Upper Clannaboy rebels

By 1596, Niall McBrian was able to resist Tyrone's pressure no longer and took Upper Clannaboy into 'confederacy with the Earl'.[13] This led him to play a minor role in an uprising in June 1597 alongside Shane McBrian,

Neil McHugh Óg, Arthur Maginnis and Owen McHugh.[14] However, after taking Belfast Castle the rising was thwarted, and in August its leaders surrendered to Sir John Chichester at Carrickfergus, professing newfound loyalty.[15] The miscreants were duly dispatched to Dublin to stand trial, where each received a prison sentence apart from Niall McBrian. He was reprieved, presumably because of his previous loyalty and his marginal role in the intrigue.

More remarkable still, Shane McBrian escaped with his life despite his merciless butchering of the English garrison during the taking of Belfast Castle. Anthony Dearinge reported that he had ordered 'their throats cut, and their bowels cut out of their bellyes.'[16] Perhaps Shane was avenging the slaughter of the men of Clannaboy at the castle in 1574 and the execution of his father, Sir Brian McPhelim.

During this period, Niall McBrian was continually courted or cajoled by either Tyrone or the 2nd Earl of Essex, who became Lord Lieutenant in 1599. Essex believed Niall McBrian might defect again:

Neil O'Neill (Niall McBrian) and the Earl (Tyrone) are almost thoroughly agreed. The only difference is as to a castle, which the said Neill has in his possession and which he wishes the Earl to let him enjoy.[17]

And sure enough, Niall McBrian joined forces with Tyrone after his victory at the Yellow Ford, when the pendulum swung in Tyrone's favour. The English saw this as going against Niall McBrian's deepest instincts, for the 'Clandeboys naturally hate Tyrone, and now only follow him for fear.'[18]

The return of the enforcer

The *Carew Manuscripts* record that in April 1599 Niall McBrian had eighty foot soldiers and fifty cavalry in the service of Hugh O'Neill, an underestimation of his strength as he was always able to bolster his ranks by recruiting Scottish mercenaries.[19] Upper Clannaboy was now in a state of complete turmoil as its septs divided, with many rallying to Tyrone's cause.

Niall McBrian's dilemma was further compounded by the return

The defeat of Sir Henry Bagnall in 1598 at the Battle of the Yellow Ford tempted Niall McBrian to join with the victorious Tyrone. (Trinity College, Dublin)

of Tyrone's arch-enforcer. Brian MacArt camped 'for a time among the creaghts' (common people) to convince 'them of the necessity of going to war' in support of Tyrone. MacArt allowed no-one wriggle room: 'any doubtful parties had a visit from MacArt who soon brought them to the test.'[20]

Tyrone then established three satellite camps in eastern Ulster to ensure that its clans remained loyal: 'one under Magennis in Lecale… a second in the Great Ardes, with the forces of South Clandeboy, in the command of Brian MacArt'[21] and a third at Glenarm in County Antrim.

Although Niall McBrian could field a force of some three hundred shot,[22] MacArt's occupation force of '600 shot, 200 targeteers, and 120 horse' considerably outnumbered him.[23] Another account suggests an even greater force had entered the Lower Ards (the northern part of the peninsula) consisting of, '900 shot, 300 targeteers and 240 horse.'[24] This huge encroachment helped to ensure that Niall McBrian, at least tacitly continued to support the rebellion. However, the fact that Niall McBrian was forced to provide MacArt with hostages as a guarantee of his loyalty suggests that he was at best a reluctant conscript.

Supplying the insurgency

Brian MacArt's considerable encampment in Lecale and the Ards was supplied by produce exacted from the local septs and by a chain of 'sundry Scottish boats and barks' arriving into the bays of Dundrum and Strangford Lough 'with munitions, morions (visorless helmets) and swords'.[25] It would appear that King James VI of Scotland had turned a blind eye to his subjects' clandestine enterprises, or had begun arming and encouraging Tyrone's rebellion:

There are two brethren at Ayre that are merchants for Tyron, and all that country trade thither… these Scottishmen send over the powder and munitions in very small boats of ten, sixteen and twenty tons… Upon complaint made by Mr. Nicolson of these Scottishmen that do furnish the enemy with powder and munitions, the Scots King did put them to the horn on the Friday, and restored them again the Saturday following.[26]

Consignments also arrived from the River Humber in England, Denmark and France:

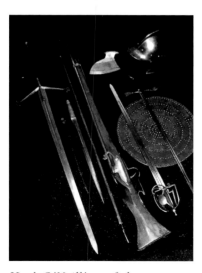

Hugh O'Neill's confederate army was well equipped with modern weaponry, supplied with the connivance of James I. (Claiomh)

a Frenchman called Petite Ognette, came last week into Strangford, with wine, salt, iron and some powder, unto Brian MacArt.[27]

Brian MacArt's camps and not Castlereagh were now the local centre of power.

Secret negotiations
Even though Upper Clannaboy had fallen completely under Tyrone's cosh, Essex had not given up on weaning Niall McBrian away from Tyrone. In June 1599, he sent one of his captains to:

parly with such rebels as... Niall McBrian Ferto and McCartan… who as we are informed inwardly hate Tyrone, of whom you shall demand what service they will do to Her Majesty if they should be taken into protection.[28]

However, Brian MacArt's agents frustrated his efforts, causing Essex to send in a female spy, 'because a man should have been suspected'. This reveals the extent of Tyrone's networks in the region but also how much he feared an alliance between Upper Clannaboy and the English. Essex reported:

if Tyrone's shot (musketeers) were gone out of his town into the country he (Niall McBrian) would come to speak with me where I would appoint at the seaside, but I was advertised that he was so waited on that he could neither send to me, nor I to him.[29]

Pope Clement VIII, who made O'Neill 'Lieutenant General of All the Catholics of Ireland'. (Private collection)

Eventually, negotiations took place and Niall McBrian did indeed change sides, placing '80 foot and fifty horse'[30] at Essex's disposal.[31] Captain Robert Bethell wrote that he could 'trust non but Niall McBrian'. But this alliance put Niall McBrian and the septs who remained loyal to him out of step with the rest of Gaelic Ulster.

Papal pressure
The Gaelic lords were also encouraged by the Papacy to back Tyrone's 'extirpation of heresy' in Ireland. Pope Clement conferred the title of 'Lieutenant General of all the Catholics of Ireland' on Hugh O'Neill and sent Matthew d'Oviedo with 'indulgences and remission of sins to all who would take arms against the English in defence of the Faith; and to O'Neill a plume of Phoenix feathers.'[32]

Tyrone's followers were offered the same cleansing of sin that had been granted to the medieval Crusaders.[33] Sir Geoffrey Fenton suggests that the Pope's offer of salvation circulated widely:

There is some bulls come over from the Pope... put forth through all Ireland. I saw one that came up, which was sent to Clandeboy.[34]

But d'Oviedo brought Tyrone more than the blessing of God's representative on earth. He also brought money. With him, in heavy chests, came 'from His Catholic Majesty, Philip III, 22,000 pieces of gold to pay the army.'[35] O'Neill used the money to recruit Irish, Scottish and English soldiers, promising,

Papal Bull from Pope Clement VIII. A Bull was allegedly sent to Clannaboy offering remission of sins to all who defended the faith. (Private collection)

'whosoever will come to serve the King of Spain under his command will have 20s. a month', which the English countered with the rumour that the Spanish coin was 'not good but forged.'[36]

The arrival of Arthur Chichester

In 1599, with war raging across Ulster, Arthur Chichester arrived from England to take up the job of Governor of Carrickfergus, rising to become 'second in command' to Lord Mountjoy.[37] Chichester was an experienced soldier who had fought against the Armada, and commanded ships under Sir Francis Drake, and Essex at the Siege of Cadiz.

He had also experienced personal loss in Ireland. His brother had been killed in a skirmish with James McDonnell, chief of the Scots. John had been beheaded on a rock and his head sent to the camp of Tyrone, where it was used as a football.[38] Given this raw, personal tragedy and heinous debasement of his brother's corpse, it is perhaps understandable that he hated the rebels with a vehement intensity. Chichester arrived in Ireland bent on revenge.

Scorched earth

Mountjoy understood that while Ulster's rich granaries and pastures were in Tyrone's control, his rebellion would be sustained. So he commanded his forces to deploy scorched earth tactics and Chichester mercilessly pursued this objective. One of his first actions was to 'waste (Con's) father's country, whence Brian MacArt and some 400 bonnaughts (mercenaries) were maintained and fed.'[39] By destroying MacArt's access to food and grazing, Chichester hoped to flush him out of the Ards.

Fynes Moryson records that Chichester:

slew all four-footed animals in the Irish farm steadings, he burned the stacks of grain… and in early summer mowed down the growing crops…[40]

famously declaring that, 'a million swords will not do them so much harm as one winter's famine'.

An 'unremitting devastation was inflicted' upon the Irish 'without compunction for age or sex.'[41] Chichester was clinical and relentless. He destroyed crops ripening in the field, harvested crops in winter storage, and disrupted the planting and setting of seed in springtime. He stole and killed livestock, particularly targeting the horses and oxen used in ploughing. Nothing could escape his hellish reach. Chichester wrote:

they starve miserably and eat dogs and mares and garrons… Starvation… is the only thing that will cut the throat of the grand traitor.[42]

These tactics were not of course an English invention. They had previously been deployed to devastating effect by Shane O'Neill, Brian McPhelim and Tyrone himself.[43] None, however, used them as systematically or to such powerful effect as Chichester, who swept the countryside, 'as with a fiery broom from hell', all the while covetously eyeing up the fish-filled loughs and rivers and fertile, tree-covered lands of Down. (As T.M. Healey astutely observed, 'The Northern war made Chichester acquainted with everything of value in Ulster.'[44]) This unrelenting assault sent a clear message to the septs of Upper Clannaboy: support Brian MacArt at your peril.

Con's coming of age

As the Nine Years War raced to a climax, an ominous cloud of uncertainty and foreboding enveloped Upper Clannaboy. In May 1600, with the

'As with a fiery broom from hell'. Both Chichester and Tyrone engaged in a scorched earth policy to bring their enemies to their knees. (Mark Pillsbury)

outcome uncertain and both sides sensing imminent victory, Con O'Neill 'and his horsemen' were received 'into her majesty's pay'.[45] Con was going to war on the side of the Crown, no doubt at his father's behest.

Was this the twenty-five-year-old's first action? And if so, why did he not 'come of age' earlier? Or was he by this stage an experienced and highly regarded commander, whose war had not been recorded because he had survived? (Only deaths tend to be recorded.) The answers to these questions are unknown. As is the question of why, at twenty-five, Con had not taken full control of the clan. Did his father dominate him? Was he reluctant to hand over power? Was it because Upper Clannaboy was at war? Again, we don't know. All that is clear is that in 1600, Con and his soldiers fought for the Queen, receiving a handsome daily stipend of twenty shillings, paid by a Captain Jephson on Chichester's behalf.[46]

9
Con at home and at war
1601

Two sudden deaths

On the 5th February 1601, the fragile stability of Upper Clannaboy was shaken to its core; Con O'Neill's father and mentor, Niall McBrian, died in Carrickfergus.[1] His mother Katherine died on the same day. Were they struck down by disease? Involved in a freak accident? The darker, but equally likely explanation is that someone had them killed. But who? Surely not Tyrone, for Katherine was his first wife? Surely not Chichester, for whom Niall McBrian was a valued ally? Or did one of them have Niall McBrian murdered to bring the callow Con to power?

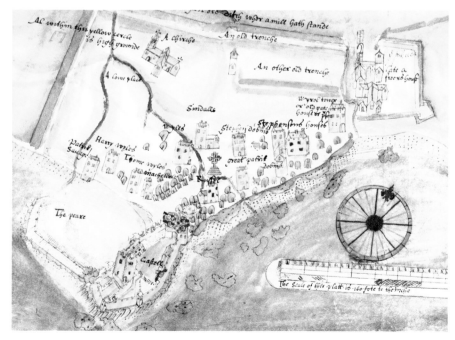

1567 Map by Robert Lythe of Carrickfergus, where Con's parents Katherine and Niall McBrian died in mysterious circumstances. (British Library)

Irish musketeer. Chichester's recruitment of some of MacArt's musketeers sapped O'Neill's strength. (Tony Barton)

Anything is possible. We can imagine Con being devastated by the sudden loss of his parents. The shock and trauma that he will have felt can only be imagined.

Con's leadership challenged

And he did not get time to grieve. Immediately after their deaths, his leadership of Upper Clannaboy was challenged by Owen McHugh, his second cousin and a fervent supporter of Tyrone. This challenge was also deeply personal. Owen McHugh had killed Con's brother, Felymy Duff at Comber in 1593.

The challenge took place against a background of intensified conflict. Brian MacArt was still in Down, and with support from 'Killultagh and Kilwarnan' his force had increased to six or seven hundred *bonnaught*.[2] However, in a decisive spring offensive, Chichester drove MacArt 'out of the Upper Clannaboy and Dufferin', causing him to save 'himself by his legs and bogs, leaving his horse behind.'[3] Upon MacArt's defeat 'the gentlemen began to revolt from him, and offer submission and obedience to Her Majesty.'[4] Their fear of MacArt melted away after the public parading of his riderless steed. Chichester was even able to recruit some of his leading musketeers to serve in the defence of Upper Clannaboy.

However, the uneasy peace in Upper Clannaboy was overshadowed by the brooding threat posed by Tyrone, 'which makes the inhabitants doubtful and timorous to become true subjects.'[5]

Con's challenger, Owen McHugh, had been Brian MacArt's strongest ally in the region. McHugh now came in from the cold, providing Chichester, the power broker, with a leadership conundrum to resolve.

The Upper Clannaboy compromise

On the face of it, Chichester should have had no dilemma. Con was Niall McBrian's anointed heir and his loyal pensioner. Owen McHugh, who had coveted Clannaboy from the days of Brian McPhelim, had a slender claim to the territory through his great-grandfather, Niall Mór, and a history of rebellion.[6]

But Chichester could not resist the opportunity to exploit the situation, and did so by provisionally dividing the territory between the rivals, under the jurisdiction of Sir Fulke Conway. Both were required to provide Chichester with pledges of loyalty which was further guaranteed by an ingenious clause stating that, 'he that did Her Majesty best service, should have… superiority over the country.'[7] This ensured that each would strive to outdo the other in service to the Crown, their prize being overall control.

Con O'Neill and Owen McHugh would now form part of a new defensive strategy for the region, with Con assigned to the open plain, and Owen to the wooded areas he had previously infiltrated. At this time, the Crown had 1,250 foot soldiers and 175 cavalry in the region. Con and Owen added some four hundred men, who served in Chichester's *bonnaught*.

English troops by John Derricke, 1581. Upper Clannaboy provided almost a quarter of Chichester's force during his Down campaign in 1601. (Mansell Collection)

However, Tyrone wasn't prepared to give up Upper Clannaboy and in April he sent reinforcements to Brian MacArt, who immediately attacked Owen's force in the wood of Dufferin, before breaking out into the plain, defended by Con O'Neill. Both men stood their ground and successfully repelled the invaders.

Hearing of the attack, Chichester sent the English garrison to their aid. During the affray, some eighty Irish were killed on either side, including Owen McHugh. Chichester's account of the affray was typically caustic, 'It was good service on both sides, for never an honest man was slain.'[8]

Great Teirne and Lord of Upper Clannaboy

Owen McHugh's death finally allowed Con to take control of Upper Clannaboy, acknowledged as chief by his clan and the Crown through Chichester. It was a significant moment. Had Owen McHugh won Upper Clannaboy, Tyrone could have had all Gaelic Ulster behind him, an alliance the English would have found hard to resist.

At the age of twenty-six, Con had finally come into his birthright. To the clan he was their *Great Teirne*, or chief, charged with governing the land on behalf of the tribe – a fact that had become somewhat blurred in the 16th century, when Irish chieftains increasingly acted as pseudo-landlords. Con would be the last Gaelic Lord of Upper Clannaboy and last Gaelic occupier of Castle Reagh.

View across the Lagan Valley to the Belfast Hills from the site of Castle Reagh.

The Eagle's Nest

Con lived in Castle Reagh with his wife Eilish. She will have been in her mid-teens, and the couple, who had probably married a year or two previously, will initially have shared the castle with Con's parents and siblings. They lived comfortably, but under threat from MacArt, McBrian and even Eilish's uncle, the Earl of Tyrone. As yet they had no family, but would go on to have four children: Daniel, thought to have been born in around 1604, Aodh Buidhe (Hugh Boy) born about 1611, Con Óg (c.1614), and Catherine, who seems to have been born around 1620. The couple are likely to have had more children, but only these four are known to have survived infancy.

Their home, the hilltop fortress of Castle Reagh, was built years before on the reputed site of an Early Christian rath.[9] Situated 135 metres (440 feet) above sea level, on one of the highest points along the Castlereagh Hills, their tower house dominated the skyline, offering panoramic views of the Lagan Valley, Knockfergus Lough and the Belfast Hills. To the east they had a fine view across the Dundonald Gap to the Holywood Hills, where Stormont stands today.

Con would have enjoyed these views, but only after the fall of the leaves, or from the upper stories of the castle, as the landscape beyond its immediate vicinity was heavily wooded. The castle stood out above a canopy of trees.

The wooded valley below it led down to a swampy, marshy plain and the winding River Lagan. At the ford of the Lagan, a speck in the distance, stood the village of Belfast or *Belfearste*, which consisted of a fort and a church, with dwellings nearby.

The Presbyterian historian James Seaton Reid, writes of the 'imposing fortress of Castlereagh… for many generations the place of inauguration and chief seat of the O'Neills, Princes of Clandeboy.[10] Locally, Castle Reagh was referred to as 'the Eagle's Nest', shorthand that reflected Con's lofty position and power.

Living in Castle Reagh

The emergence of tower houses, or *caisleán*, on the Ulster landscape, coincided with the resurgence of the Gaelic clans. Hundreds dot the countryside, making Ulster one of the most castellated regions of the British Isles.

Castle Reagh or Caisleán Riabhach seems to have been a fine example. It is thought to have been a towering stone structure, some three or four storeys high, with a surrounding bawn 100 feet square. It boasted an angled turret on each corner and was surrounded by a fosse or ditch that may have been part of the original rath, and proclaimed the power of the O'Neills of Upper Clannaboy and their young chief, Con McNiall McBrian Faghartagh.

Riabhach is normally translated as grey, but it can mean grey-brown, streaked, or speckled. Its use here is unclear. Were Caisleán Riabhach to have been built of local shale, then the translation grey would work best. Were it, however, to have included sandstone, not quite so conveniently available, but available in the upper slopes of the nearby Lagan valley, then *riabhach* meaning grey-brown, mottled or specked begins to make sense. Either way, it would appear that the castle was not 'harled' or given a white coat of limewash and crushed pebbles.

Consisting of a single, stand-alone keep, later surrounded by a bawn, Castle Reagh provided a fortified residence for Con's family and inner circle. It will have also have served as an administrative hub, a storehouse and a seat of justice.

Like most tower houses, it was probably square and four storied, with upward tapering walls and a protruding skirt, or batter, at its base.[11] The security of the entrance was paramount, so it would have had a thick door, above which there may have been an open stone box or *machicolation*, through which missiles could be launched at assailants.[12]

The main door led into a small lobby or guard room. This led on to secure inner doors, above which was the infamous murder hole. Unwelcome guests, who had breached the front door, were now musket fodder for guards positioned above on the first floor.

The ground floor was probably enclosed by a vaulted ceiling, whose stones gave strength to the upper floors. It would have been a store for sacks of grain, flour, vegetables, salt, hung meats and fowl, butter, cheese, wine, whiskey, beer and water, alongside firewood, kindling, tallow, and candles – everything necessary to sustain the chief's household from day-to-day, or in the worst case, during a siege. The ground floor may also have served as the kitchen, incorporating an oven and large iron and earthenware pots.[13] We know that the castle lacked an internal well as one of the castle's previous occupiers, Captain Barrowe, had to travel 'one quarter of a mile to fetch his water', which would have made the castle vulnerable during a siege.[14]

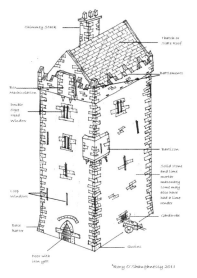

A tower house similar to Castle Reagh, though lacking its four external turrets. (Rory O'Shaughnessy)

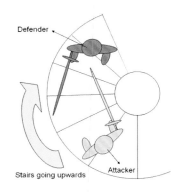

The spiral stairwell gave the advantage to the defenders.

Access to the upper floors was by *mural* stairs leading on to a spiral staircase commencing on the first floor. The spiral staircase required the addition of an external corner tower. The spiral usually ascended clockwise, providing greater stability for defenders, who could hold on to the central newel post, whilst raining down blows on any onrushing attacker. Steps were often left uneven to trip up would-be assailants.

Each storey was usually divided into main and subsidiary chambers. The first storey may have been sleeping quarters, containing simple beds of straw sacking or rushes for the chief's personal guard and servants. It may also have housed the armaments and a guard room, forming a defensive buffer for the rest of the castle.

The second floor would have contained Con and Eilish's living quarters and may have included their private chamber. The upper floor may have had a vaulted ceiling and would have been where the couple entertained guests and hosted banquets. This 'hall' would have been furnished with a banqueting table and wooden benches, and would also have had a large open fire and hearth. It would probably have been decorated with wall hangings, ornate wooden panels, and boasted larger windows than the narrow defensive windows of the lower floors.

Above this floor was the external wall-walk, affording panoramic views, protected by *crenellations*, or regular gaps, which provided cover to lookouts, archers and musketeers.

The thick walls sometimes housed mini chambers, recesses, or cupboards, used for anything from storage to dressing rooms, or mini alcoves for lights. One such chamber would have contained the *garderobes* (latrines), a rudimentary stone seat:

set over a downward flue which allowed waste matter to fall through the shaft to an opening in the external wall-face where it was jettisoned from the building'[15]

The tower seems to have been enclosed by a protective stone wall or bawn. This provided shelter for the chief's prized livestock and horses and served as the first line of defence should the castle face attack. Watchtowers and crenellations on the outer rampart may have provided cover for lookouts.

The area beyond the bawn would have been cleared and used for growing corn and oats, or for animal enclosures. The castle will also have provided a centre for settlement and trade.

The castle's structure will have contrasted starkly with the simple homes of Con's people, most of whom lived in structures consisting of heaped sods of earth, or post-and-wattle, topped by branches, sods or thatch. These single-roomed dwellings could be erected in less than a day, were windowless, had a central hearth and an opening in the roof to allow smoke to escape. Very few, if any, lived in stone-built houses.

The inner workings of a tower house, after Kilcrea Castle, County Cork. (J.G. O'Donoghue)

Con's land and people

Con O'Neill held an extensive territory, bounded to the west by the MacRory's of Kilwarlin, bounded north-west of the Lagan by Killultagh, 'the oak-wood of Ulster', controlled by Cormack McNeill, and bounded north of the Lagan by Lower Clannaboy, controlled by Shane McBrian. In the south-west his lands extended to McCartan's country of Kinelarty, and to the south he was bounded by the English territory of Lecale and the Dufferin. Con's lands stretched down the Ards Peninsula to the Blackstaff River, where they met the lands of the Savages of the Little Ards.

The septs who occupied this territory and gave him their allegiance included:

- The warlike O'Gilmores, who held lands between Holywood and Bangor
- The O'Mulcreevys of Groomsport
- The O'Flinnes de Enischargie, possessors of the mid-Ards including the townlands of Inishargy, Ballygarvan, Kircubbin, Ballyobeggan, Roddens, Ballylimp, Glastry, Fish-Quarter, etc.
- The powerful Kearneys of the Lower Ards
- The M'Gees of Portavogie
- The O'Kellys from the Lagan basin, who 'occupied one of the nine subdivisions of Upper Clannaboy' and lived around Comber and Tullynakill.

Upper Clannaboy was no mean inheritance and Con was no minnow in the Ulster pond.

MacArt seizes Castle Reagh

With matters settled in Upper Clannaboy and Con ensconced as lord in Castlereagh, Chichester marched to Massereene where he subdued Neil McHugh, taking Edendubhcarrig Castle. The Earl of Tyrone countered by sending his strong arm, Brian MacArt, back into Upper Clannaboy. Notwithstanding his recent humiliation by Chichester, MacArt was far from defeated, and exploited Chichester's absence to seize Castle Reagh.

Chichester wrote to Robert Cecil saying that he had been promised 'Castle Reagh… lost in my absence'. But this seems unlikely. Chichester could embroider the truth, especially when it came to adding to his personal estate. He assured Cecil that he would take the castle back by force.

Con, whose men may have been fighting alongside Chichester in Antrim, will have been humiliated by Brian MacArt's coup, and the familiar message it conveyed, i.e. that nowhere and no-one was beyond Tyrone's reach. He would have been equally nonplussed had he known of Chichester's designs on his castle. Losing it to an O'Neill from Tyrone was bad enough, but the idea of an Englishman residing there was unthinkable!

Though he had bested Brian MacArt on the Plain of Down just weeks before, Con did not attempt to retake his home.

Taking the fight to Tyrone

During the winter of 1600, Chichester found a new way to take the fight to Tyrone. Tyrone had avoided pitched battles, and engaging his forces had proven nigh impossible as conditions made troop movements difficult, and

Chichester's 'Queen's Boat' strikes fear into Tyrone, as recalled in the Barony Map of c.1609. (Public Record Office of Northern Ireland)

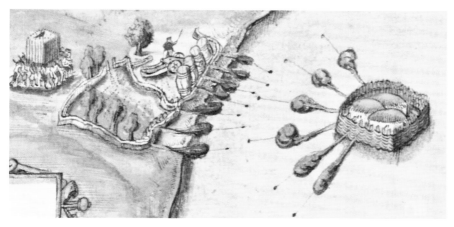

The Irish were given no hiding place. Attack on a crannog from Richard Bartlett's map of c.1602. (National Library, Ireland)

Tyrone's men had the greater local knowledge. The war had become a game of cat and mouse, in which Tyrone's mice had too many boltholes.

Chichester's answer was to commission four new ships, one of thirty tons, 'The Queen's Boat', along with a number of smaller craft. In the spring of 1601, these crossed the Lough from Chichester's naval base at Massereene, striking into Hugh O'Neill's heartland. Each attack delivered sixty troops into Tyrone, taking the enemy unawares.

Chichester, the master of euphemism, records one such raid in which over a hundred were killed:

The last service was upon Patrick O'Quinn, whose house and town were burnt, wife, son, children, and people slain, and himself, of a hurt received in flying from his house.[16]

The attack on the O'Quinns took place at Edendork, four miles from Dungannon, and inland from the shores of Lough Neagh. We should pause a moment to unpick this statement. Too often, we skim the surface of such descriptions and miss the suffering that lies behind them. Patrick O'Quinn was a top man in Tyrone and 'his people' were not fictional characters, they were real people slaughtered in a frenzied moment. Furthermore, this was not just the killing of a single family, it was carnage involving the destruction of a small community.

Imagine the barbarity of the scene as panic and screaming filled the air. Imagine the despairing attempts of parents to catch up their children, the frantic clambering to escape, or the fruitless attempts to defend against relentless blows raining down on limb and bone. Visualise the macabre aftermath, now quiet, as some lie torn apart by sword, some run through by pike, none spared, not the beasts, not the corn in the field. Chichester was letting all Tyrone know that there would be no hiding place from his sword.

Captains Bodley and Blarney reported a similar assault upon a crannog on Lough Rorcan near Newry which served as a 'magasine' or storehouse for Tyrone's allies in that country:

the shot playing incessantly upon the island, while the other delivered their arrows (wildfier), suddenly the houses fired and burst so vehemently, as the rebels lodging there forsook the island, and swumme to the further shore… (they) killed there six kerne, gaining their armes, besides churles and calliachs… eight swumme away, of which foure were shot in the water… the rest were killed or lay hurt on the island… (they) brought away some cowes and sheepe and other pillage… and a great store of butter, corne, meale and powder was burnt.[17]

With the Irish committed to guerrilla warfare and unwilling or unable to engage the English in battle, Mountjoy, Chichester and Dowcra visited atrocity after 'unheard of atrocity… upon the ancient territory of the *Hy Nial.*'[18]

The retaking of Castle Reagh
In June 1601, Chichester rendezvoused with the Lord Deputy Mountjoy near Dundrum, where he received a reinforcement of some 200 men. Now, in one of the great ironies of our story, Chichester, who coveted Clannaboy for himself, was ordered to retake Castle Reagh from McArt and restore it to Con. With MacArt occupied elsewhere, Chichester seized his opportunity and on the morning of the 6th July 1601, 'besieged' the castle in a surprise attack, retaking it that same day with minimal casualties.[19]

Con was restored in a saga which seemed to lay bare Upper Clannaboy's weakness and its dependency on the Crown. However, all was not as it seemed. There may have been method in Con's inaction. There were undoubtedly manoeuvrings behind the scenes that Chichester was unaware of.

The expulsion of MacArt freed Chichester to unleash an audacious plan to 'damnify and amaze the Traitor' by establishing a frontier garrison 'within five miles of Dungannon'.[20] The waiting game was over. Chichester was ready to launch a series of decisive, military strikes that would bring the war into Tyrone's backyard.

10
Rebellion!
1601

With the arrival of Spanish support for Tyrone imminent, the Muster-Master of Ireland, Sir Ralph Lane, was tasked with recording the number of soldiers on the Queen's payroll. His ledger lists Con O'Neill as having forty horse in service to the Crown.

However, this was Gaelic Ulster, and all was not as it seemed. Within the month, Con had forsaken the English muster. Chichester's removal of his forces to Tyrone, and the news that 'Spanish assistance' was en route to Ireland, 'caused Con O'Neill, "the young Lord of Clannaboy" to revolt treacherously' just weeks before the Spanish landing.[1]

With Chichester mired deep in Tyrone, Con and three hundred and fifty of his *bonnaught* joined forces with Hugh O'Neill.[2] Like his father before him, Con had proven a fickle ally, tilting his cap in the direction of those he thought might win the day.

His dramatic volte face did not come out of the blue. Tyrone is likely to have been working on Con ever since he took power, and probably before. Youngish, unused to exercising authority, and deprived of his father's council, Con will have been seen as eminently recruitable. And Tyrone could be persuasive. He mixed charm with bluster, and promises with threats. Brian MacArt's capture of Castle Reagh is likely to have been just the visible part of an iceberg-sized campaign to wean Con away from the Crown.

Having no recourse to a standing army, Con will have mustered his foot and horse from the ranks of the Clannaboy's numerous septs. With him too came Scottish mercenaries, lured by the prospect of payment and land.

Led by Ustian McDonnell, these Scots were formidable warriors, armed with bows, arrows, and the infamous claymore sword. A contemporary account describes them as:

pyked and scelected men of great and mightie bodies, crewel without compassion. The greatest force of the battell consisteth in them, chosing rather to dye than to yeelde…[3]

Scottish mercenaries strengthened Con's armies. (ex Barry R. McCain, The Laggan Redshanks)

With these men behind him, Con went on the offensive. The *Calendar of State Papers* records that:

In August 1601, Con O'Neale, Ustian McDonnell and McAlexander Roe, who had formerly submitted to the Governor of Carrickfergus (Chichester), went again suddenly into rebellion and possessed themselves of the Dufferin, save only the Castle of Ranahady.[4]

Ustian McDonnell now laid claim to the Lordship of the Dufferin. Con championed his cause, throwing Upper Clannaboy and the Dufferin into turmoil. The English garrison, billeted in the region by Chichester, was quickly overrun and forced to retreat to Ringhaddy Castle on the shores of Strangford Lough.[5] Con's force, which had originally been deployed by Chichester to ensure the peace of the region, now launched unrelenting

Set on a narrow, highly defensible peninsula, Ringhaddy Castle held out against Con's furious assaults.

attacks upon Ringhaddy. However, its indomitable seneschal, Edward Brookes, repelled their daily assaults.

Ustian McDonnell's involvement represented a significant coup for Tyrone and an ominous development for the English. Ustian was a grandson of the late Sorley Boy McDonnell and nephew of Randal McDonnell, the newly crowned chief of the Glens. The English had devoted much effort to keeping the Scots out of the war in Ulster. Now the Scots and Con had declared for Tyrone, the odds seemed to shift towards an Irish victory.

Rebellion crushed

Con's defection incensed Chichester, who a year previously had made Con his pensioner. He had recently confirmed Con's lordship and just two months before had graciously restored him to Castle Reagh:

for which favour he (Con) so well requited him, (and)… betrayed all trust that was committed to him'.[6]

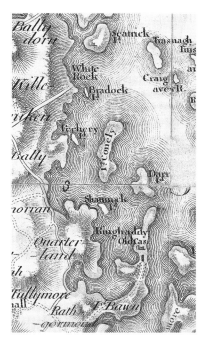

Ringhaddy Castle on Williamson's map of 1810. (University College, Dublin)

But events now conspired against Con. Unfortunately for the rebels, a secret dispatch from Ustian to Randal McDonnell requesting reinforcements was intercepted by the English. Chichester returned from Tyrone to 'banish Con out of those parts (the Dufferin)'.[7] He then placed an English garrison at Newtown to 'settle the country' and prevent the rebellion spreading to the Ards.[8]

Unaware that their message had not reached the Glens and that reinforcements would not be forthcoming, Con's forces continued their siege. Chichester now rendezvoused with Shane McBrian, Lord of Lower Clannaboy, at Carrickfergus, and a force one thousand strong descended upon the Dufferin, an army that dwarfed Con's by almost three to one.[9]

Catching Con unawares, Chichester mounted a night attack on his camp in the forest of Dufferin. The *Calendar of State Papers* records how Chichester, 'unlooked for, surprised the said Con O'Neale on the sudden when he was aslape in the woods!' suggesting that the element of surprise was complete.[10] Chichester writes that he 'charged their camp in the fastnage where they lay', suggesting that Con's camp was naturally well defended.[11] Imagine the terror that shook the camp as Con's bleary-eyed troops woke to the sight of English horsemen in their battle armour, their swords and pikes glistening in the moonlight!

On realising their camp was under attack, Ustian ran out to meet his assailants. With sword drawn menacingly, he charged straight for Chichester, 'but by a couple of bullets shot out of a pistol he was there fortunately slain.'[12] All who fought back were swiftly cut down. After much slaughter Con and McAlexander Roe surrendered, and Con was taken in chains to Carrickfergus Castle, from where Chichester boasted:

My endeavours on them have been so successful that Con is now prisoner with me in Her Majesty's castle and Ustone, the Scot and divers others are slain.[13]

English cavalrymen from c.1600, such as surprised Con's camp at night. (David Sque Illustrations)

There can be little doubt that Con was lucky to have been taken alive. We can only imagine the exchange between the two men as Con was brought before Chichester. However, if Chichester felt tempted to have Con's throat quietly cut in the dark woods of the Dufferin, he did not allow himself to do so. Like Sir Brian McPhelim before him, Con was too important a figure to be dispatched in this way, so he was arraigned and accused of conspiring to expel the English from the Dufferin. For Chichester, there was but one path to peace in Ulster – the crushing of the Celtic alliance between the Scots of the Glens and the Ulster Gaels.

Young man in a hurry

What had caused the young lord to rebel? Chichester's removal and the arrival of the Spanish have already been mentioned. Con may also have been tempted by the prospect of extending his influence by putting a client ruler, Ustian MacDonnell, into the neighbouring territory of Dufferin.

There was also the small matter of Tyrone's continued intimidation of the Gaelic clans across the region. Brian MacArt's likely role in Con's conversion has already been highlighted. MacArt suppressed dissent and extracted loyalty at the end of a bloodied sword. Con need only have looked to Westmeath and the 'burning, killing and spoiling the O'Carroll's and Sir Theobald Dillon's tenants… for no other reason than that their landlord had refused to join him (Tyrone)',[14] to know that the threat was real.

Tyrone also used religion to further his cause, increasingly pitching his rebellion as a 'fight for the catholic religion', a fight for the extirpation of protestant heresy, freedom of worship, and the establishment of Catholic supremacy in Ireland.[15] Religious convictions may also have helped persuade Con to side with the self-styled Catholic champion.

But the most plausible reason for his rebellion was that Con believed Hugh O'Neill might win. The English military machine had been unable to defeat Tyrone in almost a decade; indeed he had inflicted significant defeats on the English at Yellow Ford (1598) and the Curlew Pass (1599). Chichester recounts that Con, 'drew many loose rascals with him', suggesting that his septs probably supported his stand.[16]

Until this point, Con had shown every sign of being not just loyal to the Crown, but dependent on it. However, late 16th century Ulster politics was a cut-throat business. In turning on his allies, Con had demonstrated that he had what it took to survive in this dog-eat-dog world. However, before Con and Ustian could make any impact, their 'perfidious revolt' had been crushed and the fresh-faced lord now found himself in shackles in Carrickfergus Castle.[17]

He 'made dainty to hang him'

Con was now living on borrowed time. Sir Robert Cecil wrote to Mountjoy warning that Chichester 'made dainty to hang him' after some sham display of justice without the Lord Deputy's permission, and was itching to see the

The infamous Three Sisters Gallows outside Carrickfergus, where it was feared Con might hang. (National Museums of Northern Ireland)

Lord of Upper Clannaboy twitching breathlessly from the 'Three Sisters' gallows outside Carrickfergus's walls.[18]

This prompted Mountjoy to intervene, deeming it preferable to spare the rebel chief and to restore him to his lands and title rather than add fuel to the Clannaboy fire. By showing Con clemency, Mountjoy hoped other Irish chieftains would likewise betray Tyrone and fall on the mercy of the Crown.

Chichester found the decision difficult to swallow and wrote back acknowledging that Con had 'already suffered so much, that he wishes to be received' into the Queen's grace and favour.[19] But he also pointed out that as Con had:

been with Tyrone, Brian MacArt, and all the rebels of these parts practising to draw them upon us, I think it is dangerous to trust him.[20]

Carrickfergus Castle, where Con was incarcerated. (Tourism Northern Ireland)

The crannog on the Clea Lakes near Killyleagh, where Brian MacArt's store of victuals was seized. (Mark Stronge)

Chichester suggested that Con should be deposed and the Crown's ally in Lower Clannaboy, Con's second cousin Shane McBrian, should replace him. However, it seems that Chichester changed his mind or was overruled, as Con was released and returned to Upper Clannaboy. Having a leader who was legitimate and compliant in the area would allow him to concentrate on his struggle with Hugh O'Neill.

Con had rebelled in late August 1601, and as a result of his capture would play no part in the catastrophic Battle of Kinsale, a fortunate, if unplanned by-product of his defeat. When the Spaniards arrived, Brian MacArt returned to the Dufferin with all his forces. Chichester went out to confront him, allowing Hugh O'Neill a relatively clear corridor south to join the Spanish at Kinsale.

Edward Brookes was sent after MacArt, who had laid up a store of butter, corn and munitions at his crannog on the Clea lakes, just outside Killyleagh, on the roadside between Derryboye and Shrigley. Brookes bribed the local priest, Patrick McCrossan, with £20 to get thirty of his men onto the island, which he took without resistance. MacArt withdrew to his impregnable fort of Ennisloughlin in Killultagh.[21]

Clannaboy laid waste
Con had made a massive misjudgement when he aligned himself with O'Neill. Although his restoration spared Upper Clannaboy from devastation, the war continued to be played out over his lands. His people were imposed upon, and their food and crops were destroyed or confiscated by hungry troops from both sides.

This led to terrible suffering. As Mountjoy's secretary, Fynes Moryson, was pursuing Brian MacArt he came across:

a most horrible spectacle of three children (whereof the eldest was not above ten years old) all eating and gnawing with their teeth the entrails of their dead mother upon whose flesh they had fed twenty days past, and having eaten all from the feet upward to the bare bones, roasting it continually by a slow fire, were now coming to the eating of her said entrails in like sort roasted, yet not divided from the body being as yet raw.[12]

Another account describes the region as:

waste and destroyed and terrible want and famine oppressed all so that many were forced to eat dogs and whelps… many not having even these, died… wolves, coming out of the woods and mountains, attacked and tore to pieces, men weak from want… dogs rooted from the graves rotten carcasses partly decomposed.[23]

It was not only Upper Clannaboy that suffered in the wake of Tyrone's defeat. English captains wrought havoc upon the rebels' lands all across Ulster, spoiling or stealing an 'incredible amount' of grain, without which the Irish had 'no other means to keep their *bonnaughts*, which are their hired soldiers.'[24]

Restored to power, Con, his wife and young family returned to Castle Reagh to try to rebuild their depleted kingdom. Until, that is, the fateful Christmas of 1602, when the castle would provide the backdrop for the next act in the unfolding drama, an act that would result in Con's downfall, and usher in the coming of the Scots.

Brian MacArt retreated to his impregnable fort of Ennisloughlin, set among the underwoods and bogs of Moira. (Trinity College, Dublin)

11
How are the mighty fallen
1602-03

There are two accounts of the events of that fateful Christmas. Both were written by Scots, years afterwards, and so came to the page as well-crafted stories, the object of which, in part at least, was to legitimise the Scottish presence on Con's lands.

Christmas on the hill

At Christmas 1602, three months before the death of Elizabeth I, Con hosted a 'grand debauch' or wild party at Castle Reagh, attended by his friends and followers and his brothers Hugh Mertagh (the Pockmarked), and Tuathal (Toole).

In the windows of the castle, glowing candles welcomed the 'blessed couple' and weary strangers.[1] The chill night air rang to the chime of *cruit* and *clarseach* harps, the rumble of *bodhrans* and *timpans,* and the haunting swirl of *cuislenna* pipes could be heard in the humble cottages nearby. Waves of laughter and raucous jests filled the room. Jigs and reels were danced upon the wooden boards, while guests feasted on wild boar, goose and freshly caught salmon. Minstrels and poets regaled the merry assembly with tales of Epiphany, of the Clann Aodha Buidhe's former glories, feeding 'with song the patriot's fire' and of course, orations in praise of their illustrious host, Con McNiall McBrian Faghartagh O'Neill.

However, with the party in full swing, a cowed servant approached Con with the unwelcome news that the wine had run out and his cellar was dry. This was a source of great embarrassment to the chief, who, not wishing to end the merriment nor to appear miserly, sent his men off to retrieve a consignment of wine he had recently smuggled in from the continent. The servants set off in the darkness to retrieve the barrels, which may have been stashed near the estuary of the Connswater River. With their runlets packed onto a cart, Con's 'merry' men began the unenviable uphill trek back to the castle.[2]

Music will have filled the banqueting hall during Con's Christmas feast. Harpist by John Derricke, 1581. (Mansell Collection)

The quarrel of the barrels

However, on the return journey they were intercepted near St. Columbkille's Church, beside what is now the Clarawood estate, by soldiers from the Belfast garrison.[3] In what must have been a very confusing exchange between the English-speaking soldiers and the Irish-speaking servants, a fracas broke out, during which Con's men took a severe beating. To add insult to injury the soldiers confiscated the wine, 'until Con should pay a lately imposed duty'.[4] The servants returned empty-handed to Castle Reagh, battered and bleeding, complaining that soldiers were demanding payment of duty before Con could be reunited with his wine.

Con, however, was in no mood to think about such niceties, and he became enraged at the insolence of the English troops. Not only had they seized his wine, but they had belittled his men and disrespected his position. For a second time that festive evening, Con had been embarrassed in front of his guests.

Probably the most expensive wine in Irish history

When he discovered that his men had been beaten, although they outnumbered the soldiers by two to one, Con is said to have sworn 'by his father, and the souls of his ancestors, that they should never more be servants of his nor his family till they had beaten the "*Boddagh Sasonagh*" soldiers' and taken back his wine.[5] Con's wine would soon prove to be the most expensive consignment of wine in Irish history.

With their master's words stinging in their ears, Con's chastened men armed themselves and set off towards St. Columbkille's, then followed the dirt track down towards the village of Belfast. Within a short distance, they caught up with the English soldiers and engaged them. In the ensuing melee a soldier was mortally wounded, but the English got the upper hand

Con's empty chalice triggered a chain of events that would have far-reaching consequences. (Graeme Anthony Pewter)

Runlets of the type Con's men will have carried to the castle. each held a fourteenth of a tun of wine. (Portugal Wine Corporation)

Sir Arthur Chichester, the Governor of Carrickfergus, whose interference in the affairs of Upper Clannaboy would prove cataclysmic. (Belfast Harbour Commissioners)

and chased off their assailants, pursuing Con's men back towards Castle Reagh and killing several on the way, deaths that are often overlooked in this narrative.

As the chase approached the lights of Castle Reagh, the soldiers halted, fearing the dispatch of reinforcements from the castle. The *Montgomery Manuscripts* add that Con and his guests witnessed the drama from the turrets of the Eagle's Nest, their party mood well and truly dampened.

Banged up in Carrickfergus

Within a week, Arthur Chichester had established an 'office of inquest', which determined that Con bore responsibility for the affray. Then, accompanied by an escort of towards a hundred men, he rode out to Castle Reagh, where he arrested Con and members of his inner circle.

Con and his co-accused were taken to Carrickfergus Castle, Ulster's strongest prison, for Con's second stretch in its jail in just over a year. This time he was arraigned on a charge of 'levying war against the Queen' under a law established by Henry VII which stated:

whatsoever person… cause assemble, or insurrection, conspiracies, or in any wise procure or stirre Irishry or Englishry to make warre against our sovereign lord… be deemed traytour, atteynt of high treason, in likewise such as assemble an insurrection had been levied against the king's own person.[6]

This was an act of treason, which carried the death penalty. But could this minor affray be considered an act of war? Could Chichester make the charge stick? Quite possibly. He was used to getting his way. The Constable of Ringhaddy had recently beheaded a 'loose knave' and hanged his three accomplices on Chichester's orders. And Chichester had designs upon the fertile lands of Upper Clannaboy. For Chichester the incident was manna from heaven, and he would inflate it out of all proportion to serve his own ends.

Chichester's friends would have been amused at the idea of him using the pretext of unpaid taxes to try to unseat Con. As a student at Oxford, he had robbed the Queen's Purveyor of Taxes and escaped justice by absconding to Ireland, then going to France where he had distinguished himself as a soldier.[7] This would seem to be a classic case of the pot calling the kettle black!

The wine tax conundrum

Had Con avoided paying import tax? Did the Gaelic lords, like the French nobility, see themselves as above taxation? Was it a cross-cultural misunderstanding on the part of a people who made few monetary transactions and for whom coinage was an alien concept? Such interpretations seem naïve. A Gaelic chiefdom was a busy and significant economic unit, and Con received regular cash payments as Chichester's pensioner, so he and his staff will have been well versed in fiscal matters and the workings of a coin-based economy.

We also know that large quantities of wine were then imported into Ireland, with vessels regularly arriving at Carrickfergus from the Continent to trade wine for local produce. However, then as now, no-one was particularly keen to pay duty, and there were regular, high profile prosecutions.[8] So great was the problem of illicit trading that the authorities kept a pinnace called 'The Merlin' in Knockfergus Bay to deter would-be smugglers and pirates. In 1598, the sums raised from the sales of illegal wine imports seized by the Crown raised enough to largely offset the wages of the garrison.[9]

Records show that 'Hoggesheads' of wine from Bordeaux were then exchanged at a rate of one hundred and fifty litres for '9 cowes skinnes'. Furthermore, a duty of four shillings per tun was levied on French wine and six shillings per tun on Spanish wine, Spanish duty being higher to deter trade with England's enemy. The Royal Exchequer had been all but

A pinnace was a manouverable, well-armed ship used to hunt down pirates. From Ortelius's Map of Ireland c.1572. (University College, Dublin)

bankrupted by the war with Spain and the ongoing military campaign in Ireland, so the payment of duty was a sensitive matter and tax avoidance was a serious crime.

Excise collection was a lucrative business. Chichester controlled its collection at Carrickfergus, the foremost port in Ulster, and received one-third of the customs duty paid on exported or imported goods passing through the port.[10] But a small port also existed at Garmoyle near the mouth of the Connswater River, which would have been the perfect place for Con to land his 'duty-free'.

The death of Elizabeth

By this time Elizabeth I was near to death and would soon be succeeded by James VI of Scotland. In failing health, Elizabeth had returned to Richmond, where she became increasingly withdrawn and weak. On the morning of Thursday, 24th March 1603, Elizabeth fell into a deep sleep from which she did not awake. She was sixty-nine years old and had reigned for forty-four years. As the old Queen lay dying, Hugh O'Neill surrendered and the nightmare that was the Nine Years War finally drew to a close.[11]

Robert Carey witnessed Queen Elizabeth's death and saw opportunity to win favour with her likely successor. Disobeying the orders of the Council, he set out on horseback for Edinburgh, determined to be first to inform King

For two generations Elizabeth I had had a powerful influence on Clannaboy. She died on the floor, after refusing to go to bed or to sleep. Elizabeth's death as visualised by Paul Delaroche, 1828. (Musée du Louve, Paris)

James of Elizabeth's death. Carey made the 400 mile journey in less than three days and arrived at Holyrood House late on Saturday 26th March. Ushered into the King's bedroom, he imparted his news.

Ten days after Carey's arrival, James rode out of Edinburgh in royal procession to make the journey to Westminster. Among the many Scottish lairds and nobles who travelled in his entourage was one Hugh Montgomery, Laird of Braidstane, of whom we shall hear more. In July 1603, with the constitutional arguments resolved, the crowns of Scotland and England were united as James VI of Scotland became James I of England, or 'James the VI and I'.

James I, King of Ireland

James I by John de Critz, c.1606. James massively extended Scottish influence in Ulster. (Dulwich Picture Gallery)

Catholic Ireland greeted James I's accession with 'a delirium of joy'. The people 'forced open the gates of the ancient churches, re-erected the altars and used them for the public celebration of worship.'[12] Catholics believed James would be more sympathetic to their religion, after all, he was a direct descendant of the Irish prince, Fergus Mór, and son of the Catholic champion, Mary Queen of Scots. Furthermore, during the Nine Years War, he had covertly supported the McDonnells of the Glynnes, 'connived with the Ulster insurgents', and 'sent supplies secretly from Scotland'. Indeed, at one point Hugh O'Neill had offered to march on Dublin to proclaim James King of Ireland![13]

Although more liberal than his Tudor predecessors, James viewed his Catholic subjects cautiously. He reminded the Irish peers that they viewed the Pope as their father '*in spiritualibus*' while the King was merely their father '*in temporalibus*', which led to 'an uncertain acceptance of the authority of the Crown'.[14] Put simply, James was wary of his Catholic subjects, anxieties that would soon be confirmed by the Gunpowder Plot.

Con's genteel incarceration

Elizabeth's death inadvertently loosened the noose around Con's neck. After James I's coronation in July 1603, Con's confinement became more relaxed. He was allowed to walk freely in the street, and to entertain his friends in the 'victualling house within the towne, having only a single sentinel to keep him in custody.'[15] It was a very genteel form of imprisonment, and meant that Con was probably able to continue to run Upper Clannaboy from behind prison bars. Having spent the day entertaining and seeing to his affairs, he would return to prison in the evening, under the custody of the Town Marshall, probably Thomas Dobbin, who lived behind the county gaol.[16]

At the time of Con's incarceration, the town was a vibrant, thriving settlement, a garrison town, a religious centre, a fishing port and a trading town with its distinctive market cross, a farming community with cattle reared on its commons, a prison town, and a place of refuge for English and Irish alike, visited by traders from across Europe. It was the nearest thing Ulster had to a cosmopolitan centre.

Dobbin's Inn stands on the site of the Town Marshall's house. (Dobbins Inn)

No longer held in flesh-chaffing irons within the damp confines of a prison cell, Con enjoyed relative freedom within the ramparts of the town, which he will have known well, having probably attended school there. He had also the *caché* of being one of the town's most distinguished residents, hugely respected in its Irish quarter, and, Greeves has suggested, maybe even made welcome in 'the castellated houses of the followers of de Courcy... Savage Castle, Russel Castle, Sendall Castle, Wilks Castle, Dobbin Castle etc.'

He will have visited Niall Mór's friary and the tombs of his ancestors. His daily constitutional would have taken in the meandering path of the Woodburn River, with the heady aromas of the garrison's brewery, the sweet savour of its bakery, the pungent smoke of its pottery kilns mingled with the putrid stench of the town's open sewers, and the sea breeze rolling in from the Lough. He would have watched as trading ships offloaded their cargoes on the quayside, and perhaps listened as sailors regaled the townsfolk with tall tales in the town's various inns. Carrickfergus of 1603 was a vibrant, happening town, a tough, soldier's town, a fisherman's town and centre of commerce.

The constable at this time was Roger Langford, who had arrived with Chichester in 1598 and been appointed on his recommendation.[17] The garrison then numbered 685 men, so its presence would have had a huge impact on the life of the town; except when Chichester was on manoeuvres and only a skeleton guard remained.

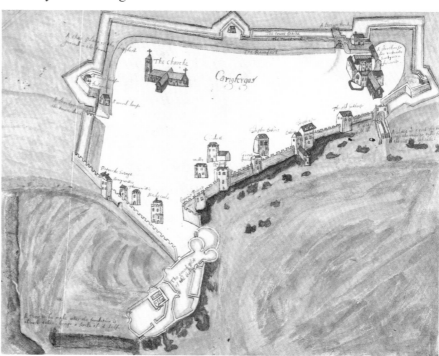

Carrickfergus, where Con was imprisoned. Dobbin's house is shown on the foreshore, with a little annex extending towards the sea. (Trinity College, Dublin)

However, despite the relative ease of his confinement, everything he had remained under threat from Chichester, who as this letter to Lord Cecil shows, in his mind had already moved past Con's disposal to the redistribution of his lands:

concerning the Clandeboys, the Lords of which I left prisoners in the castle of Knockfergus, being taken by me in actionable rebellion. May it please his Majesty to pass lands to the Captains that have served in those wars.

12
The great escape
1603-05

The lady, the laird and the entrepreneur
During Con's imprisonment, his wife Eilish spent considerable time in Carrickfergus, perhaps even lodging there. It seems that she was able to meet and talk freely with her husband, not least about how to secure his freedom. Perhaps it was during one of their walks down by the harbour that she had become acquainted with Thomas Montgomery from Blackstown in Ayrshire. Thomas was an entrepreneur who traded grain with the English garrison using his own 'sloop' or ship, and was well known in the town. The *Montgomery Manuscripts* describe him as 'a discreet, sensible gentleman', and he would play a pivotal role in the coming events.

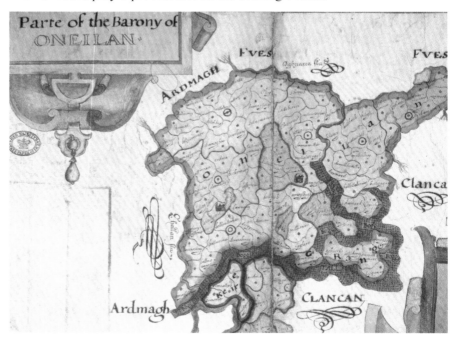

Eilish O'Neill grew up in MacBaron's Country in Oneillan. She was a teenager at the time of the negotiations. 1609 map of Oneillan by Josias Bodley. (National Archives, Kew)

When Thomas learned of Con O'Neill's plight, he immediately informed his kinsman, Hugh Montgomery. This was the opportunity the Scottish laird had been waiting for. With Thomas acting as a conduit, contact was established between Eilish and the Laird of Braidstane.

Born in Loughgall, County Armagh, in around 1585, Eilish was of noble stock, being the daughter of Art MacBaron, the brother of Hugh O'Neill.[1] She was also a granddaughter of the Earls of Tyrone and Kildare. Her brother, Owen Roe, would lead the rebellion during and after 1642. Her marriage to Con had been of great political and military significance, uniting two warring factions, the O'Neills of Tyrone and the O'Neills of Upper Clannaboy. In addition, it established a link with the great Geraldine dynasty of Leinster. In short, Eilish was a lady of great standing. She was also astute, and feared the intervention of Chichester in her husband's future trial. She and Con would work ably together to secure his release.

There are two accounts of what happened next, one in the *Hamilton Manuscripts* and another in the *Montgomery Manuscripts*. I have drawn from both to describe the most likely course of events.

The Sixth Laird of Braidstane
With time of the essence, Thomas acted as an intermediary conveying correspondence back and forth between Carrickfergus and Ayrshire. Some records suggest that Eilish travelled to Scotland to deal directly with the laird. But Eilish was more than an intermediary, she was a full partner or more in this endeavour, and her tenacity and clear thinking would eventually secure the laird's assistance.

Hugh Montgomery was a Protestant landowner from Ayrshire, who was connected to the noble House of Eglinton. He was also an experienced soldier, having fought against the Spanish. The *Montgomery Manuscripts* describe him as:

of middle stature, of ruddy complexion and had a manly, sprightly and cheerful countenance... strong and agile... had a vigorous constitution, seldom being sick... temperate in meat and drink... well educated.

Montgomery was well placed to help Con, having long-established trading links with Ulster. More importantly, he was also a close ally of King James, who had recently restored Montgomery to favour, following his bloody feud with the Cunninghams. Montgomery had also provided the King with intelligence concerning Elizabeth's failing health, via secret communications from his brother George in London, and was in a position to petition the King on Con's behalf.[2]

The Montgomerys were also interested in settling lands in Ulster. To all intents and purposes, this was a marriage made in heaven.

Hugh Montgomery, Laird of Braidstane and friend of King James VI, who came to Con and Eilish's aid, but not purely for altruistic motives. (Ulster Scots Agency)

What price freedom?

Although Eilish was a capable woman, Montgomery held all the aces in their negotiations and drove a hard bargain. The price he set for Con's freedom was astronomical. In exchange for Montgomery's assistance in springing Con from prison and getting a pardon from the King, Con would relinquish half of his ancestral lands to Montgomery. The sheer magnitude of the transfer shows just how seriously Con and Eilish took his predicament, and how difficult they believed it would be to win Con's freedom.

But were they right? It is possible that if Con had held his nerve, he would have been pardoned and restored to his lands? James had already pardoned numerous Irish leaders, including Elizabeth's arch-nemesis, Tyrone, and restored most to their lands under the Act of Oblivion.

An article in the Dublin Literary Gazette states there was 'no probability of him ever being prosecuted' and refers to his incarceration as an 'unblushing villaney'.[3] The *Montgomery Manuscripts* suggest the same:

Carrickfergus Castle, a bastion of the Crown, but no match for the wiles of an Irish lady and a Scottish laird. (Northern Ireland Explorer)

his words at his grand debauch were reputed very pardonable… greater offences would be remitted by his majesty's gracious declaration of amnesty.[4]

But there was a difference between the pardoning of the defeated Irish lords, which Chichester had worked for, and the possibility of a pardon for Con.[5] Pardoning the Irish lords had cost Chichester nothing. Pardoning Con could cost him Upper Clannaboy. How brazenly would Chichester have pursued his 'villaney'? Were Con and Eilish actually prudent rather than foolish to cut a deal? We will never know.

Weighing the risks
From Montgomery's perspective, the agreement was an astounding triumph. But he had yet to effect Con's escape, and this would be no simple undertaking. Carrickfergus was a formidable fortress and springing Con would not be easy. Were the plan to be uncovered and traced to him, Montgomery could be arrested. Then there was the problem of petitioning the King on behalf of a man charged with insurrection who had absconded from prison. Moreover, were they to gain an audience, there was no guarantee that the King would show mercy. The wily Scot would have to use all his influence and powers of persuasion if he was to win the new King's favour.

Over the ensuing months, a daring escape plan was devised. Montgomery himself probably had a hand in its creation, having as a young man escaped from Binnenhof Prison in The Hague. Hugh Montgomery was not averse to taking risks.

Into the lion's den
The first part of the plan involved winning an influential ally inside the castle. To that end, Thomas Montgomery was tasked with romancing Anna Dobbin, daughter of the castle gaoler. This went well, indeed went very well, and within a short time Thomas and Anna were very much in love. Their feeling for one another went far beyond the cynical use of Anna intended in the plan. Whether Anna's father knew of the plan we cannot be sure, however, it would seem likely that he did and was committed to its success. Thomas and Anna would eventually marry and go on to live in Montgomery's town of Newtown.

As we have seen, Con's confinement was infinitely more pleasant than that usually experienced by prisoners on 'death row'. Many experienced the hopelessness of imprisonment in the 'Oubliette' (from the French *oublier*, to forget), a windowless dungeon in the castle's Sea Tower, accessible only via a trapdoor in its ceiling. Con's quarters befitted his high position, which in turn made escape more achievable. It is likely that he was confined in the cell known as the 'Lion's Den' in the East Tower, 'as it is the only tower that has a wall shelving down to the water.'[6] Positioned at the back of the castle, it lay outside the secure inner ward and keep and some distance from the garrison.

It was now July 1604, and Con had been a prisoner for approximately eighteen months. With phase one an unbridled success, it was time for phase two. Once more Montgomery called upon the assistance of his nephew, who was 'furnished with instructions and letters to the said Con', outlining the details of how the breakout would be effected, by whom and when.[7]

The jail house rocks

With the jailer's support secured, phase two unfolded. Wealthy prisoners then relied upon family to bring them clothing, blankets and food parcels, so they did not have to depend on prison cuisine. Eilish managed to smuggle in a rope, said to have been concealed in a hollowed-out cheese.

On the appointed evening, the gaoler plied the prison guard with alcohol, then Anna or her father unlocked Con's cell to effect his escape. Alternatively, given the relaxed terms of his captivity, is it possible that Con had attended what was effectively his own 'leaving party,' and during the merriment escaped undetected. Whatever the truth, under cover of darkness he made his way to the perimeter wall, secured the smuggled rope and, heart thumping, hid in the shadows awaiting the signal from the rescue boat.

Then, just as planned, a light flickered momentarily as Thomas's sloop moored in the castle's shadow. As the 'drunken revelry' proceeded in the guardroom, Con descended the seaboard wall. Clearly, he was fit and strong, as the descent would have required considerable strength and not a little courage. Landing on the rocky foreshore, he swam or waded out to the

Under cover of darkness, Thomas Montgomery's sloop anchored close to the castle. Carrickfergus Castle by John James Syer. (Mid and East Antrim Council)

awaiting boat, and unceremoniously clambered aboard. As silently as it had arrived, Montgomery's sloop weighed anchor and made the short journey across the Lough to Bangor.

I am sure a wry grin crossed Con's face as he sailed over the Lough. The rescue had gone like clockwork.

The false trail

The next day, Con's followers spread the worried rumour that their master had been abducted at knifepoint. This minor detail is often passed over but is important for several reasons. Firstly, it established the notion that Con had been kidnapped, deflecting blame from Con and the Clannaboy. Secondly, it ensured that any subsequent search would probably centre on Tyrone or Antrim and not Upper Clannaboy, and certainly not Scotland.

For three nervous days and three haunted nights, Con hid in the tower of the ruins of Bangor Abbey, awaiting favourable weather to make the crossing to Ayrshire, where Eilish planned to join him. At any moment his presence could have been discovered, for we can be sure that Chichester was hunting him down. Bangor lay within Con's territory in the Great Ards, making it unlikely that he would be handed over by the locals.

The medieval abbey was an ironic choice of bolthole, as Con's predecessor, Sir Brian McPhelim, had burned it back in 1572. Today the tower is the only part of the original abbey that remains. We can imagine Con scanning Bangor Bay from its arched windows, awaiting the all-clear.

Scotland beckons

When conditions were right, the comrades made their way down to the shoreline, where the sloop lay anchored. Their journey to Scotland would have been a straightforward run past Ailsa Craig into the Firth of Clyde and berthing at the Port of Largs.

On arrival, they were met by a 'welcoming party led by Hugh's brother-in-law, Patrick', 'well mounted and armed'.[8] Con breathed easy for the first time in four days. He and Eilish were among friends. From Largs, they travelled twelve miles inland to Braidstane Castle to meet Hugh Montgomery. Coincidentally, and somewhat ironically, considering the fate of Con's fortress at Castle Reagh, not a single stone of Braidstane Castle remains today!

The *Montgomery Manuscripts* tell us that Con was 'joyfully and courteously received by the Laird and his Lady with their nearest friends' and was 'kindly entertained and treated with due deference to his birth and quality, and observed with great respect by the Laird's children and servants'. However, the Scot was keen to cement their contract, so the two men travelled to Ayr, where their agreement was 'endorsed and registered in the Town Council Book of the Royal Burgh of Ayr'. This made it a legally binding contract, leaving Con no room to manoeuvre out of his side of the bargain. There remained but one obstacle, the King.

The original tower of Bangor Abbey, where Con O'Neill hid following his escape. The steeple was added later.

Or did it?

Not all historians are content with this explanation of events. Michael Perceval-Maxwell has suggested that the story of Con's 'grand debauch', incarceration and escape is 'more colourful than true'.[9] He thinks it likely that Con was just imprisoned once, following his part in Tyrone's rebellion.

It is an interesting idea, but it discounts the evidence for Con's release by Chichester at the behest of Mountjoy, after his besieging of Ringhaddy Castle in the summer of 1601. It also discounts the evidence provided in the *Hamilton Manuscripts* and *Montgomery Manuscripts*, and offers no explanation of subsequent events. Why would Con have divided Upper Clannaboy with Montgomery if he had no reason to do so? Why would Con have felt obligated to Montgomery's nephew Thomas in his subsequent granting of land to the Scot?

Perceval-Maxwell is not the only sceptic. Local historian Keith Haines has suggested that Con's escape was not so much a rescue as a kidnapping.[10] Haines argues that Con was kidnapped by Montgomery, detained under duress in Braidstane Castle and plied with alcohol until he agreed to part with half his lands.

However, this idea is not supported by evidence from contemporary or secondary sources. And if Con was kidnapped, why had he never protested about it? Furthermore, why did his son Daniel not refer to his father's kidnapping in his many petitions for the return of his father's lands?

To London, to the King!

In Scotland, Montgomery continued to, 'entertain and subsist (Con)... in the quality of an esquire and also his followers in their moderate expenses.'[11] In August 1604, this unlikely band of brothers travelled to London to meet the King.

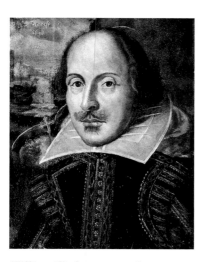

William Shakespeare, who was writing and performing in London at the time of Con's visit. The Flower Portrait of Shakespeare, 19th century. (Royal Shakespeare Company)

Montgomery may well have tried to disguise Con's appearance, accent and manners, as he moved among the upstanding ruffs, slashed doublets and manicured beards of London society. Con and Eilish must have found the vast metropolis a place beyond imagining. A city of wooden houses built in a labyrinth of streets on either side of the mighty Thames, united by that most astonishing of structures, London Bridge, whose mighty houses seemed almost to float on water.

London was a city of merchants and commerce, of guilds and street traders, of tall ships and exotic goods, a city to overload the senses with incredible sights, smells and sounds. It was a city in mourning, the Black Death having claimed 31,000 lives in the previous year. It was a mecca of culture. Seven of William Shakespeare's plays were performed in 1604-05, including the premieres of *Measure for Measure* and *Othello*.[12] Had Con inherited his family's long-standing love of the arts? Might he have been tempted to attend one of these plays?

London was also a place of political intrigue, where Scottish nobles vied

Con's senses must have exploded as he took in the architectural megastructure that was London Bridge. Visscher, Panorama of London, 1616. (Peter Harrington)

for power with their English counterparts. It was a place of religious fervour, where the puritanical strains of Protestantism faced down the prohibited practices of Catholicism. And as Con was suing the King for clemency, Guy Fawkes and friends were meeting in St. Clement's Inn, conspiring to 'roll back' the Protestant tide by blowing up the King and his government at the state opening of parliament.

Of course, Montgomery was already well known to the King and had powerful allies at court in the forms of the Earl of Eglinton and his brother, George Montgomery, Dean of Norwich. George was greatly respected by James, having spied for him in Dublin and at Elizabeth's court. Now as a result of their combined intercessions and negotiations, Con was eventually received into the King's presence.

King James meets Con
The charge sheet against Con was damning. He stood accused of rebellion alongside Tyrone, tax avoidance, sanctioning an attack on the Queen's troops in the course of which a soldier had been killed, not to mention being an 'on the run'. This must have been a tense meeting for the young chief. Con was contrite. He acknowledged his crimes, sued for mercy and surrendered his lands to the King in return for a royal pardon. James accepted Con's plea and offered his hand, which Con kissed with due deference, as he had kissed the

'Up the road' from Con and Montgomery, Guy Fawkes and Robert Catesby were working on detail of what would become The Gunpowder Plot. (Getty Images)

hand of Elizabeth's representatives in Ireland. All charges against him were 'taken off the file in the King's Bench Court'. Con's relief was palpable, and I will vouch that a delighted smile stretched across Montgomery's face.

However, this was no free pardon. Con's liberty would come at a heavy price. Upper Clannaboy would be divided in two, half to be given to Montgomery and the other half to be returned to Con by letters patent. Sir Hugh was about to become a powerful player in Ulster.

13
Enter James Hamilton
1604-05

In a scene reminiscent of a Shakespearean drama, another powerful Scot observed events from the wings. He was the Machiavellian James Hamilton, 'a very clever and well-educated agent of the king.' Originally from Dunlop in Ayrshire, Hamilton was an academic with a Master of Arts degree from the University of St. Andrews, who went on to gain a reputation as a fine scholar and wit. Like Montgomery, he was keen to acquire land in Ulster.

Game of Thrones

In 1587, James VI sent Hamilton and James Fullerton to serve as his agents in Dublin. Their task was, 'to spy on the doings of the Elizabethans',[1] to inform James VI of events in Ireland, 'to quiet the suspicions of Protestants as to Scottish intrigues with O'Neill and to promote a Stuart succession to the Crowns of England and Ireland.' Hamilton also acted as a conduit for correspondence from the 'Lords of England' to James's court in Edinburgh.

In his secret communications, Hamilton was known by an angular symbol, and Fullerton by 'No. 88'.[2] The pair concealed the true nature of their mission by establishing a Latin school in Great Ship Street. Both were talented teachers and the school flourished under their leadership, producing many luminaries including James Ussher, later Archbishop of Armagh and Primate of Ireland, and the man who calculated the first day of creation as Sunday 23rd October 4004 BC.[3]

When Trinity College Dublin was founded on the site of the monastery of All Hallows in 1591, Hamilton and Fullerton were among its first Fellows. Trinity had been established to allow Ireland's gentry to be educated in a Protestant institution in place of the Catholic seminaries of Paris, which – not without foundation – the Crown saw as fermenting 'undutifulness and treason'.

The Scottish King of England and Ireland

In the summer of 1600, with the Queen's life nearing an end, King James recalled Hamilton from Dublin and reassigned him to espionage duties at Elizabeth's court in London. There, Hamilton witnessed Essex's failed rebellion first-hand.[4] He writes extensively of it in his letters, although he

James Ussher, later Archbishop of Armagh, one of Hamilton's star pupils at the Great Ship Street school. (Durham University)

Dublin c.1610 by John Speed, showing Trinity College far right (number 12). Hamilton became one of its early Fellows. (University of Texas)

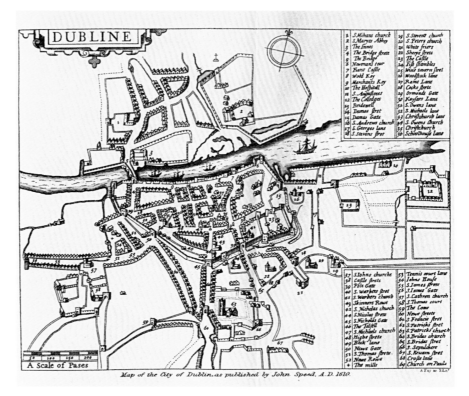

took no part in it. Was Hamilton perhaps a little too close to the London insurrection for comfort? This point is worthy of further investigation, as it suggests that James VI and Essex may both have been working for a Scottish succession.[5]

As an emissary of the Scottish King, Hamilton would have been a prominent figure at court, relaying confidential information back and forth between Edinburgh and London.[6] He also used his time there to ingratiate himself with the Queen and her circle. In a letter to Secretary of State, Sir Robert Cecil, he writes of, 'Her Highness being the king who, next his Master, he doth most honour and is desirous to serve.'[7] His letters also reveal pre-conditions imposed by Elizabeth in return for her support for James VI's succession, namely that James VI must promote the Protestant faith and must induce the Scottish mercenaries to withdraw their support from Tyrone.[8]

These positions gave Hamilton an intimate knowledge of the workings of the Scottish, Irish and English courts. He watched and listened, biding his time for 'the destiny that he knew would be his when James of Scotland would become King of England'.

Although James VI was 'heir apparent' to the English throne, he was still uncertain of a seamless succession, for other nobles opposed him and claimed the throne. Consequently, King James commissioned Hamilton to write a treatise asserting his claim to the English throne.[9] His erudition and clear thinking ensured that James' case received broad acceptance. Hamilton then acted on James' behalf in the negotiations following the Queen's death. Clearly, Hamilton was a significant player in the succession and could expect a king's bounty for his service.

Drawn towards Ulster

Events also conspired to increase James Hamilton's growing preoccupation with Ulster. In November 1603, he had been granted a monopoly for the export of 1200 packs of linen yarn from Ireland to Britain.[10] This opened Hamilton's eyes to the prospect of making a fortune here.

Then, as a favoured Scot with a keen legal mind, Hamilton was asked by William Smith, a nephew of the adventurer, Sir Thomas Smith, to petition the King for the restoration of his patent to the Ards. However, according to Smith, Hamilton misused his employment to solicit the King to grant him the land instead![11] Hamilton was also determined to gain a slice of the Clannaboy pie. The already cloudy waters were about to run opaque.

Hamilton's hieroglyph. This symbol identified Hamilton the spy, (Ulster Journal of Archaeology)

Intrigue at the Half Moon Tavern

When in London, Hamilton boarded at The Half Moon Tavern in Bow Lane, a lodging house frequented by Scotsmen and owned by one Thomas Irelande.[12] Thomas Allen describes it as 'the place of resort of the most celebrated wits of the 16th century.' (Incidentally, Half Moon Road was where David Bowie recorded *Ziggy Stardust,* and a restaurant of that same name still exists today!)

As the two men became more closely acquainted, Irelande agreed to procure extensive monastic lands in Upper and Lower Clannaboy on Hamilton's behalf. On the 6th December 1604, for the huge sum of £1,678 6s. 8d., Irelande acquired: [13]

our Castles, Manors etc., which will come to us by surrender, forfeiture, attainder, etc., as shall amount to the clear yearly value of £100 English, wherof the Manor of Moygare, and so much land of the Two Ardes… as he or his nominee shall think fit to parcel.[14]

He then signed over title of these lands to Hamilton, who through the employment of a phantom purchaser had avoided drawing attention to his acquisition of the land.[15]

Significantly, Irelande's transaction took place several months before Hugh Montgomery and Con O'Neill made their agreement with the King – for some of the same lands!.

Armed with two letters from the King, one formerly assigned to Thomas Irelande, and a second previously in the name of John Wakeman Esq., Hamilton travelled to Ireland to claim his new lands.[16]

The Half Moon Brewhouse formerly Tavern, c.1890. James Hamilton roomed here when he visited London. Remarkably, the building survived the Great Fire. (Mrs Pepys' Small Change)

Chichester comes onside

News of Hamilton's good fortune did not sit comfortably with the Lord Deputy, Sir Arthur Chichester. Chichester's Devon estate was bankrupt, and his future prosperity depended on success in Ireland. In 1603, as Governor of Carrickfergus, he had received titles to Belfast Castle, the River Lagan and control of the River Bann and Lough Neagh and their lucrative fishing rights.[17] Indeed, Chichester now went by the grandiose title of, 'Admiral and Commander-in-chief of Lough Neagh'. He even had the temerity to rename it, 'Lough Chichester'.

He had also long coveted Con's lands, which with Con's confinement in Carrickfergus, must have seemed to him to be within his grasp. One can imagine the jaw-dropping moment when he read Hamilton's letters. This cannot have been a happy day in the Chichester household! Chichester records that he felt as if 'a stranger had struck a sickle in the corn he had sown.'

Determined to prevent Hamilton from realising his grant, Chichester complained to the Secretary of State, Sir Robert Cecil, that:

There is come thither one Mr James Hamilton with two letters from the King... if he have his desires, he will have more lands than the greatest Lords in that Kingdom.[18]

However, just one month later something changed; almost overnight Hamilton and Chichester were reconciled and the King's patent was honoured without halt or hindrance. Healey suggests Hamilton and Chichester had arrived at an accommodation that would see each man accrue vast swathes of territory. They would use the letters as an open chequebook to claim land well in excess of the grant's original scope.

Robert Cecil by John de Critz, 1602. Cecil was cultivated by Hamilton as he sought to win influence at court. (National Portrait Gallery, London)

The tripartite division

Around this time Hamilton got wind of the deal struck between the King, Montgomery and Con O'Neill. With Hamilton having secured the patent to great tracts of land in the Ards, his close associate Fullerton, who was now a Gentleman of the King's Bedchamber, brought the conundrum to the attention of the King. The Crown had unwittingly granted the same lands twice, to different people. A large part of the land recently promised to Montgomery and Con O'Neill had already been given to Hamilton, via the

Amongst Chichester's 'nice little earners' were the fishing rights to Lough Neagh, which he tried to rename Lough Chichester. View of one of Lough Neagh's seven crannogs.

Part of the illuminated text of a royal indenture. The seated figure is King James. (Public Record Office of Northern Ireland)

King's letters to Irelande and Wakeman. If the King was not to be left with egg on his royal chin, the circle would have to be squared.

James acted decisively and revised the grant, deciding instead upon a three-way split between Hamilton, Montgomery and O'Neill. To sweeten the pill, James made Montgomery a knight and granted him additional lands which formerly belonged to the abbeys. As the *Montgomery Manuscripts* noted:

In the King's letter of the 16th April, the Laird of Braidstane is styled Hugh Montgomery, Esq.; but in the grant to Hamilton of the 5th of November following, he is styled Sir Hugh Montgomery; so that he must have received the honour of knighthood in the interval between these dates.

Con was the big loser. Caught up in high level power plays that he could not influence, at a stroke he was deprived of a further sixth of his lands. He had no option other than to accept the King's decree.

Con's feelings about Hamilton's intrusion are unknown. Montgomery's assessment is crystal clear. The *Montgomery Manuscripts* describe it as 'that killing dart' and 'that great hurt'. It stirred a deep and lasting hatred for the interloper, which would blight relations between the families for generations to come.

Almost immediately, an inquisition directed by Chichester was established to survey 'the state, contents and limits of the territories' and to oversee the redistribution of land between the three protagonists.[19] Montgomery and Hamilton were required, 'to inhabit the said territory and lands with English or Scotchmen'.[20] The Scottish settlement of Down had begun.

Let the enmity begin

The *Hamilton Manuscripts* provide a different slant to this story, suggesting Hamilton had come to the aid of Montgomery as he sought a favourable hearing from the King. They argue that Hamilton's influence at court paved the way for Con's pardon and restoration to his lands. However, as we have already noted, Montgomery had his own voice at Court and is unlikely to have required Hamilton's intervention.

The *Montgomery Manuscripts* draw a clear distinction between Hamilton and Montgomery's dealings with and attitude to Con O'Neill:

The conduct of Hugh Montgomery contrasts very favourably with that of others who profited also by the confiscation of Con O'Neill's estates. Had it not been for his prompt and able interposition, Con would have no doubt met the inevitable doom of all landowners… found guilty of treason… Con had no means and no friends; and when Montgomery began to expend money on his behalf, the prospect of recompense must have been very faint, seeing Chichester was all-powerful in Ulster. [21]

Whilst there is undoubtedly some truth in this claim, it would be naive to conclude that Montgomery acted solely from compassion. However, there can be little doubt that Hamilton's intervention was almost entirely about his personal advancement. In this narrative, James Hamilton is portrayed as a manipulative, conniving fox, whose moral compass was monumentally out of kilter.

The age old rivalry between Clannaboy and Tyrone had been replaced by a new rivalry between Montgomery and Hamilton.

The Clannaboy carve up
But Hamilton was now the lead player, and in April 1605 an indenture outlined a tripartite agreement in which letters patent would shortly issue to James Hamilton for lands identified as belonging to Con's grandfather, Brian Faghartach and his late father, Niall McBrian:

James Hamilton, academic, diplomat, spy, and now a magnate in County Down. (National Trust)

JAMES, by the grace of God, of England, Scotland, France, and Ireland, King, Defender of the Faith, and so forth : To all to whom our present letters shall come, greeting:—Whereas, we (on the humble petition of Con McBrian Fertagh O'Neile, as for and in consideration of the faithful service of our beloved Hugh Montgomery, Knight, and James Hamilton, Esq., our serjeant, rendered to us), by our certain letters, signed with our proper hand and under our seal, dated at our manor of Greenwich, the 16th day of April, in the third year of our reign of England, France, and Ireland, and of Scotland the thirty-eighth, enrolled in the rolls of our Chancery of our said kingdom of Ireland, signified our will and pleasure to be—That the aforesaid James Hamilton, his heirs and assigns, should have of our gift or grant the countries or territories of the Upper Clandeboy and Great Ards, and all castles, manors, lands, tenements, and hereditaments in the said country of the Upper Clandeboy and Great Ards, of which Neal McBrian Fertagh O'Neale, or his father, Brian Fertagh O'Neale, in their lifetimes were possessed of, and received any rents, duties, or impositions (in English, "cuttings,") with all and singular their members and appurtenances, together with a market on Thursday in every week, and one fair on the feast of St. John the Baptist, and for two days next following the said feast annually, and together with courts leet and courts baron, to be annually held at Castlereagh, parcel of the premises, and together with two other fairs, both to be held for the like time, with courts leet and courts baron, to be held within the said territories and lands, rendering to us, our heirs and successors, £100 good and lawful money of Ireland annually, at the receipt of our Exchequer there, at the two usual annual feasts, as by our said letters patent more fully and at large appears.[22]

In the course of my research at the Public Record Office Northern Ireland, I had the privilege of prising open a faded yellow, vellum parchment, an indenture, dated 30th July 1605. At that moment, I was touching history, staring down at the scratchy signatures of Hugh Montgomery and Con O'Neill, my eyes welling up, knowing the unhappy outworking of this initial division of Con's territory.

Inquisition at Ardquin

However, nothing could proceed until the extent of Con's lands had been determined. The enormity of this task cannot be overstated. The division of land in Ulster was problematic, to say the least. Boundaries regularly shifted in conflict. Reliable maps were few and lacking in detail. River bends, streams, hills, tree stumps, loughs and rocky outcrops often marked out territory. Land enclosure was almost non-existent. Determining who held title to land could be a difficult task.

This job was eventually assigned to Hamilton, and that same month an Inquisition was established at Ardquin, 'to ascertain the boundaries of Sir Con MacBrian O'Neill's estate and to declare the ecclesiastical confiscations within.'[23] The Inquisition brought the old Anglo-Norman landowners of County Down together to confirm the extent of their estates and investigated the unfulfilled patents of Sir Thomas Smith.

Con's original territory

Con's original territory is established by the Ardquin Inquisition, and tied down by reference to local geographical features such as the Bog of Dorney, the Ford of Annagh, Glemymiter, and the Rocks of Carnanleagh. Some of these places are now difficult to identify. However, the record is clear enough to allow us to trace the borders of Con's kingdom.

The inquisition describes Con's lands as stretching for eight miles from Malone to Blaris (just before Moore's Bridge), along the River Lagan, which formed its northern boundary, until it reached Lambeg, when it crossed the river to encompass the modern city of Lisburn, most of which falls within the parish of Blaris. From there it followed the Ravarnet River in a south-westerly direction to Lough Henney, near Boardmills. This area was particularly marshy, consisting of a series of mini loughs.

From Lough Henney, the territory extended south-east through the Parish of Killaney to Listooder Hill, overlooking the village of Kilmore. From there, his land followed the Ballynahinch River towards Strangford Lough, passing the 'Church of Killinchinickille' (Killinchy in the Woods) in Killyleagh Parish. To the east, Con's lands were bounded by the territory of the Dufferin, extending up through Glasswater and Raffrey, towards the 'Hill of Teochrum', possibly Scoggy Hill, which rises 400 metres above sea level. From here, the border followed the Owen Mullen River (Blackwater River) to where it enters Strangford Lough at Ardmillan.

On the Ards Peninsula, Con's territory ran to the Blackstaff River, which enters the Lough at the Saltwater Brig one mile south of Kircubbin, and forms the border between the Great Ards and the Little Ards to the south.

The territory known as the Great Ards was reserved for Montgomery and Hamilton, along with half each of the Baronies of Castlereagh Upper and Lower. The remainder of Castlereagh Upper and Lower was returned to Con.

Con's third lay in the Baronies of Upper and Lower Castlereagh, shown here in purple and orange on John Savage's map of 1855. (Public Record Office of Northern Ireland)

The tripartite indenture of 5th November 1605 granting James Hamilton Upper Clannaboy, the Great Ards and Killultagh. (Public Record Office of Northern Ireland)

Scottish portions

Letters patent for Con's territory were issued to Hamilton on the 20th July 1605. On October 1st, Montgomery paid Hamilton £106. 5s. for the abbey lands of Newtown and Greyabbey, and the abbey lands of Movilla, namely Movilla, Ballyhaft, Loughries, Ballyalicock, Ballyreagh, Ballyharry, Drumhirk and Ballygromeherry.

Then, on the 5th November 1605, the day the Gunpowder Plot was uncovered, Hamilton was granted sole control of all of Con's lands.[24] Following the three-way split, he received fifty-one townlands, mostly in east Down. His grant included the coastal parishes of Bangor (where he hoped to create a great port), Holywood, Craigavad, Ballywalter, Ballyhalbert and the landlocked but strategically situated parish of Dundonald.

Hamilton became a major landowner, having already received title to extensive lands formerly attached to religious houses, namely Rathlin, the Copeland Islands, lands around Coleraine, and in Dublin, Meath, Galway, Trim, Wexford and Mayo. In addition, Hamilton would later purchase the Barony of Dufferin, including Killyleagh, from the White family – all in all quite a portfolio.

Hamilton owned four ports, Holywood, Bangor, Portavogie and Groomsport. The importance of ports cannot be overstated. There were few roads or bridges, and the land was made impenetrable by dense forests, tangled underwood, bogs and marshes inhabited by wood kerne; all of which made sea journeys safer and faster.

On the 7th November, Montgomery received his third, which included the parishes of Donaghadee (soon to contain one of the most significant ports in Ulster), Greyabbey, Kircubbin, Newtownards and Comber. Comber parish was shared between the two Scots, with almost two-thirds going to Montgomery. The two Scots then traded townlands in order to create coherent landholdings.

The dispossessed

These lands were relatively thinly populated. Raymond Gillespie has estimated the adult male population of Antrim and Down at this time as being around 12,000. Another estimate puts the total population of Ulster at 'no more than 200,000'.[25] Dividing this by the nine counties would yield an average of some 20,000 per county, which would suggest that in the wake of the Nine Years War, Upper Clannaboy was lightly populated.

But it *was* populated, and Con's deal impacted on the wider clan. The territories of many of the leading septs of Upper Clannaboy – the Sleught Durnings, Sleught Owen McQuinn, Sleught Hubricks, Kelly, Mulcreevy (Rice) and Bryan Boy – fell within the new Scots polity. Families who had lived on their lands for generations suddenly found themselves dispossessed, without consultation or recourse to legal redress. Their years as wealthy, quasi-feudal gentry had abruptly come to an end.

There was fear. Some are said to have fled to the wooded Barony of Dufferin and the drowned drumlin islands along the western coast of

Strangford Lough. However there is no evidence of an exodus or refugee crisis. Most of Con's people seem to have stayed where they were, and attempted to adapt to the new system. Its demands were very different to those of the old order of coyne, livery, and coshering.[26] The endless hostings also ended, as did the obligation to provide military service, formerly an integral part of holding land. These changes were far-reaching. Two thirds of Upper Clannaboy moved from a semi-feudal to a market economy, and did so at almost break-neck speed.

There is some evidence of friendly relationships between Montgomery and Clannaboy's gentry. His will stated that:

James O'Dornan, Manus O'Hamill of Ballyholm and Tohil Og O'Gilmore of Ballysallagh were to pay little or no rent for good land.[27]

This suggests that something of the old, Gaelic social hierarchy managed to write itself over into the new regime. However, even though they seem to have maintained some of their social standing, the lives of families such as the O'Dornans and O'Gilmores would have been very different, for they now existed within a social structure in which their culture was no longer dominant, and a legal structure which denied them basic rights.

Petty's 'census' of 1659, reveals that the 'Irish' comprised 40% of the population of the Baronies of Castlereagh and the Ards. Indeed, his survey shows that the Irish were in the majority in five of the baronies of Down. In Con's third, the Irish found themselves in a minority, albeit a substantial one. However, numerical strength cannot be equated with authority or power. That had decisively passed to the Scots.

14
The return of the Chief
1605-06

On the 6th November 1605, a third of Con's lands were returned to him by Hamilton. It is difficult to say precisely how many townlands he received due to duplication and contradictory records. Gordon McCoy has identified their modern names as:

Ballynagnockan	Ballynagarrick	Ballymacbrennan
Ballycowan	Ballycarn	Clogher
Crossan	Cargacroy	Creevy
Ballynagarrick	Ballycarngannon	Ballydullogan
Drumbo	Hillhall	Balliderimore
Drumbeg & Ballygowan	Ballynagarrick	Ballylenaghan
Ballynahatty	Lisnastrean	Ballycloghan,
Lisdalgan	Lisbane	Tonaghmorey
Listooder	Mealough	Milltown
Taghnabrick	Monlough	Ballynavalley
Ouley	Ballyskeagh	Drumbeg
Blaris	Killeen	Tullywascunagh
Lessans	Ballyhanwood	Carricknaveigh
Knockbracken	Cahard	Lambeg
Ballentine	Craignasason	Carricknavegh
Tullycarnet	Ballymacaramery	Ballyaghlish
Drumgiven	Duneight	Carsonstown
Leggycowan	Breda	Ballynafeigh
Knock	Lisnabreeny	Ballymacarrett
Crossnacreevy	Ballyrushboy	Galwally
Cregagh	Castlereagh	Balliholiwood*
Ballylischan*	Ballylimebrenye*	Ballecrumen*
Ballycloinemore*	Ballymaltane*	

modern equivalent unknown

Con's third

Con now held some sixty-seven townlands where once he had controlled two hundred and twenty-four. His new territory extended over nine parishes:

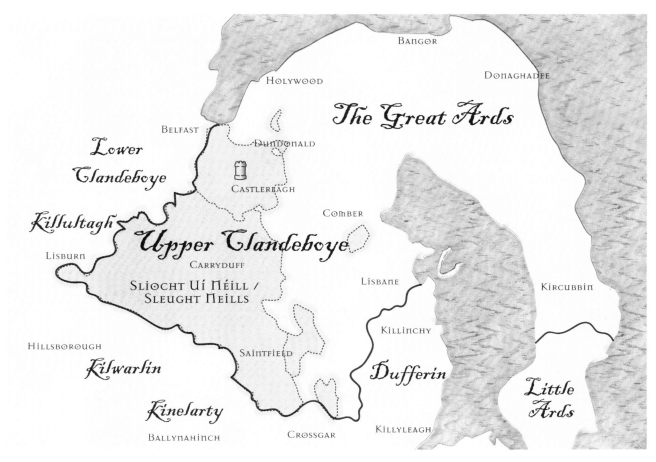

Knockbreda (8,098 acres), which includes the modern districts of Ormeau, Orangefield, Newtownbreda, Belvoir, Knockbreda, Gilnahirk and Braniel; Drumbo (9,629 acres), which includes the Giant's Ring; Lambeg (1,567 acres), which straddles the River Lagan; Blaris (10,697 acres), which lies on both sides of the Lagan and includes the city of Lisburn; and Drumbeg (2,704 acres), just north-east of Lisburn, which also lies astride the Lagan and contains the church of Saint Patrick with its famed Lychgate and Sir Thomas and Lady Dixon Park.[1]

To the south, he held the parishes of Saintfield (13,330 acres); Kilmore, which lies south-west of Crossgar; and Killaney (2,859 acres), a watery region of lough and marsh to the south-west of Saintfield. He may also have retained a portion of the parish of Comber, but was excluded from any townlands that opened onto Strangford Lough.

Whilst the boundaries of 1605 do not exactly mirror those of Lewis's *Topographical Survey* of 1837, Lewis's figures show Con's townlands equate to 67,538 acres.

Map showing Con's original territory (red border) and the third he received in the tripartite agreement (shaded green). (Gordon McCoy)

Drumbo Round Tower. Drumbo was part of Con's Sleught Neill heartland.

It is interesting to note that had his case been brought after the Gunpowder Plot, obtaining a deal might have proven more difficult. Technically, Con could even have been refused an audience with the King, since Catholics were prohibited from coming within ten miles of London in the security clampdown that followed the attack.

Con landlocked

Con retained three sites that were of great symbolic and personal importance to him, his tower house at Castle Reagh, the nearby mound of inauguration, and the church of St. Columbkille at Knock. His portion centred on the traditional lands of his close family. Was he able to win these in negotiation? If so, it will have been in part because the Crown wished to secure the sea coasts for 'Scottish men, who would be traders as proper for his Majestie's future advantage.'[2]

Con's portion was almost entirely landlocked, which probably played to his strengths as his networks were mostly internal and connected with the rest of Ulster. Those of the Scots were external, linking with Scotland and England. Through the new settlers, the Crown sought to control imports and exports to and from Upper Clannaboy. Indeed, the King's original grant to Hamilton gave him sole permission to import and export to and from the territory.[3] Con did, however, retain access to the sea via the estuary of the Connswater River, between Samson and Goliath and Victoria Park in what is now East Belfast.

The tripartite agreement required Con to permit Scottish tenants to populate at least one-third of his territory.[4] Another stipulation required Con

Con's only port now lay at the mouth of the Connswater River, near what is now the site of these two famous cranes. (Curious Ireland)

Little remains of the ancient church of St. Columbkille at Knock. Con is said to have wished to have been buried here.

to ensure that these tenants could live peaceably and without harassment. Were there to be any threat of attack from the Clannaboy, Con would forfeit land.[5]

This clause could work either for or against Con. On the one hand, it could provide him with additional income at a time when he was 'evidently penniless'.[6] On the other, it reduced the amount of land available to the Clannaboy by sanctioning a mini plantation within Con's third, setting his interests against those of the clan.

The lands Con retained were fertile and prosperous. He held them under free and common *soccage* at an annual rent to the Crown of £33. 15s Irish, or one shilling per hundred acres. Were Con able to fully tenant the land, setting rents at a shilling per acre as Montgomery did, he could expect an annual income of £3,300, minus his small head rent to the Crown. Despite losing two-thirds of his territory, Con stood to become a very wealthy man.

But to prosper, he would have to adapt. Con may have returned believing he could continue a version of his former way of life. But would that be possible in the context of the aggressive, frontier-style market economy that now surrounded him? The settlement presented Con with challenges at least as great as those it presented to Hamilton and Montgomery. The position of all three, while very privileged, was also very insecure.

Eggs and game. Con was given the right to hold a weekly market every Thursday at Castlereagh. (National Gallery, London)

Explaining the fine print

The agreement granted Con:

one market to be held at Castlereaghe every Thursday, weekly, forever; one fair to be held at Castlereaghe on the Feast of St. John the Baptist, (24 June) yearly, for ever, with court of pie powder, free warren and chase, court leet, and court baron to be held for ever of the king, at the rent of £23 16s.

The market was granted to encourage trade, and the circulation of the King's new coinage. Farmers would cart their produce here early every Thursday morning, the breath of their horses steaming in the cold early morning air. Craftsmen and traders in wool, leather, and metal would lay out their goods. Others entertained or sold food and beer. The hope was that the fair and market might lead to the creation of a small town.

The other items mentioned in the grant are more obscure, but were nonetheless important to the smooth working of local life. 'Pie Powder Courts' settled disputes between merchants and customers at markets.[7] Con or his nominee would preside, ruling on whether someone had been sold a lame horse or a faulty plough. Justice was dispensed on the day, as cases often involved traders who did not live locally and may have been tempted to abscond. In the Pie Powder Court, we see the forerunner of trading standards and consumer law.

'Free Warren' licensed the holder to keep and breed game animals within a defined area, in which hunting by others was prohibited. 'Chase' refers to an enclosed park, where the lord could hunt boar or deer. The 'Court Leet' was an annual court in which the lord heard disputes in criminal cases. The 'Court Baron' or manor court dealt with the management of the lord's estate. It met every third week to deal with land disputes, tenants' rights, rents, grazing rights, straying cattle, defective hedges, etc.[8]

Con was also required to supply, 'two horsemen and four footmen, well equipped, to attend the hostings of the chief governor in Ulster for forty days each year'. This essentially symbolic military render speaks volumes about the completeness of the Crown's new control.

What is clear in all of this is a conviction that the new arrangements would be enduring, and that Con would succeed in his new role. There is absolutely no suggestion that he could fail.

Caught between two worlds

On first reading, these privileges appear to have provided Con with considerable autonomy.

He was being invited to live like an English lord and inhabit an English identity, in other words to re-invent himself, and become not just culturally plural, which was a big enough ask, but also abandon the feudal mindset he had grown up with and become a player in a modern, market economy. Indeed, he almost *had* to do this in order to make his new, mini-kingdom work.

And while the thirty year-old may have been young and adaptable enough to make the change, it seems that he did not embrace this new identity. The events of the next few critical years make that clear. Maybe he tried and failed. Maybe it was too big an ask. Maybe – unlike Sir Brian McPhelim – he simply didn't want to. His English would by now have been equal to it, though spoken with a distinctly Scottish twang. In terms of psychology, outlook and culture, however, Con seems to have remained an Irish prince, unreconciled to the new world around him. As such, he will have found some of the conditions of his grant profoundly uncomfortable, not least the prohibition on 'granting any estate… to any of the mere Irish.'

The Christmas Eve agreement
In his original agreement with Con and Eilish, Montgomery had agreed to cover 'the proper expenses, cost and charges' pertaining to Con's escape and the upkeep of his entourage while procuring his pardon.[9] Now, however, Montgomery requested recompense for these. As if a third of Con's kingdom wasn't enough!

Con was unable to pay. Consequently, on Christmas Eve 1605, Montgomery appears to have used the leverage of this 'debt' to enter into Articles of Agreement with Con whereby Con agreed that, should he suffer misadventure, and have no heir, his land would revert to Montgomery.[10]

The Agreement is an ambiguous document, into which various meanings can be read. D.A. Chart and George Hill have viewed it as an attempt to protect Con's allocation.[11] However, it could equally be seen as a cynical move by Montgomery to ensure he would hold legal title to Con's lands in the event of any future forfeiture to the Crown.

The *Hamilton Manuscripts* state that following the settlement, Con O'Neill and Montgomery left London together, travelling back to Braidstane via Edinburgh, then journeying to Ireland. Hamilton made his way to Dublin where he informed Chichester of the tripartite agreement.

Con O'Neill and Montgomery appear to have continued to enjoy friendly relations. The same cannot be said of Hamilton and Montgomery. Their mutual hatred was such that Hamilton wrote a clause into his will stating that if any of his heirs should marry any of Montgomery's, they would forfeit their inheritance. Likewise, Montgomery felt nothing but acrimony towards Hamilton, whom he believed had swindled him out of one-sixth of what he was originally due.

Return of the Teirne
Con now made a triumphant return to Castlereagh. His homecoming inflicted a 'double whammy' on Chichester. Not only had Con escaped his clutches, but he had also been restored to a part of his lands and given the added security of the King's blessing. Once more, Chichester must have been incandescent with rage!

Con got a hero's welcome. The Clannaboy had remained loyal to their *Teirne*, and his return occasioned great joy. The stories of his courageous

The tripartite agreement invited Con to become an English-style lord. 'The Civil Irish', detail from John Speed's map of 1611. (British Library)

'Dublin equipage'. Con returned in triumph, dressed in the garb of an English gentleman. (Private collection)

escape and parley with the King will by then have been the stuff of legend. Con and his entourage processed up the hill to Castle Reagh in '*Dublin Equipage*'. In other words, he chose to present himself to his people in the attire of an English palesman – a sign that at this point he fully intended to become the esquire envisaged in the tripartite agreement.

He was 'met by his friends, tenants, and followers', most of whom came on foot, with the wealthier attending on *garrans* (horses), ridden bareback or on saddles of cloth stuffed with straw. While the majority who crowded around him will have been bareheaded or perhaps worn skull caps against the cold, his most important kinsmen will have looked striking in their traditional *wosle barrads*, tri-cornered woollen hats in the Phrygian style, dyed purple, blue, and green.[12]

Why had Clannaboy remained loyal? Did no-one curse Con for having abandoned them? If they did, such anger, or disappointment, is misplaced. Behind the tripartite agreement lay huge historical forces that not even the Lord of Upper Clannaboy could resist. Clannaboy was the low-hanging fruit. It lay close to the northern pale; no other Gaelic kingdom had such a long and difficult history of attempted colonisation. For decades it had been coveted. The wonder is that it did not wholly disappear.

Con stood before his people as their undisputed leader. The jubilant crowd showered him with gifts and tributes – *beeves* (steers), *colpaghs* (two-year-old heifers), sheep, hens, *bonny clabber* (thickened milk), *rusan butter* (wooden casks of fermented butter, similar to cheese), *greddan meal strowans* (large measures of oatmeal), *snush* (marrow) and *bolean* – tribute from a hitherto leaderless people, a people now filled with hope.[13]

15
By earth and twig
1605-11

'An excellent bargain'

The received wisdom is that Con lost out substantially in the tripartite arrangement. However, he had rebelled on at least two occasions, and like others who had joined with Tyrone, could have lost everything. In retaining one-third of his lands he bucked the trend. The going rate for land retention among the 'deserving Irish' was around one-fifth. He also differs from the others in that he gave up his lands to obtain his freedom, and not as a result of punitive military action by the Crown.

Con had emerged from turbulent times with his life, his liberty, and a considerable territory. He had also eluded the trap set for him by no less a figure than the now Lord Deputy Chichester, who boasted that he had exiled some six thousand Irish rebels to Sweden.

Timothy McCall goes further; suggesting that far from being a victim, Con did well to obtain a legal title to his ancestral heartland around Castlereagh, and the territory of the Sleught Neills. McCall argues that Con knew that, despite his genealogy, his legal claim to Upper Clannaboy was tenuous, having been negated by the 1569 Act of Attainder, the surrender of Con Óg to Elizabeth I in 1586, and his and his father's rebellions. As the *Hamilton Manuscripts* put it:

Brian Fertagh O'Neill, Con's reputed grandfather, and father were intruders as he himself also was unto the Queen's right and possession.[1]

Essentially, 'the pickle wherein Con was soused' was that because his title derived from Brehon and not English law, Con had no legal patent to validate his claim to Upper Clannaboy.[2] McCall argues that it was prudent of Con to make 'an arrangement by which he would give a spurious legality to the Hamilton and Montgomery claims, while safeguarding and consolidating his own interests in Castlereagh.' The Clannaboy carve-up was, therefore, a partnership and 'the product of mutual interests.'

From medieval times lands had been transferred through the symbolic giving of a clod of earth and a twig.

Strafford also argued that Con won 'an excellent bargain' as 'it was very doubtful if the Irish Council would have sanctioned such a large demesne if the matter had come before them.'[3]

The tripartite agreement
The outworking of the tripartite agreement was a three-way-split of Upper Clannaboy between Hamilton, Montgomery and Con O'Neill. Each man would pay a nominal rent to the Crown and would then lease parcels of land for twenty-one years to Scottish and English tenants, and in Con's case to the 'deserving Irish' as well.

As de facto landlords, the cosignatories looked to be set up for life, holding title to substantial lands with the prospect of amassing a vast income from their rents. Their lessees also had opportunity to accumulate land and to sublet these lands to a secondary tier of lessees.

In addition, the provision for each landowner to hold weekly markets and courts within his third encouraged the establishment of market towns, where commerce could flourish. This was a project for the pacification and development of Upper Clannaboy by social engineering.

A fresh start
Reinstated in Castle Reagh, with his wife and young son by his side, Con looked forward to a fresh start. But he would retain his lands intact for just six months. Instead of seeking stability and putting his affairs in order, Con entered into a series of reckless land deals.[4]

These began innocently enough with what seems to have been the clearing of a debt of honour. On 25th April 1606, Con granted the 'lands of Ballyrosboye, in the Galliugh, between Castle Reagh and Belfast, to Thomas

Montgomery', the man who had helped him escape from Carrickfergus Castle. Today, this corresponds to lands at the junction of Grand Parade, Ladas Drive and the Castlereagh Road. Now, probably by prior agreement, Con acknowledged his debt to the Scot.[5]

The transfer of this land was guaranteed in a symbolic ceremony of 'livery and *seisin*', whereby Con provided 'a clod of earth and a twig' to signify the sale of the land and its contents to the new owner.[6]

A family drama

In May 1606, Con granted lands to his brother, Hugh Mertagh. This grant was larger (five and a quarter townlands lying between Carryduff and Saintfield) and at first sight looks relatively innocent:

We find that the said Con did by writing under hand and seal, demise unto his brother, Hugh Mertagh O'Neale, the townes and lands of Ballynalessan, (whereof Tulloure is a quarter), Ballyaghley, Ballykillenure, Ballycarricknasassanagh, Ballylistowdean, and the mill of Ballyknockan, for 99 years, to begin the 1st May 1606, at the rent of two shillings sterling…[7]

until that is we realise that Hugh Mertagh almost immediately:

conveyed his interest in said lease to sir Fulk Conway, who, for these 17 years last past was, and is yet, in possession thereof.[8]

Hugh Mertagh had received the lands for a song and looks to have turned a quick profit. Did Sir Fulke use Con's brother as a tool to prise lands from Con? Was Hugh Mertagh prepared to deceive his own brother? This land deal is of itself a mini family drama.

Hugh received a further lease for:

Clontinakally, for the term, and under the rent aforesaid, who demised the same to sir Moyses Hill… and that said Hugh Mergagh did, by Indenture, dated 27th June, 1614, assign his interest in Clontinakally to sir Fulk Conway.[9]

The 400 year old signature of Con O'Neill. (Public Record Office of Northern Ireland)

Joymount, Sir Arthur Chichester's great house in Carrickfergus (r) as detailed on a map of c.1680. It was built on the site of Niall Mór's friary

Although Hugh seems to have held these lands for a little longer, they too ended up (via Moyses Hill) in the hands of Sir Fulke Conway. These acquisitions did not content Sir Fulke. He would soon be back for more.

The Drumbracklyn deal

The Manor of Drumbracklyn was next to go. In August 1606, it was sold to Montgomery 'for the only consideration of £317' and an annual rent to the Crown of forty Irish shillings.[10] It comprised the townlands of Duneight, Lisnoe, Ballyaughlis, Ballycarn, Ballylesson, Mealough, Knockbracken and Clogher, an area of some 3,200 acres in the parishes of Blaris and Drumbo. Montgomery paid about £40 per townland. Con O'Neill's son, Daniel, who would later attempt to recover his father's lands, claimed that Drumbracklyn's true value was £15,000. This exaggerates its worth, but Daniel is right to claim that the land was sold cheaply.

Included in the deal were lucrative timber and mining rights over the Sleught Neill and Sleught Kelly lands between Ballylesson and Drumbo. This timber in part explains Daniel's high valuation. These lands were reportedly carpeted by a swathe of forest so dense it was said that 'a man might almost make his way from MacArt's Fort (Cavehill) to Lisnagarvey (Lisburn) on the top of the trees'.[11]

Montgomery's tenants were given the right of 'ingress and egress thro' Con's lands to fell the 'timber, trees, woods, underwoods, and all other trees lying or growing'.[12] They even had the right to erect temporary houses on his land during the harvesting of the wood. Con's Irish tenants were permitted to cut wood for the building of their homes, 'oak excepted'! Oak was to be the sole preserve of the newcomers and we read that five hundred oak trees were cut to build Chichester's new houses in Belfast and Carrickfergus. Logging represented a massive bounty to Sir Hugh. It also represented a massive loss in earning potential to Con.

Clearing the forests of Breda and Ballynafeigh

The tripartite agreement and Con's subsequent land deals opened the forests of Upper Clannaboy to the market for the first time, and would lead to wholesale woodland clearance. At a time when England's woodlands were

Forest clearance made the new loggers rich, not Con. (Scientific American)

being cut out, this huge reserve of high-quality timber had great value. Con had something akin to a gold mine on his land – had he only known it.

Some of Con's leases seem specifically timber-oriented. In October 1608, for example, he leased the townlands of Breda and Galwally to Michael White of Carrickfergus for twenty-one years, and let Ballynafeigh to Thomas Hibbotts, also of Carrickfergus. In turn, Hibbotts sub-let all woodcutting rights to a tanner called Walter Hillman and a carpenter called John Spencer. Between them, they felled the trees along the banks of the Lagan, floating the logs downstream to Belfast and on to Carrickfergus, from where they were exported to Scotland and England.

This woodcutting deal made Hillman and Spencer very rich men. There was no such thing as sustainable forestry in those days. The forest of Ballynafeigh was almost completely cleared during the period of the lease, making way for what would eventually become the Annadale and Ormeau demesnes.

Hibbots would also gain the lucrative rights 'to transport yearly 10,000 quarters of grain, 300 packs of wool, 200 packs of flock, 500 lasts of hides, 100 tons of tallow, sheepskins and beef' out of Ulster, allowing him to amass a fortune.[13]

Riches to rags, rags to riches
Another of the four major beneficiaries of Con's willingness to sell his leases was Moyses Hill. A native of Devonshire, Hill had arrived in Ulster in 1573 with little more than his sword and a reputation for soldiering. However, he was able and ambitious and went on to serve under Devereaux, Chichester and Mountjoy, who appointed him Governor of Olderfleet Castle to protect the 'harbour of Larne from the invasion of the Scots.' Hill was knighted in 1603 for his military service and made provost of

Sir Moyses Hill, founder of the Downshire dynasty. (Hillsborough Castle)

Carrickfergus. Miskimmon records that he resided in the house of William Dobbin, later Dobbin's Inn, a name that carries on to this day.

Hill's first marriage was to Alice McDonnell, a sister of Sorley Boy McDonnell of Dunluce – an unexpected alliance, given that he had narrowly escaped death at the hands of the McDonnells in 1597. It was during this ill-conceived affray that Arthur Chichester's brother, Sir John Chichester had lost his life. Hill, the Commander of the Horse, escaped to Islandmagee where he hid in a cave.

In 1607, Hill leased Con's manor estate of Castle Reagh, in the parish of Knockbreda, along with eight townlands in the parish of Drumbo, including Killaney, Carryduff, Temple, Ballynahinch, Annahilt, Legacurry and Hillsborough.[14]

Hill established 'a brave plantation' of settlers from Lancashire and Cheshire along the fertile Lagan valley. As Con descended from riches to rags, Hill ascended from rags to riches, becoming one of Ulster's wealthiest landowners and founder of the Downshire dynasty. Moyses Hill would represent County Antrim at the Irish Parliament of 1613, and by 1617 had risen to the lofty position of Provost Marshall of Ulster. One of Hill's descendants, Arthur Wellesley, Duke of Wellington, became one of Britain's greatest military leaders. Soldiering was in the blood. Nevertheless, however much we may gild the lily, Moyses Hill 'built his fortune on the ruin of Con O'Neill of Castlereagh.'[15]

The Flight of the Earls

September 1607 was a seismic period in Irish history; the Earls of Tyrone and Tyrconnell left Ulster for the continent of Europe. Ulster was left bereft of a Gaelic hierarchy. Great tracts of land were forfeit to the Crown, paving the way for the Plantation of Ulster.

1608 saw the once-loyal Lord of Inishowen, Sir Cahir O'Doherty, in violent revolt against the Governor of Derry. However, his initial successes were soon overturned and within three months, his head had been unceremoniously displayed on a pikestaff. With Gaelic Ulster leaderless, broken, and in turmoil, the Crown further tightened its grip on power.

The departure of these powerful figures elevated Con's relative importance. Resident at Castle Reagh, and with much of his third intact (notwithstanding his string of disastrous land deals), Con O'Neill remained a substantial and influential figure. He is also described as disaffected.[16] In April 1608, in a well-informed appraisal of the fragile mood of the Gaelic nobility, Sir Henry Dillon included him on a list of the, 'great men of the North, who in their hearts are haters of all Englishmen and English laws'.[17] There was concern that he could become a rallying point for disaffection in eastern Ulster:

Con M'Neyle M'Brian Fertaghe O'Neyle, commonly reputed Lord of Clanneboyes, who is discontented, and has a great many knaves at his command..[18]

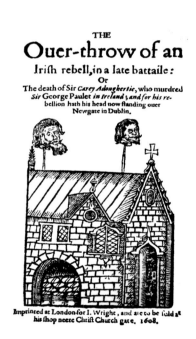

Grisly end. Sir Cahir O'Doherty's severed head was displayed in Dublin. Con chose not to rebel. (Trinity College, Dublin)

Statue at Rathmullan commemorating the Flight of the Earls in September 1607, by John Behan.

Con had good reason for discontent. His class was being swept from the pages of history. He may also have been personally disillusioned. He had come back apparently intent on making the new settlement work. But he had not been able to do so, and had conspicuously failed to find – or be afforded – a place in the new order. He had lost an empire and not yet found a role, and disillusion may have followed. However, unlike Sir Cahir O'Doherty, Con did not go so far as to rebel.

Ballymacarrett goes

Con continued to make profligate land deals. Several involved Montgomery, who appears to have exploited his friendship with Con to advance his own interests. In 1607, we see him using his influence with Con to secure townlands for third parties:[19]

Sir Hugh Montgomery of Newtowne… and Con O'Neale of Castlereagh… to Sir George Sexton of Dublin esq., Grant of the townlands of Ballyneahaughty[20] and Ballyvollvally, in the country called the 'Slught Neales Country'… Ballydollaghan… at an annual rent of 18/8 to the Crown and of 40/- to Con O'Neale.[21]

In 1609, Con sold the townlands of Ballymacarrett and 'Strone Moore' excluding the Church of St. Columbkille to a Colonel David Boyd. The indenture contains the statement that he did so with the 'consent of his superior' (Montgomery), an extraordinary phrase that suggests they did not deal as equals.[22] Montgomery was pulling the strings.

Sir Fulke returns

In 1609, Sir Fulke Conway came back for more. This time he felt emboldened enough to approach Con directly. He found Con willing to parley, and was able to purchase four townlands near Hillhall and Ballyskeagh from him for £200 English. This included the townlands of Largymore, Ballyonenillan, Ballytooleconnell and Ballymullan (in Blaris), by the Lagan.

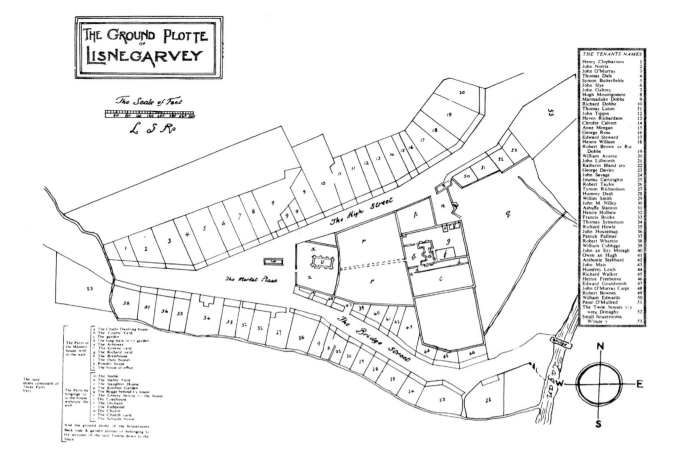

THE GROUND PLOTTE OF LISNEGARVEY

The Scale of Feet

L S R⁰

THE TENANTS NAMES	
Henry Clopharison	1
John Norris	2
John O'Murray	3
Thomas Dale	4
Symon Butterfielde	5
John Slye	6
John Galtrey	7
Hugh Mountgomrie	8
Marmaduke Dobbe	9
Richard Dobbe	10
Thomas Luton	11
John Tippin	12
Heven Richardson	13
Chrofer Calvert	14
Anne Morgan	15
George Rose	16
Edward Steward	17
Henrie Willson	18
Robert Brown or Ric Dobbe	19
William Averne	20
John Lillworth	21
Kathrin Bland aro	22
George Davies	23
John Savage	24
Jounie Cartirighte	25
Robert Taylor	26
Tymon Richardson	27
Humrey Dash	28
Willim Smith	29
John M. Nilley	30
Ashuffe Stanton	31
Henrie Holbete	32
Francis Bricke	33
Thomas Symonson	34
Richard Howle	35
John Housemap	36
Patrick Pallmer	37
Robert Wharton	38
William Cubbege	39
John an Ery Meragh	40
Owen an Hugh	41
Anthonie Stabbard	42
John Mais	43
Humfrey Leich	44
Richard Walker	45
Hernie Freeborne	46
Edward Gouldsmith	47
John O'Murray Carpt	48
Robert Bownes	49
William Edwards	50
Peter O'Mullred	51
The Twoe houses t/y were Donaghy	52
Small houserooms w'oute v	53

The High Street

The Market Place

The Bridge Street

The Lagan

This 'ground plotte of Lisnegarvey', now Lisburn, dates from the 1620s. The tenants' names are almost all English, with a few of Welsh origin, reflecting the background of the Conway family, the owners of the estate. (Irish Linen Centre & Lisburn Museum)

These lands adjoined the territory Sir Fulke already possessed on the north side of the Lagan. Eventually, he would gain ownership of most of the Barony of Killultagh, and reside at the fortress of Ennishalaughlin, near Moira. This Welsh soldier and adventurer would found the town of Lisburn, and his descendants would go on to become Marquesses of Hertford. In addition to introducing Welsh and English settlers to the Lagan Valley, Sir Fulke is credited with developing the Lisburn linen industry and planting apple orchards using pips from the Severn and Avon valleys.

Sir Fulke closed out the year by adding Ballydownconner and Ballymoney to his flourishing Hillhall estate. He bought out the leases two weeks later.[23]

Montgomery's endgame

Montgomery also seems to have picked up on the rumours concerning Con's disloyalty, and in 1610, in the wake of O'Doherty's rebellion, reaffirmed his earlier Christmas Eve agreement with Con, by which Con agreed to transfer his lands to Montgomery, should he ever fall foul of the law. In the context of the rebellion, this extraordinary arrangement reads like an invitation to Montgomery to get Con arrested, as Chichester had done just eight years before. What benefit could Con derive from such a deal? Did he see the older Montgomery as a father figure or protector? We have no way of explaining Con's apparent naivety. All we know is that Con signed.

The signature of Sir Hugh Montgomery. (Public Record Office of Northern Ireland)

Montgomery was positioning himself for a windfall. But as we shall see, he had reckoned without his old nemesis, James Hamilton.

Con loses Castle Reagh

The vultures were now circling the beleaguered Con, who continued to offload territory in what seems to have been a despairing attempt to remain solvent. He also continued to support his family. In 1610:

We find the said Con O'Neale by deed, 23rd July 1610, demised unto Toole O'Neale, his brother, the three towns of Ballytannymore, Ballyrichard, Ballydughan, and half towne of Drumhirk, for the term of 21 years, paying 28 shillings yearly.[24]

In 1611, a milestone on Con's road to ruin was reached when he leased his ancestral seat at Castle Reagh to Moyses Hill. For Con and the wider Clannaboy, this was a deeply tragic moment. It will have brought the extent of Con's fall from grace into public view for the first time.

The letting also exposed the poor conditions Con's family had been living in. Carew's survey of 'voluntary works' notes that when Hill took on the castle it was not fit to move into:

Moyses Hill hath repayred Castle Reagh neere the Foorde of Bealfast and made up the Bawne with an addition of flankers.[25]

It may have received a mauling when it was captured by Brian MacArt and retaken by Chichester. It is also likely to have been neglected during Con's years of imprisonment and exile. In 1608, Con's name had appeared on a list of great men of the north. By 1611 it had become conspicuously clear that he was a great man no longer.

16
The coming of the Scots
1606

In 1606, Montgomery and Hamilton began settling their new territories with Scots, changing the character of Upper Clannaboy forever. They were men in a hurry. Their enterprise was time-bound and the clock was ticking:

Mr. Hamilton and Sir Hugh were obliged in ten years' time, from November 1605, to furnish British inhabitants (English and Scotch Protestants) to plant one-third of Con's lands granted to himself.

Were they to fail to reach their settlement targets they would forfeit the patents to their lands as Thomas Smith had done thirty years before.

The incoming Scottish tide

The new settlers came in through Donaghadee, the importance of which in these first critical years cannot be overstated. Situated just eighteen miles

Donaghadee - the Staten Island of County Down, where the Scots would enter their promised land. (Kyle Thompson Photography)

from Belfast, and a similar distance from Portpatrick in Scotland, 'the Dee' became the beachhead for the Scottish immigration, making it one of the busiest and most important ports in Ulster.

Montgomery got in on this too. In 1608, he traded lands in Ballymena for Portpatrick, gaining control over the two ports that would be most crucial to the migration. In 1611, James I granted Montgomery control of all trade between Donaghadee and Portpatrick, thus enabling the Crown to collect excise duty and berthing levies. In 1626, Montgomery's income was such that he could justify expanding and improving the harbour.[1]

With lands to settle and serviceable ports available, Montgomery and Hamilton recruited would-be settlers from the Scottish Lowlands and Borders. They attracted thousands of Scots willing to put down roots in County Down, many of whom were Presbyterian. They also moved their own families and business interests to Ulster. They would be resident lairds, not absentee landlords, and County Down would become their land of opportunity.

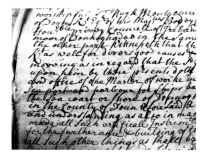

Document authorising John Moore to make improvements to the harbour at Donaghadee. (Public Record Office of Northern Ireland)

The promised land?

Before uprooting the wife and bairns, the wary Scotsman will have asked, 'What's in it for me?' Why did Scots leave the Lowlands for the drumlins of Clannaboy? What did they stand to gain?

Powerful 'push' and 'pull' forces were both at work. The late 16th and early 17th centuries had witnessed the mass-migration of Scots to Poland and Scandinavia. Now the forces that had pushed them out of the Scottish borderlands began pulling them towards Down.

Many moved because of difficult circumstances in Scotland. In the late 16th century, Scotland had witnessed a population explosion, which made land expensive to buy or rent. Inflationary pressures were another driver. The cost of living had soared, with the price of a pint of ale trebling to 16d. and the price of bread more than doubling. These demographic and economic factors made resettlement in Down an attractive proposition, and we read that:

Scotland (like the painfull Bees) did every yeere send forth swarmes.[2]

Many who came were crofters from the west coast, and labourers or farmers from the Lowlands and Southern Uplands looking for a brighter future in County Down. They were a hardy bunch, well used to sweat, toil and bad weather. Their know-how and physicality would clear the scrubland and make the sodden earth productive.

Others saw the investment potential of settling in Down. These proto-capitalists saw a 'land that would repay the emigrant's toil.'[3] They had prospered during the recent peace, 'when trade had expanded and improvements had been made in agriculture' and were attracted by access to cheap and fertile land. Montgomery hoped that these modest landowners would form a superior class of tenants who would in time become gentlemen. These better off settlers brought capital, not labour. He saw that the success

The Border Reivers, who had outstayed their welcome along James I's new 'soft border' with England. (Angus McBride)

of his plantation would in large part depend on the self-interest of those investing from their own pockets.

So it was in 1606, that many Scots packed up their earthly belongings, paid their eight pennies and bought a one-way ticket to Donaghadee. They arrived in their droves, the majority hailing from Ayrshire, Kirkcudbright, Lanarkshire, Renfrewshire, Dumfries and the Rhins of Galloway.

The Border Reivers
The Rev. Andrew Stewart, who decades later would minister to the new arrivals, disparaged them as:

generally the scum of both nations, (Scotland and England) who, for debt or breaking or fleeing from justice, or seeking shelter, came hither hoping to be without fear of man's justice in a land where there was nothing, as yet, of the fear of God.[4]

While partly true, Stewart's remarks did not reflect the rich tapestry of folk who 'crossed the narrowest of seas'.[5] Perhaps the minister was just 'too heavenly minded' to see the rough diamonds glistening beneath the surface of their earthy grit.

The Border Reivers represented a formidable and intimidating presence among the newcomers.[6] They were frontiersmen, who for centuries had repelled English incursions along the Scottish border and had orchestrated attacks and counterattacks into England. Their way of life involved raiding, marauding, burning and thieving, and they were not averse to drawing blood. Immediately after the death of Elizabeth I, for example, the Graham, Elliot and Armstrong clans had invaded Cumbria, where they plundered 5000 livestock.

James I wanted the lawless Reivers gone from Scotland to stabilize the new 'soft' border between his two kingdoms. So on acceding to the English throne, he conducted a pogrom against them, which resulted in seventy-nine executions in 1605, and many more thereafter. Many went into foreign service in Poland and Scandinavia or escaped across the sea to Ulster.

Among their ranks were the Humes, Croziers, Bells, Grahams, Armstrongs, Elliots, Bateys, Johnstons, Kerrs, Maxwells, Robsons, Scotts and Nixons, many of whom were Catholic. This warrior breed, with their trademark steel bonnets, quilted jackets, lances and sturdy hobbler ponies, would provide military muscle for the new settlements in Down.

A microcosm of rural, Scottish society transplanted itself from one side of the North Channel to the other. The rough and the smooth, the saint and the sinner; swordsmen, labourers, farmers, shepherds, herdsmen, gentry of 'gud fashion', ministers, stonemasons, merchants, 'weavers, carpenters, butchers, shoemakers, millers, tailors, tanners, ditchers, coopers and smiths'.[7] Men, women and bairns from every walk of life joined the Scottish exodus. According to the celebrated Ulster poet, John Hewitt, this was:

a transplantation of Scots from not very far away to a climate and an economy very like home, and to which the language, folk culture and lore had been carried without dilution…[8]

A re-peopled landscape

A.T.Q. Stewart wrote that, 'Hamilton and Montgomery… did not wrest a fertile, cultivated and prosperous region from Gaelic proprietors. They came instead to a country devastated by war and famine.'[9] The *Montgomery Manuscripts* go further, painting a picture of eastern Clannaboy as a wasteland:

In the springtime (1606) those parishes were now more wasted than America (when the Spaniards landed there)… for in all those three parishes aforesaid, 30 cabins could not be found, nor any stone walls, but ruined roofless churches, and a few vaults at Gray Abbey, and a stump of an old Castle at Newton, in each of which some gentlemen sheltered themselves at their first coming over.[10]

One could argue that it suited the planters to paint such a picture. However, this perspective cannot be dismissed. All the indications are that the conflict had decimated the population, the consensus view being that over the previous decade Ulster's population may have as much as halved as a result of war and famine. Other indicators, such as the number of troops that Con and his fellow chiefs could raise, paint a similar picture of a low population density.

Scots of all hues arrived with a steely determination to succeed.

Michael Perceval-Maxwell has estimated Ulster's post-war adult population at between 25,000 and 40,000. If this is correct, County Down's adult population could have numbered less than ten thousand.[11]

This population, which had suffered so much, now faced mass inward migration. O'Laverty states that some of the Clannaboy in the planted lands sought 'asylum' in the Little Ards.[12] The English chronicler, Fynes Moryson, says that others took refuge in the forests and islands dotted along the coast of Strangford Lough.

However, the 1659 'census' suggests that the overwhelming majority of Upper Clannaboy's population stayed put.[13] For example, in Newtown, the census recorded 125 adult Irish alongside 207 Scots. Remarkably, the Irish outnumbered the Scots and English in each of Ulster's nine counties, and across the province, 63,272 Irish are recorded as opposed to 40,651 Scots and English.

The names of some of these Scots are known to us. The Rev. George Hill, editor of the *Montgomery Manuscripts*, compiled a list of the earliest settlers on Montgomery's estates:

Gilbert Adare of Ardehine; Quitene Moore of Aughneill; James Cathcart of Balirogane; David M'Ilveyne of Ballelogan; James Cowper of Ballichosta; Thomas Nevine of Ballicopland; Hector Moore, William Hunter, John Peacocke and Patrick Allen of Ballidonan; John Maxwell of Ballihalbert; Uthred M'Dowgall of Ballimaconnell; Patrick Shaw of Balliwalter; Patrick Montgomerie of Ballycreboy; William Caderwood of Ballyfrenzeis; Andrew Sempill of Ballygrenie; Thomas Kelso of Ballyhacamore; John Wyle and John Harper of Ballyhay; William Shaw of Ballykilconan; John Montgomery of Ballymacrosse; John Barkley of Ballyrolly; John Thompson of Blackabbey; Andrew Agnewe of Carnie; David Anderson of Castlecanvarie; Hugh Cunyngham of Castlepick; James Williamson of Clay; Thomas Boyde and John Mowlen of Crownerstown; William Crawford of Cuningburn; Nynnan Bracklie of Newtown; William Cuninghame, John Harper, John Fraser, John Moore, James McMakene, John Aickin, Claud Conygham, Robert Mongomery, William Mongomery and Matthew Montgomery of Donoghdie; Robert Boyle and Hugh David Cunyngham of Drumfad; John Marten of Dunnevilly; David Boyde of Glasroche; David Kennedy of Gortvillan; Hugh Montgomery of Granshaghe; James Maxwell of Gransho; Thomas Agnew and Alexander Speire of Greyabbey; Willam Moore and Robert Wilson of Milntowne; William Wymis, Allen Wilson, Rev. William Moore and Thomas Harvie of Newtowne; Robert Harper, Walter Logane and Charles Domelstone of Provostoun; John Cuningham of Rinchrivie; and John Montgomery and Michael Craig of the Redene.

Other names found among the first Scottish settlers include:

Abernethy, Agnew, Barr Boyd, Bryson, Burgess, Busby, Cally, Campbell, Carr, Carson, Catherwood, Chalmers, Clark, Cleland, Corbet, Coulter, Cregg, Creighton, Davidson, Dunlop, Dunwoody, Ferguson, Frame, Gamble, Gerrit, Gray, Grier,

Gumming, Hamilton, Hanna, Harris, Irvine, Jackson, Jamieson, Jennings, Johnson, Kennedy, King, Lament, Lindsay, McBirney, McCaw, McCleary, McClement, McConnell, McCormick, McCreary, McCullock, McCullough, McGarock, McGee, McGowan, McKee, McKibben, McKinning, McKinstry, McMunn, McQuoid, McRoberts, McWhirter, Malcolm, Malcomson, Martin, Matthews, Maxwell, Miller, Milling, Minnis, Moore, Moorehead, Munn, Murdock, Neilson, Orr, Patterson, Patty, Pettigrew, Pollok, Porter, Rea, Reid, Riddle, Rodgers, Shannon, Shaw, Smith, Stewart, Stevenson, Taylor, Thomson, Todd, Walker, Wallace, Watson, Wilson, Winter

a list that includes the author's own ancestors. These people fanned out and settled on a land that in Jonathan Bardon's words, was 'underpopulated and underdeveloped' and had been devastated by years of attritional warfare, endless hostings, famine and disease.[14] Hardly a picture-postcard destination, yet the Scots saw beyond this and made Clannaboy their home.

The Clannaboy as Gibeonites

As we have seen, despite the prohibition, elements in the upper tier of Clannaboy society continued to hold land, and enjoyed friendly social relations with Hamilton and Montgomery. The lower ranks became, or more accurately remained, tradesmen, farm hands and labourers. The early flight to the woods meant that the 'meere Irish' were at first only partially integrated in the new economy. This is hinted at in the *Montgomery Manuscripts*, which record that during the repair of Newtown House, Montgomery did 'not withdraw his own planters from working for themselves, because there were Irish Gibeonets (labourers) and Garrons enough in his woods to hew and draw timber for the sanctuary.'[15]

This notion that some of the Clannaboy took refuge in the forests casts new light on the idea that the landscape was empty. Perhaps it was 'empty' because a number its people were in hiding, afraid of the incoming Scots. However, any such dislocation was temporary. Most returned – they had few other options. Some may even have had hope of the new system, for life had not been perfect under Con. From now on, survival would mean working for and with the Scots. Pragmatic and adaptable, the Irish came out of hiding and made a place for themselves within the new order. But the sense of dispossession galled. In 1610, Chichester wrote that the Irish 'hate the Scottyche deadly', a hatred that in 1641 would lead them to take a terrible revenge.[16]

17
Upper Clannaboy refashioned

The transformation of Clannaboy

One striking result of the settlement was the remoulding of the landscape. In 1586, Marshal Bagenal had described Upper Clannaboy as 'for the most part a woodland', with huge mosses or bogs that were dotted with islands.

This changed with the arrival of the Scots, many of whom had a Calvinistic work ethic, and a burning desire to build a better life and escape the privations they had faced in the Lowlands. They cleared Clannaboy's oak forests and drained its unaerated soils to create land that could be grazed and planted. The sweat and toil of these Scottish pioneers and human 'earth movers' would lay the foundations of modern agriculture in County Down.

Trees were felled at such a rate that the 1623 Inquisition was moved to catalogue their rapidly diminishing number, noting that:

there were then standing trees of six inches square at the butt, at least, upon the lands of Lisdalgan 342, Carricknesassanagh 534, Tawnaghmore 290, Lisdromlaghan (now Lisban) 475, Killany 162, Tullywastekenna 56, Creevylouggare 221...

The report goes on to describe how one settler by the name of John King:

did cutt upon Lisdalgan and other inland timber townes, with sundry workmen with him, for a year and a-half great store of timber trees, converting the same to pipe-staves, hogshead-staves, barrell-staves, keeve-staves, and spoakes for carts, of which wares there was transported 5 barque loads from Owen O'Mullyn (near Island Mahee in Strangford Lough)[1]

The clearance of the ancient forests was a lucrative business. The timber was put to use in shipbuilding, house construction, furniture making, spokes for carts and the production of strips of wood called staves which could be used to make wine casks, hogsheads, wainscoting and wooden panelling.

Wood also provided the fuel that fired the kilns of the developing iron, glass-working, cooperage and lime industries, and was burned as charcoal in the blast furnaces producing bricks for new houses. Every part of the tree was put to good use, with the bark of the oak used in the tanning of

Datestone from Newtown Priory, carved just one year after the Scots arrived.

The ruined Priory of Newtown, where Hugh Montgomery made his first home.

hides and Montgomery grazing his hogs on the acorns on Con's lands.[2] The timber that was not used locally was exported to England and Scotland to meet the same needs there.

Montgomery's Newtown

Montgomery made his home in Anglo-Norman Newtown (Newtownards) in 'the stump of the old castle… beside the Priory in Court Street'. This tower house had been built by the Clannaboy when they seized the Dominican Priory after its dissolution in 1541.[3] Sir Hugh repaired the church roof, burned down in Brian McPhelim's uprising, employing:

Newtown's early seventeenth century Market Cross. (Ulster Scots Agency)

One John Makinlas… (who) made roofes for the church of Gray Abbey and old Cumber, and some other store of tymber for his lordship's buildings at Newtowne and Donaghdee… all which could be no less than 100 trees

The cloister and tower house became Newtown House, the laird's new home:

Some of the priory walls were roofed and fitted for Sir Hugh and his family to dwell in… with coins and window frames, and chimney-pieces, and funnels of freestone, all covered… floors beamed with main oak timber, and clad with boards; the roof with oak plank from his Lordship's own woods, and slated with slates out of Scotland; and the floors laid with fir deals out of Norway, the windows were fitly glazed and the edifice thoroly furnished within.[4]

The luxurious restoration did not win universal approval. Writing in 1643, Father McCana, a Franciscan friar, deemed it an impious heresy.[5] The truth, however, is quite the opposite. Montgomery restored the roofless chancel of the priory for sacred use.

Walter Harris recounts that the shoreline of Strangford Lough then came further inland and 'the old house of the Montgomery family stood pleasantly seated on the edge of the Lake'. Newtown House was an idyllic setting for Montgomery's first home in Ulster.

The restoration of the old castle provides a prophetic metaphor for the changes that would sweep Upper Clannaboy. The Scots were in it for the

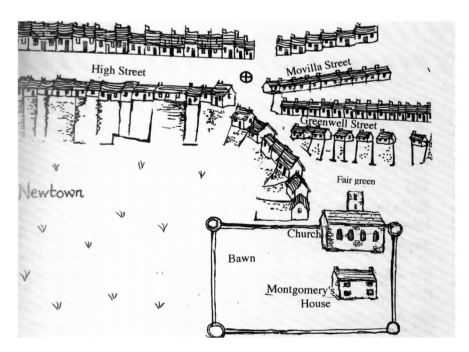

By 1611 Newtown had become 'a good town of a hundred houses... all peopled by Scots'. (Trevor McCavery)

long haul, a fact writ large in their preference for permanent, stone-built houses. By 1611, Newtown had become, 'a good town of a hundred houses or thereabouts all peopled by Scots', equating to a population of between four and five hundred.[6]

In 1613, Newtown became a Royal Borough, sending two members to Parliament. Montgomery became its first provost, selecting twelve burgesses to help him administer the affairs of the flourishing town.

Montgomery also built a residence in Donaghadee, where he would 'wait for the wind' when travelling back and forth to Portpatrick. It is thought to have stood on the site of the Manor House. Another possibly early building here was Grace Neill's Bar, which stands to this day and is reputed to have been built in 1611.

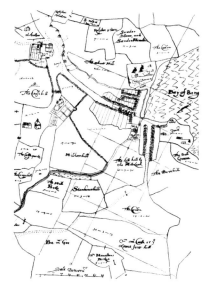

Hamilton's Bangor, 1625, showing the beginnings of Main Street and High Street. (After Raven)

Urban renewal

James Hamilton was 'followed over by a posse of relations with their tenants in tow,' including four of his five brothers – this was a family enterprise.[7] He settled in Bangor, and built a fine new home there:

Sir James Hamylton, Knight, hath buylded a fayre stone house at the towne of Bangor... 60 foote longe and 22 foote broade; the town consists of 80 newe houses, all inhabited with Scotyshemen and Englishmen.[8]

By 1611, his new town and port were prospering. His Scottish craftsmen were joined by twenty 'artificers' from England, who dressed stone and carved wood for the new buildings.[9]

The *Montgomery Manuscripts* talk of a housing boom, with:

streets and tenements, regularly set out, and houses rising as if it were out of the ground (like Cadmus's Colony) on a sudden so that these dwellings became towns immediately.[10]

Towns also provided security for the settlers, offering them safety in numbers.

Not all the new settlements succeeded. Raven's map shows a place known as New Comber which does not exist today – or rather exists only in ghostly form. Archaeologists who scanned the site using geophysical technology uncovered a street layout under the surface of the soil.[11]

Did Con visit these new settlements? And if so, what did he make of them? If he was indeed 'discontented', then he may well have resented them.[12] However, he could do nothing to prevent them. The world was changing. Urban life was reviving. Long dormant settlements were rediscovering their purpose and new ones were being founded, laid out around a green or market square, a main street, kirk and session house.

The towns of Bangor, Holywood, Newtownards, Donaghadee, Dundonald, Comber, Carryduff, Saintfield and Portavogie all exist today on

The lost village of New Comber. (North Down Museum)

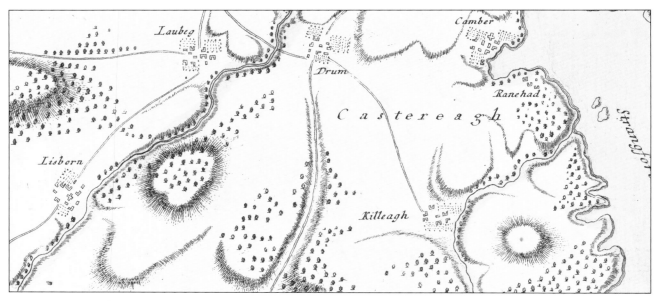

Lisburn in 1760, showing substantial forests remained along the Lagan and in the vicinity of the town. (From Raspe's Schau Platz des gegenwärtigen Kriegs)

what were then the lands of Upper Clannaboy. Substantial parts of two cities also lie within its boundaries. East Belfast, and much of South Belfast grew up on the lands of Upper Clannaboy, as did Lisburn, originally Lisnagarvey, which was founded by the Lagan in the west of Con's kingdom, and in 2002 became the first city to be created on his lands.

Buildings of sod give way to buildings of stone

The ordinary planters could not stretch to the luxury that Hamilton and Montgomery enjoyed. They lived in, 'huts of the roughest kind (built) from sods and saplings with rushes for thatch.'[13] However, increasing numbers of stone dwellings and farmsteads began to appear across the planted parts of Clannaboy.

New sounds and smells now filled the County Down air: the clamour of the quarryman's hammer and chisel, the shaping of stones, the thunder of saltpeter rending rock faces asunder, the bellow and braying of ox and garron teams dragging carts laden with freestone, the acrid smoke of coal-burning lime kilns, all accompanied by the unmistakeable and distinctive burl of Lallans Scots.

The materials for these buildings were often taken from wherever they could be found. This included stones from ruined abbeys and churches, purged in 1541 and burned in 1572. Father McCana, this time with justification, lamented the fact that there was no longer any trace of Comber Abbey as the Scots had used its stones to build their houses. Montgomery used stones from the Abbey to build Mount Alexander as a wedding gift for his son.

Copies of the 'democratic' Geneva Bible were placed in the new Protestant churches.

New churches

Religious worship in Upper Clannaboy was likely to have been regularly conducted outdoors, at recognised religious sites, particularly after Brian McPhelim's wholesale burning of religious houses in 1572, and the absence of any attempt to repair them. This now changed. The settlers quickly established places of worship. The priories at Newtown and Bangor were repaired and new churches were built, often in the rustic 'barn' style. Hamilton 'placed "learned and pious ministers from Scotland" in the six parishes of his estate'. Montgomery did likewise in Newtown, Comber, Kilmore, Greyabbey and Donaghadee, with the help of 'money… handycrafts and… labouring' from his tenants. He also placed copies of the new Geneva Bible and Book of Common Prayer in their pulpits, and provided bells to summon the faithful to the kirk.[14]

These ministers were Presbyterian. And they ministered to mostly Presbyterian congregations, but did so in Anglican churches, hence the description of the period as Prescopalian. This process began with the arrival of the Rev. Edward Brice in Ballycarry in 1613 – a radical minister who had been driven from Scotland. In the ensuing years, Montgomery and Hamilton sponsored the arrival of increasing numbers of Presbyterian ministers, who travelled the length and breadth of Ulster establishing new meeting houses.

James I tried to compete by sending over an Episcopalian minister, the Rev. John Gibson, who ministered in Bangor Abbey Church and became the Deane of Down, but Gibson was heavily outnumbered. The settlers were warmed every Sunday by Presbyterian fire.

Schooling becomes secular

Upper Clannaboy had its own ways of teaching and passing on knowledge, but the fact that Con had probably been educated in Carrickfergus suggests that it had no first rank school. This changed in the wake of the plantation. Education was important to both Hamilton and Montgomery, who founded a 'great school' in Newtown to provide a classical education for the next generation of would-be landlords and merchants. Montgomery endowed his academy with:

twenty pounds yearly salary, for a Master of Arts, to teach Latin, Greek and Logics… and further paid small stipends to a master to teach orthography and arithmetic, and to a music master, who would be also precentor to the church (which is a curacy), so that both sexes might learn all those three arts; the several masters of all those three schools having, over and beside what I mentioned, wages from every scholar under their charge.[15]

It is interesting to note that provision was made within his school for the teaching of girls and boys; quite a forward-thinking institution!

Lallans thrives alongside Irish

Irish had long been the everyday language of Upper Clannaboy. After 1606, however, it acquired not one but three challengers, for the new settlers variously spoke Scots Gallic, English, and Lallans or Lowland Scots, which was the everyday speech of the immigrants from Ayrshire who formed by far the largest part of the new population.

With the 'hamely tongue' came a new literary tradition. The more educated newcomers would have been familiar with Scottish authors such as Robert Henryson, William Dunbar and Gavin Douglas, and perhaps court poets such as Alexander Scott (1525-84), Mark Alexander Boyd (1563-1601) and Alexander Montgomerie (1545-1611).

Irish was displaced but was not extinguished. For decades the four language communities co-existed, with Gallic being by far the smallest and Lallans apparently becoming dominant in the later seventeenth and early eighteenth centuries. By this time Irish was very much in retreat, to the point that when John O'Donovan toured the parishes of what was once Upper Clannaboy in 1837 on behalf of the Ordnance Survey, he could find very few Irish speakers to provide him with Gaelic versions of the territory's place names.[16]

Lallans too would fall into disuse on the lands where it had once been almost universal, but not before leaving behind a rich folk literary tradition, that of 'Weaver Poets' such as Robert Huddleston, Bard of Moneyreagh, Hugh Porter, Bard of Moneyslane; John Meharg, Bard of Gilnahirk; James McKowen, Bard of Lambeg; James Orr, Bard of Ballycarry; Samuel Thompson, Bard of Carngranny; John McKinley, Bard of Dunseverick, and more recently in the novels of Philip Robinson and the poetry of James Fenton.[17]

'Oneals point' off the Copeland Island, a forgotten place name from the days of Upper Clannaboy. The port of Portavo is also marked, where in the seventeenth century there was a lively fish market. (Glens of Antrim Historical Society)

Writing in 1875, Alexander Knox noted:

The Scottish idiom is most observable in the Baronies of Ards and Castlereagh… spoken as broadly as in Ayr or Wigtownshire.

By then it was becoming something of a curiosity. Denigrated as uncivilised and unsuitable for polite discourse, it was relentlessly mocked, trivialised and marginalised. Mass education delivered through the National School system not only did a huge amount to drive it out of public life, but challenged it around the hearths and in the homes of its beleaguered speakers, with the children of the family feeling they could not make their way in the world unless they abandoned the language of their parents.

The arrival of football

The invention of curling, shinty, football and golf are all ascribed to Scots. It is therefore unsurprising to find that Montgomery created a large 'green for recreation at goff, football and archery'[18] at his school in Newtown – 'effectively the first recorded golf course and football pitch in Ireland'.[19]

Hamilton also set aside an area for recreation in his settlements. A 'Ball Greene' is clearly shown at Comber and Bangor on the Thomas Raven Maps. Today football is probably the number one sport in Northern Ireland, bowls are played in every village, and almost every child wants to be the next Rory McIlroy. Quite a sporting legacy, all begun by these Ulster Scots.

Open pasture gives way to fields

Numerous small farms replaced forest and pasture. Hedging and ditching became a priority. Each lease included a requirement to enclose 'the premises from ye adjoining lands by ditching and quick setting 20 perches each yeare till the whole be ditched'.[20] Notwithstanding these measures, many disputes arose around land boundaries, not least between the top two landowners.

This situation was not helped by the fact that three different systems of measurement were in widespread use. For example, the Irish *perch* was almost a quarter longer than the equivalent English measure. Hamilton's mapmaker, Thomas Raven, produced 'A scale proportion to the English, Scotch and Irish acres, whereby acres of eyther kinde are redely reduced into acres of ye other with the compasses only.'[21] A clever chap indeed! Raven mapped the new landholdings in 1625, drawing the new settlements, villages and towns that were springing up across eastern Clannaboy. His glorious maps of the Hamilton estates are a must see for history enthusiasts, and worthy of a place at the top table of plantation artefacts![22]

Farming replaces grazing

Under Montgomery's guidance, Donaghadee, Newtown, Greba (Greyabbey) and Comber prospered. In the first years, the Scots were also blessed with

Bountiful harvests in 1606 and 1607 got the new settlement off to a good start. (Ulster Folklife)

bumper harvests of oats and barley, possibly because the largely uncultivated land was bursting with nutrients.

The settlers grew bere barley, which was 'distinguished from ordinary barley by having four rows of grain instead of two', so doubling the yield. This crop was also less likely to 'lie down in wet weather and could thrive on poor land.'[23] Fruit trees were set. Orchards were established. Kelp fertilised the newly turned soil.[24]

During harvest time, or when undertaking new building projects, the settlers 'neighboured' or helped one another bring in the crops, cementing the cohesion of what at first were very ad hoc communities. Those bountiful early harvests are also likely to have encouraged more Scots to pour into the region.[25]

The huge herds that had once grazed Clannaboy disappeared. New breeds of cattle and sheep grazed on the freshly minted fields, but in small numbers, as few farmers were able to afford anything approaching a herd. The barter economy continued in that these animals were often paid as rent to landlords. 'Garden-plot' tenants paid as little as two hens rent for their land. The Raven Maps also show a 'Coney Burrow' or rabbit warren in Bangor, near where Pickie Fun Park stands today. Rabbits were bred for meat and fur.

The increase in grain growing led to the building of new watermills. Mills were not new to Clannaboy, but their number greatly increased. Each community had its own corn mill, usually belonging to Montgomery or Hamilton. Tenants were obliged to grind their corn at the landlord's mill, paying him a sixteenth of the grain as a toll or *soccage*. Tenants who took their corn elsewhere had to pay the landlord two shillings per barrel as a penalty.

Mill owners became increasingly important and wealthy. One such family were the Andrews, first recorded in the Muster Roll of 1630. They acquired milling rights in Comber and went on to become Comber's first

Water mills, like this one at Boardmills, ground the harvested grain into flour. The Clannaboy hated mill-ground flour. (Lisburn Borough Guide)

Grace Neill's in Donaghadee may have provided a welcome stop off for traders before they returned to Stranraer.

family, with Thomas Andrews designing the *Titanic* and his brother John becoming Northern Ireland's second Prime Minister.

The Clannaboy 'hated the mill ground flour because it was heavy and soggy'. They preferred to roast their oats, prior to grinding them in a stone hand mill or quern. This circumvented the use of the landlord's mill and avoided payment of the levy. Charles II eventually declared the hand mill illegal and his bailiffs broke them up. However, no amount of laying down the law could root them out of Ulster.

Clannaboy tentatively embraces the market economy

In the early days, the settlers relied upon the import of produce from the *hameland,* and during the summer it was commonplace for Scottish traders to make two trips per week from Portpatrick and Stranraer to Donaghadee to sell their produce in Newtown market.

in June, July and August, 1607, people came from Stranraer, four miles and left their horses at the port, hired horses at Donaghadee, came with their wares and provisions to Newton, and sold them, dined there, staid two or three hours, and returned to their houses the same day by bed-time, their land journey but 20 miles. Such was their encouragement from a ready market, and their kind desires to see and supply their friends and kindred…[26]

The ample harvests of 1606-07 provided an economic boost to the new settlement. Not only was there enough food to feed the family, there was a surplus to sell in the markets that now dotted Upper Clannaboy. On market day, hundreds of deals were done, often using coin stamped with James I's likeness. All this helped nudge Clannaboy towards a monetary economy.

Trade also increased with the rest of Britain, with timber, horses, cattle,

Lady Montgomery encouraged spinning in the cottages. (Dulwich Picture Gallery, London)

skins, wool, wood, tallow and butter being exported in large quantities. Merchants also developed trading partnerships with 'France, Flanders, Norway etc.'. The well established trade in wine continued apace – not withstanding the fact that Montgomery was teetotal!

Lady Elizabeth Montgomery

We have already noted the key role Eilish O'Neill played in her husband's escape from Carrickfergus. Eilish's Scottish contemporary was another highly capable woman, Lady Elizabeth Montgomery (nee Shaw), the wife of Sir Hugh. Much of the success of his settlement was down to her talent and effort. Always innovating, and decades ahead of her time, she was the driving force behind many of the agricultural improvements that took place on the Montgomery estates.

She established model farms at Greyabbey, Newtown and Comber. She employed 'poor labourers (newly) arrived from Scotland with little money but some livestock'.[27] She provided them with 'grass and so much grain per annum, and a house and garden-plot to live on, and to graze a cow or sheep and enough space to plant with flax and potatoes', going out of her way to ensure her tenants would succeed.[28]

Elizabeth Montgomery also encouraged the spinning of wool and linen. These homespun textiles, called *breakin,* usually took the form of a 'tartan' or 'shepherd check'.[29] Perhaps she deserves to share the credit with the Huguenots for nurturing Ulster's textile industry.[30] Her initiatives ensured each smallholding became a productive unit based on tending animals, growing crops and making textiles.

The Comber spud and other political hot potatoes

In 1606, Lady Montgomery introduced seed potatoes in Comber. The crop flourished and some four hundred years later potatoes are still grown here. Red sandstone and light, gravelly soils, plus a favourable microclimate allow 'Comber Spuds' to be planted and harvested early. In 2012, 'Comber Earlies' were afforded Protected Status by the European Union, placing them on a par with French Champagne, Parma Ham and English Stilton. Not so humble now!

Sir Walter Raleigh, credited with introducing the potato to Ireland. (National Portrait Gallery, London)

The potato was introduced to England in the mid-1580s by Walter Raleigh, who may have introduced them to Ireland on his Youghal estate. Some, however, say they arrived with a nameless Spanish sailor, via the Armada. The idea that an Englishman may have introduced the potato to Ireland sits uncomfortably alongside England's lamentable role in the Great Famine. History, of course, is laced with such ironies, sometimes amusing and often poignant.

Was it Raleigh or some unnamed Spaniard who brought the potato to Ireland? Whichever is true, if either, Ireland got a new staple food, and Irish folk since have enjoyed their fill of potatoes – mashed, champed, boiled, roasted, chipped and even sautéed! Hail to the humble spud,' King o' the Crop'!

The Plantation Commissioners' Report

In 1611, with the 'official' Plantation underway in the six escheated counties of Ulster, the Plantation Commissioners visited the Hamilton and Montgomery settlements in Upper Clannaboy.[31] Their report provides a glowing account of progress, indeed, the settlement of Upper Clannaboy was considered a model of good practice. This was largely down to Hamilton and Montgomery:

had the two men on whom devolved the colonisation of south Clannaboye and the Great Ards been chosen by the most exhausting of Civil Service examinations, it is somewhat doubtful whether our modern system of discovering administrators would have put forward men so well fitted for the work as Hamilton and Montgomery.[32]

Neither Montgomery nor Hamilton had been scrupulous in their dealings with Con O'Neill. But they were transformative figures, whose tenacity, energy and creativity enhanced the prosperity of the region. Their settlement touched every aspect of society; civil life, law and order, political representation, religion, education, construction, urbanization, commerce, international trade, agriculture, textiles, diet, language, sport and culture. The character of northern County Down today is testament to their industry, and the dour determination of their Scottish kith and kin.

It took him a while, but in time King James recognised this and rewarded his enterprising compatriots. In 1622, Sir Hugh Montgomery was made Viscount of the Great Ards, and the next day, Sir James Hamilton was appointed Viscount of Clandeboye. Clannaboy's historic names had been carried over, but by this point, the political entities they described were no more.

18
The ould King
1611-19

The fallen lord

In 1611, Con rented Castle Reagh to Sir Moyses Hill. In December 1616, the castle was 'formally transferred... to Hill' along with a further twenty townlands for the miserly sum of £60 and an annuity of £160.[1] This pattern was repeated in transaction after transaction. First, the land was leased for an annual rent, then a little further down the line, the lease was bought out and the land sold. For example, on the 24th December 1609, Sir Fulke Conway:

obtained a lease from Con, for 21 years of the townlands of Dunconnor and Ballymoney, in the territory of Slutneale, at the rent of £1 sterling for each towne… on the 7th of November 1615 Con sold to Sir Fulk… Ballydownconnor alias Ballynafeigh and Ballynamoney alias Lisderry in consideration of £100 sterling.

Why did Con sell off his lands for as little as a fiftieth of their market value? Why did he put short-term gain before long-term security and prosperity? At first sight, Con's apparent foolhardiness is astonishing. But it is too simplistic to suggest that Con was simply feckless. He may have been naive, he may have acted rashly, however he was also subject to significant pressures, and rather than receiving help, he got no quarter from Moyses Hill, Sir Fulke Conway, Hamilton or Montgomery. Excited by Con's evident vulnerability, they seem to have worked themselves into a kind of feeding frenzy, driven by an insatiable appetite for land.

Spinning in a vortex

Con's apparent fecklessness was not unique, and he was not alone in his predicament. R.J. Hunter observes that, 'the demands of adjusting to a market economy proved difficult' for the Irish lords. Hiram Morgan develops the idea:

Gaelic Ireland was losing out to a new capitalist spirit of landholding which they simply couldn't cope with.[2]

All across Ulster, the Gaelic nobility found it difficult to adapt to:

managing their estates and financial affairs… Native proprietors were to be found mortgaging much of their land, selling off townland after townland, and many became hopelessly indebted.[3]

This happened on numerous occasions. The *Carew Manuscripts*, for example, inform us that Carbry McCann, a minor chief in Orier, sold out cheaply and moved to lands previously owned by Con O'Neill.[4] In South Down:

Edward Trevor's acquisition of Crogary was by way of payment for a loan of £28 to Donal Murtagh Magennis.[5]

In Kilwarlin, to the west of Upper Clannaboy, Brian Óg Magennis had inherited 28,000 acres after the death of Ever McCrory Magennis. Finding himself with mounting debts, Brian Óg was forced to sell the leases on his territory acre by acre to Moyses Hill.[6]

Again and again we find Irish lords, who were intelligent people, apparently behaving irrationally. Like South Sea islanders in the age of exploration, they exchanged precious things for the equivalent of beads and mirrors.

Indentures leasing townlands in Upper Clannaboy. (Public Record Office of Northern Ireland)

It is not enough to explain this in terms of personal weakness. Something much more fundamental is going on. These men behaved as though they were caught in a vortex, or trapped within something they could not navigate their way out of. Perhaps they were simply caught in the front line as the market destroyed this remote outpost of feudalism. If this is so, then it was not England or 'Englishness' that destroyed the Gaelic system, it was capitalism, and England was merely the midwife. Con was caught as tightly in its net as anyone, and his life careered off into a downward spiral that would eventually leave him destitute.

Aggravating circumstances?

In Con's case, however, there was more. In the only pen portrait anyone offers of him, the *Montgomery Manuscripts* characterise Con as a 'drunken, sluggish man'. As ever, we must be cautious. It was in the interests of the newcomers to paint Con as a wastrel. But his son Daniel appears to allude to something similar, many years after his father's death, when he wrote that in their dealings with Con, Montgomery, Hamilton and Hill, took 'advantage of a weakness and inexperience of the laws of the Kingdom'.

Daniel is the soul of discretion, but it is clear that something is amiss. What was his father's 'weakness'? Anxiety? Insecurity? Or is the description of Con as drunken and sluggish a way of describing alcoholism, a condition for which no term existed at the time? Again we can only speculate, but note that the blight that afflicted Irish lords in general was aggravated by something very personal in Con's case.

Feudal authority disappears

Another dilemma Con faced was that he was used to receiving dues from his vassals in the form of *ceart,* or gifts in kind. There 'was little use of money' in Upper Clannaboy, where cattle were the currency of commerce, and Con's under-tenants held their land from him through cessing and coshering rather than monetary payments.[7]

After 1605, these exactions were no longer legal. In that year, James I abolished the authority of chiefs over their tenants, declaring that they were 'the free, natural and immediate subjects of his Majesty' and not 'the natural followers of any lord or chieftain whatsoever'.[8] This freed the O'Gilmores and O'Kellies etc. from their obligation to pay the tribute that Con and his predecessors had formerly demanded.

Con was also forbidden from leasing land to any 'mere Irish' other than his immediate kin. However, they, like Con, were also mostly insolvent. Unable to accrue sufficient revenue from rents and *ceart*, Con's already significant debts mounted.

Cash flow crisis

Debt is a recurring feature in Irish lordly dispossession. Over a three-year period as a prisoner and then as a fugitive living with Montgomery, Con had accumulated personal debts of upwards of £1000, most of which was

James I by Paul Van Somer. In 1605, James freed the Irish people from all obligations previously owed to their chiefs. (Royal Collection Trust)

owed to Montgomery.[9] This is confirmed in a letter from Montgomery to Hamilton in which he discloses:

> I can directly prooue that befide this Con hath receaued contynuall and daily benefits from me in money, horfes, cloathes, and other prouifions of good value, and allfoe hath bene chardgeable vnto me in diuers other difburfements [10]

Following his imprisonment and rescue, Con appears to have been able to draw only limited funds from his estate, and seems to have been financially dependent on Montgomery. When his erstwhile 'benefactor' sought reimbursement, offloading his lands may have seemed the natural course.

Lost in legalese

Selling land involved entering into legal agreements. To understand the contracts he entered into, Con would have needed specialised legal advice. In addition, the transactions appear to have been conducted under Scottish law, which would have been foreign to Con and his advisors. Noting the use of terms such as:

letters patent, indentures, feoffment, re-enfeoffment, endorsements, boundaries, crown rents, patronage, superior, amercements, sojourners, lessors, lessees, grantor, halfendales, quittance of obligations, hereditaments, freehold, free and common soccage, livery and seisin, moieties, articles of agreement, attorneys, fee and heritage, covenants etc.[11]

D.A Chart concludes that the 'phraseology, both legal and general, is Scottish', and indeed suggests that some of the deeds were 'probably drawn up there'.[12]

Chart also notes that many, though not all, of the attorneys and witnesses to these transactions were Scots. One of these, Patrick Montgomery, was a relative of Sir Hugh and another, John Shaw, was Sir Hugh's brother-in-law. What were the chances of Con receiving impartial legal advice from such people? Both attorneys had a vested interest in acquiring his land on the most favourable terms for their kin.[13]

Language differences may also have disadvantaged Con. He spoke Irish, Hamilton and Montgomery spoke Lallans, and Hill and Conway spoke English: there was much room for confusion. While we know that Con was literate and educated, and that he signed his leases in his own hand, we do not know whether he could read English, Latin, or Scots.

The mystery of valuation

In Con's world, land was not bought and sold, it was taken and held by force, and redistributed occasionally within the hierarchical structure of the clan, under a system of 'gavelkind'. Con did not understand the monetary value of his lands and does not seem to have obtained any independent

Abstract of Letters Patent granting lands to James Hamilton. These fiendishly complicated documents conformed with Scottish, not Gaelic law. (Public Record Office of Northern Ireland)

valuation. How should they be valued? Used to them as open pasture, how could Con even conceive of their settled value at a point in the future when they supported a population of double the size or more?

There may also have been confusion as to the relative values of the Irish, Scottish and English currencies. At the beginning of the 17th century, one English pound equated to twelve Scottish pounds. In addition, the debased Irish coinage introduced towards the end of Elizabeth I's reign, 'was so unpopular that the merchants either refused it altogether or only accepted it at far below its face value.'[14] Could Con's path to ruin have been accelerated by confusion over currency?

The feeding frenzy reaches its climax

In 1611, Con appears to have defaulted on his Crown rents, and turned to Montgomery for help. Montgomery agreed to foot the bill, and in a 'deed of release' dated March 1612, also cancelled the £1000 bond which Con was required to pay to him.[15] He even waived his long-standing £1000 claim for expenses. But this was no free lunch. In return, Con 'conveyed to Mountgomery all his estates in Upper Clannaboy' excepting a limited number of townlands, a clause that apparently gave Montgomery a retrospective claim to lands that had already been sold on to others.

The cards were seemingly falling into Montgomery's lap; upon Con's demise he might now inherit all. But there was one final twist. Montgomery had reckoned without his old nemesis, James Hamilton, and on 2nd December 1616, Hamilton and Moyses Hill intervened to outflank him by persuading Con to give them a similar claim to almost all of his entire landholding, 'upon the only consideration of paying for him a fine of £60 and the yearly rent of £160.'[16] Montgomery had been outmanoeuvred for a second time, his backstop overturned.

Montgomery thought he had Con's third sewn up. Hamilton and Hill believed likewise. Furious legal battles ensued as Montgomery and Hamilton tugged at the rotting carcass of Con's kingdom. 'The tangled relations of O'Neale, Hamilton and Mountgomery' had reached a point of Byzantine complexity, not to say total insanity.[17]

The court cases bled and exhausted Hamilton and Montgomery, which in the circumstances seems like no more than poetic justice. No-one understood where right lay, least of all the participants. It would take the Earl of Abercorn's intervention and the Inquisition of 1623 to determine the legality of the myriad of contradictory claims.

The wild rover

From the year 1608 onward, the O'Neills were a family on the move. They had left Castle Reagh long before Moyses Hill leased it, indeed the expense of its upkeep may have prompted the leasing. Young Daniel and his brothers Aodh and Con Óg had an itinerant childhood, moving from place to place.

Hillsborough Castle. Moyses Hill turned his back on Castle Reagh.

The castle fared no better under Hill than Con O'Neill. Not long after the transfer, Hill's interest turned to the development of his new lands at Hillsborough, and the castle was allowed to fall into decay. The result was that today Hillsborough boasts a fine Georgian mansion, the official residence of the Queen in Northern Ireland, while Castlereagh and East Belfast have been left with little to bind them to the history of the Clannaboy.

In 1609, Con is reported as living in 'Downaregan, in the Upper Clannaboy', probably Ballyregan in the parish of Dundonald.

Dundonald can claim a substantial connection with Con in his latter years. In 1613, we find him living at Ballyhennocke, (probably Ballyhanwood), where his 'chestnut coloured mare' was stolen from him, one Tirlagh Oge McBryne being tried for the theft, but acquitted.[18]

The land transactions continued, but there was little left to sell. In 1615, Con leased 'the half towne of Kilduffe in Slut Neales' to Tool McCormick.[19] In one of his last transfers, he leased Ballynacrossan, near Drumbo, to John William Moore for twenty-one years at an annual rent of twenty-six shillings. The 1616 sale of Castle Reagh to Sir Moyses Hill marked Con's point of no return.

The end beckons

Con was now a spent force – in debt, unable to collect his dues, his castle lost, bamboozled by 'legalese', and unaware of the true value of his lands, which he had now almost completely alienated on 'most unfavourable terms'. As Donal Cregan put it, 'the fortunes of other families were being founded on the ruins of his own'.[20] Con had been swept aside. Fourteen years after his pardon, he was yesterday's man. The impact of this on his well-being can only be imagined. And if he was indeed an alcoholic, the lives of Eilish and the children must have been bleak indeed.

By 1615 he had moved to Tullycarnet near Dundonald. Nearing the end of his life and worn out by its travails, Con set about ensuring that his wife and five-year-old son, Hugh Boy (Aodh) were provided for. The Inquisition of 1623 states:

We find a lease of Con O'Neale's to Eilish Neal his wife, and Hugh Boy O'Neale his son, of the lands of Ballycarngannon (in Drumbo parish), Bressage (in Saintfield parish), and Crevy (in Drumbo parish), dated the 1st of June, 1616, for 101 years, at 8 shillings rent during said Con's life, and after his decease his wife to give as much to his heir during her life, and after her death, yielding 20 shillings to his heir, out of every of the said townlands.[21]

The death of the 'ould King'
Sometime in the year 1619, at the age of just forty-four, Con O'Neill passed away. He died in relative obscurity, and there is no record as to the cause of death, which is recorded without comment in the *Leabhar Cloinne Aodha Buidhe* or *History of Clannaboy*:

Conn, mhac Neill, mhac Bhriain Fhoghartaigh d'fhaghail bhais, 1619

an entry that is in sharp contrast to the accolades lavished on his predecessors. At the time of his death, the 'ould King' is believed to have held at most eight

Raven's view of Dundonald (1625), a village which, in his latter years, Con will have known well. (North Down Museum)

of his sixty-seven townlands. By some accounts he had just two, Gilnahirk and Tullycarnet. According to the *Montgomery Manuscripts,* the Scottish settlers spoke affectionately of Con as 'the ould King', and tradition tells us that they held him in high regard.[22]

Who delivered his oration? Who carried his funeral board? What tokens were placed with his body? Was there any dignity afforded him on his last journey? Was the occasion passed over with something close to embarrassment, or did his people turn out in vast numbers to mourn not just his passing, but the passing of a way of life?

Eilish will have been with him. His kin will have come to share their stories and to pay their last respects. However, by far the greater part of Con's extraordinary life as a leader, father, husband and man will never be known about or recovered. The book of his life has gone to the grave with those who knew him. Mary Lowry adds a salutary epitaph:

Con O'Neill died in abject poverty in a small house at Ballymenoch, near Holywood... all the land as far as the eye could see once belonged to him, but at the end of his life, he could claim only a grave in the old church that once stood at Ballymachan.[23]

Ballymaghan, on the tranquil slopes of the Holywood Hills, overlooking Belfast Lough, where the last Lord of Upper Clannaboy was buried. By J.H. Connop, 1864. (Belfast Harbour Commissioners)

19
One last hurrah
1619-64

Con and his wife Eilish had four children: Daniel, Hugh (Aodh Buidhe), Con Óg, and Catherine. Only the lives of Daniel and Con Óg are to any extent known about, and in terms of their politics at least, these lives could not be more contrasting. Daniel was a firm royalist, who repeatedly risked his life in the service of Charles I. Con Óg rejected the plantation and everything it entailed, and would become a colonel in the Confederate army that arose out of the 1641 Rebellion.

It was as if the two competing parts of Con – the part that embraced Englishness and the part that spurned it – had been abstracted and been given individual personalities, fully realised in the lives of his sons. Their lives set Con's life within an ongoing history.

Con's heir Daniel
Daniel O'Neill, Con's eldest son and heir, is thought to have been born in or around 1603-04, the period of Con's captivity. Upon his father's death in 1619, he inherited a small estate and an annuity of £160, an inheritance that was almost demeaning for an heir to Upper Clannaboy.

Fortunately Lord Conway, the brother of Sir Fulke Conway, made him a Ward of Chancery, allowing him to be introduced as a page into the household of Charles I, a remarkable stroke of good fortune. At this point, his story bears remarkable similarity to that of the youthful Hugh O'Neill, who received his wardship as part of an attempt to anglicise the leading sons of Gaelic Ulster.

In London, Daniel received an excellent education and converted to Anglicanism. Clarendon described him as, 'a great observer and discerner of men's natures and humours' and, 'in subtlety and understanding much superior to the whole nation of the old Irish.'[1] Daniel was quick-witted, resourceful, courageous and charming – a credit to the clan of which he was the uncrowned prince. Though resident at court, Daniel did not lose his Irishness, and maintained close contacts with his family and peers, who of course included the remaining leaders of Gaelic Ulster.

The 1623 Inquisition found that twenty-seven townlands were still held in Con's name. (Public Record Office of Northern Ireland)

The Chancery Inquisition of 1623

One of Daniel's abiding interests was to get back what he could of his father's lands. This was not a fool's errand. The leases, transactions, ownership and boundaries within Upper Clannaboy were often contradictory and had been the subject of numerous disputes. In 1623, a Chancery Inquisition was established at Downpatrick:

> to distinguish the lands severally held by Sir Hugh Montgomery… Sir James Hamilton… Sir Foulke Conway… Sir Moses Hill; Donell (Daniel) O'Neale, son and heir of Con O'Neale, late of Castlereagh…[2]

The Inquisition would provide a definitive register of ownership and put an end to all contention and debate.[3] The inquisition was independent and rigorous, and its findings astonished everyone. It found that Daniel O'Neill held legal title to twenty-seven townlands in the environs of Castle Reagh that had been part of his father's estate. These twenty-seven townlands were the de facto possessions of Montgomery, Hamilton, et al, but they were still legally Con's because the new 'owners' had failed to file for legal title.[4]

Daniel did not act on these findings until 1635, when his position at court had become strong enough to give him the confidence that he could obtain their return. His suit detailed how his father had been tricked by Montgomery, Hamilton and Hill, who took 'advantage of a weakness and inexperience of the laws of the Kingdom and made (him) to believe that he had committed some capital offence against the Crown.'

William Laud, Archbishop of Canterbury. Supported Daniel O'Neill's case. (National Portrait Gallery, London)

He accused Montgomery of taking eight townlands from his father 'to the value of £15,000... upon the only consideracion of £317.' He accused Hamilton and Sir Moyses Hill of procuring 66,000 acres:

by many undue practices, insinuacions and circumvencions... upon the onlie consideracion of a £60 fine then paid, and the yearly rent of £160 Sterling.

According to Daniel's calculations, this represented less than one per-cent of their true value.

His suit would be decided by the Lord Deputy, Thomas Wentworth. Armed with affidavits from the great and the good, Daniel pursued his case with fervour. His claim was endorsed by none other than the Elector Palatine, Maximilian I of Bavaria, and his royal patron Charles I, who wrote to Wentworth:

As Daniel O'Neill is conformable in religion we order you to call these people (Montgomery & Hamilton) before you and take steps to give him fair provision.[5]

Even the Archbishop of Canterbury, William Laud, asked Wentworth to 'see if in a fair way you can help him to a subsistence'. This pressure left Wentworth with no choice but to call on Hamilton and Montgomery to treat with Daniel. Laud's letters make clear that the Scots sought to concede as little as possible:

These Lords taking into consideration the young gentleman's small means, at his last coming out of Ireland, were willing to give him some increase; but so small that all will not make competency.[6]

But Wentworth had huge reservations about Daniel. Indeed, he doubted Daniel's loyalty, given his close and continuing ties with Con Óg, Owen Roe O'Neill and Randolph McDonnell of the Glens, believing him:

in his heart and affections a traitor, bred no other, egg and bird as they say.[7]

He also saw a revived Upper Clannaboy lordship, even in diminished form, as a potential threat to stability in Ulster. Wentworth, who was closer to Charles than Daniel was, threatened to have him imprisoned if he did not drop his case. For now, Daniel was forced to back down, but when Wentworth was being attained would bring his claim again to the Long Parliament.

Daniel the brave
Grievously disappointed by Wentworth's dismissal of his claim, Daniel travelled to the Netherlands, where he and Lord Conway (who somewhat

ironically, continued to hold what had been Daniel's father's lands in Upper Clannaboy) fought with the Dutch at the Siege of Breda in 1637. There he received a serious leg wound.

When the Bishops' Wars broke out between Charles I and the Scottish Covenanters, O'Neill fought on the Royalist side. Indeed, it is recorded that at the Brig O'Dee in 1639, Daniel remained in the field, despite the panicked retreat of the English infantry, one of only 'six of our troops' to make a stand. By this time he had also become active in politics. In 1640, at the Battle of Newburn Ford, he was captured by Alexander Leslie's Scottish Covenanters on the banks of the River Tyne and imprisoned in Newcastle. Presuming Daniel had been killed, Lord Conyers retorted he, 'owed me thirty-three pounds' and requested 'a good horse of his' to cover the debt! In the same year Daniel was made a Freeman of the Borough of Belfast, an honour which highlights his continuing connection with Ulster, just a year before the 1641 Rebellion.

Thomas Wentworth, 1st Earl of Strafford. Scuppered Daniel's claim. (National Portrait Gallery, London)

Rebellion and imprisonment
After his release in 1641, Daniel returned to London, and became involved again in politics at the highest level, both in England and Ireland. He secretly met with his brother, Con Óg, then disaffected, to discuss the unrest brewing in Ulster. Con Óg would go on to become one of the leaders of the infamous 1641 Rebellion. Several years later Daniel was even offered command of the rebel forces, on condition that he converted to Catholicism, something he was not prepared to do.

Under the code name 'Louis Lanois', Daniel also acted as an agent for the King in his uneasy dealings with the Long Parliament. In May 1641, Charles sent Daniel to York to persuade the army's leaders to bring their troops south to 'protect' the king and royalist parliamentarians. However, Charles' arch enemy, the leader of the Long Parliament, John Pym, uncovered the plan, and Daniel was forced to flee to the continent. With him went all hope for his second claim to his father's lands. A few months later, he returned to England in pursuit of a pardon, only to be arrested and sent to Gatehouse Prison in Westminster.

Charged with High Treason
Like his father before him, Daniel was charged with High Treason, albeit against Parliament and not the Crown. He was also in poor health, and petitioned for release in order to recuperate on the continent. This ambitious request was rejected, but he was transferred from the Gatehouse to the more congenial surroundings of the Tower of London. As befitted a person of standing, Daniel received better treatment in the Tower, and his health recovered. Here he lived in relative luxury, enjoying sheets on his bed, a cloth for his dining table and towels for his daily ablutions.

With his strength restored, Daniel determined to make his escape, just as his father had some forty years before. On 4th May 1642, assisted by

The Tower of London. The strongest prison in Ulster couldn't hold his father, and the strongest prison in London couldn't hold Daniel O'Neill.

Dennis, his Irish manservant, and disguised as a woman (in a dress acquired from a Mrs Sanders), 'he did delude his keepers' apprehension', and scaled the outer wall using knotted bed linen, tablecloth and towel, before fleeing into the countryside.

The Lords summoned the Lieutenant of the Tower, Sir John Conyers for questioning. He reported that O'Neill had been visited earlier in the day by Herbert Price and an Irish gentleman, called Robert Walsh.[8] He was able to confirm that O'Neill had been seen at five pm, but when his gaoler returned in the evening to lock his cell, Daniel was gone. Conyers protested at the 'great liberty, Mr O'Neill had at the Lord's order' which had made possible his flight.

Daniel's daring escape created a stir in the city and caused uproar in Parliament. A sensational pamphlet entitled, *O'Neale's Escape out of the Tower of London* was published and quickly sold out. A bounty was placed on his head, and an arrest warrant issued describing him as:

of sanguine complexion, of a middle stature, light brown hair, about the age of thirty years, little or no beard, and of late hath been sick…[9]

The House of Lords ordered the Lord Admiral, Lord Chief Justice, Justices, Sheriffs, and Lord Warden of the Ports of London to apprehend 'O'Neale'.

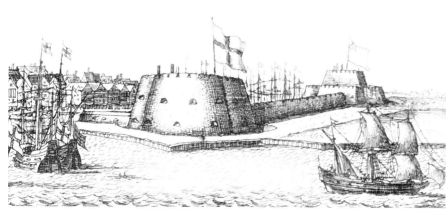

Daniel O'Neill, gun-runner for the King, brought a shipment of arms up the River Humber to Hull. (Wenceslas Hollar)

But Daniel escaped to Holland, where, along with Queen Henrietta Maria, the king's unpopular French wife, he recruited troops and acquired armaments for the royalist cause. It is claimed that the Queen sold some of the crown jewels to finance their enterprise. Daniel was irrepressible. In July he was back in England, sailing a shipment of guns up the Hull Estuary.[10]

The ultimate cavalier
By August 1642, armed conflict between the King and Parliament seemed inevitable. On the 22nd August, 'in the evening of a very stormy and tempestuous day,' Charles I unfurled his standard at Nottingham, signalling the commencement of the English Civil War. Standing resolutely 'among the fairly meagre turnout of cavaliers who witnessed this brief and unimpressive ceremony… was Daniel O'Neill'.[11]

Throughout the ensuing struggle, O'Neill stood four-square for the King, serving as a Lieutenant Colonel in Prince Rupert's Regiment of Horse, and fighting against Cromwell's New Model Army at Edgehill, Chalgrove Field, Newberry, Marston Moor and Naseby – most of the important battles of the Civil War. In 1644, he returned to Ireland as the King's emissary in an attempt to raise an army to oppose the Parliamentarians. After Naseby, he was rewarded for his loyalty by being made a Groom of the King's Bedchamber.

October 1647 found Daniel in Paris, where he became embroiled in a duel between Lords Digby and Willmot, which saw him wrestling an opposing second to the ground, before Digby wounded Willmot on his sword hand and the duel was halted.[12]

Irish connections
During the Civil War, Daniel continued to act as Charles's ambassador in Ireland. His relationships with the main protagonists, the Duke of Ormonde, Lord Antrim, and the commander of the Irish Catholic Confederation, his

The Battle of Naseby, by Charles Landseer. Daniel was there, as part of Charles' inner circle. (Alte Nationalgalerie, Berlin)

uncle, Owen Roe O'Neill, coupled with his proven diplomatic acumen, made him a powerful advocate for the King's cause. He made three missions to Ireland. During these he sought to broker a peace treaty, and to raise a royalist army of 10,000 men, complete with 4000 muskets, 300 barrels of gunpowder and enough victuals to supply them. However, in the factionalised Ireland of the 1640s, not even Daniel was able to achieve this goal.

Even so, he remained a respected and popular figure here, being offered command of the Confederate forces in Connaught, and later, the role of Major-General of the combined forces of the Confederacy, both of which he declined. Next to the Duke of Ormonde, O'Neill was arguably the most influential Irishman of his time. He would go on to obtain the reversion of two Irish estates forfeited in 1641, and represent County Down in the Dublin Parliament.

Exile and reward
On Charles's execution in 1649, O'Neill did not abandon the Royalist cause. During the Interregnum (1649-60) he spent much of his time with Queen Henrietta and her son Charles in their exiled court in Europe. There was no glory and little comfort in this, but at a time when many deserted the royalist cause, Daniel remained true. During this period he spied for the Prince of Wales 'under the appropriate cover-name of Subtle', and in 1651 joined the Prince in a forlorn attempt to invade England from Scotland. In 1658, he travelled incognito to London alongside the Marquis of Ormonde to discuss a plan for the overthrow of Oliver Cromwell.[13]

When the monarchy was restored in 1660, Daniel's years of living and working, 'in a dangerous and treacherous world of suspicion and fear' came to an end. Having 'combined an unflinching loyalty to the Stuart cause, with the qualities of resourcefulness and courage', he returned to England where he had the joy of seeing Charles II crowned.[14] Daniel, first son of Con O'Neill, was a Royalist to his bones.

The young King did not forget his old friend and mentor Daniel O'Neill. Lucrative honours were showered upon him. He was made a Captain in the Horse Guards, became Member of Parliament for St. Ives (somewhat ironic for one who had fought so resolutely against Parliament!), and was admitted to Gray's Inn. He was also given valuable mining rights in Wales and the north of England, became Warden of St. James's Palace, was made the Accountant for the Regulation of Ale Houses, and most lucrative of all, was given the monopoly for supplying gunpowder to the Ordnance.

Despite his many rewards, O'Neill was dissatisfied with his position at Court. He wrote to Ormonde in October 1662:

I know that I shall be but a porter still unless I have it from your favour, which I doubt not to come by the earnest you give me... You know my melancholy humour makes me apprehend more than there is cause for.[15]

Charles II, 'the Merry Monarch', who amply rewarded Daniel for his loyalty. (Royal Collection, Hampton Court)

The signature of Daniel O'Neill from his last will and testament. (Public Record Office, Kew)

He had no cause for apprehension; in March 1663 he was granted the highly lucrative post of Postmaster General. The former pauper had become a very wealthy man, who dined out with the chief men of London, including the diarist, Samuel Pepys.[16] His father's ruin in Ulster had been reversed on English soil.

Daniel and the foundation of the British Army

After the Restoration, Charles II purged the armed forces, re-naming the Commonwealth Regiment (the only standing regiment then in existence) the Royal Regiment, and replacing its Cromwellian officers with royalists. Daniel O'Neill was appointed its first colonel.

Shortly afterwards, nervous about the idea of a standing army, Parliament made the King stand the army down. However, following the insurrection of the Fifth Monarchy Men – knowing the weight his opinion carried with the King – the Privy Council sent Daniel O'Neill to urge Charles to reverse his decision and to establish a standing army 'for the security of his Person and Government'.[17] Charles signed the Royal Warrant, thus creating the first standing army.

The Royal Regiment was reconstituted as the Royal Regiment of Horse. Daniel was given the prestigious position of troop commander. From its inception, the regiment's kettledrummers and trumpeters wore heavily embroidered, gold-laced frockcoats, broad-brimmed black hats sporting an extravagant feather, not dissimilar to the regiment's state dress today.

Belsize House. Daniel O'Neill's English mansion was very different from his first home back in Clannaboy. (Jan Siberechts, Tate Britain)

How mind-blowing is it to think that the little boy who had played on Castlereagh's hills, who had learned the Gaelic tongue on his mother's knee, and had called Castle Reagh home should be so closely involved in the establishment of the British Army? Unlikely as it seems, in 1661, an Ulster Gael, indeed a lord of Gaels, was a key player at a seminal moment in British military history. Daniel O'Neill could be seen as a unionist before his time, and was the first Irishman to hold a position of influence at Whitehall.

Marriage and a mansion

In 1662, Daniel married his long-time friend, Catherine Wotton, Countess of Chesterfield, 'a powerful figure in the dynastic politics of Stuart and Orange', and a lady renowned for her numerous *amours*, who included Sir Walter Raleigh's son and the painter, Anthony Van Dyck.

This was Catherine's third marriage. Her second husband, Lord Henvliet, had known of her close friendship to Daniel but seemed reconciled to it, in spite of the scandalous rumours that raced around the exiled court. Like Daniel, Catherine was a loyal servant to the Stuarts, serving as governess to Charles I's daughter.

At sixty, Daniel's zest for life remained unabated. He used his new wealth to build Belsize House 'at vast expense' at Hampstead, then just outside London, which was to serve as his new family seat.[18] But he did not live long to enjoy it.

On the 4th October 1664, knowing that the end was near, Daniel made his will. His house and fortune were left to his wife Catherine, who was charged with looking after his sister Catherine's children, Charles and Honora O'Hara. He bequeathed any Irish land interests due to him under the Act of Settlement to his nephew Cormack O'Neill, Con Óg's boy; and as a man of faith, left £100 towards the repair of St. Paul's Cathedral, shortly to be razed to the ground in the Great Fire of London.[19]

Daniel died on the 24th October 1664, possibly of stomach cancer. On hearing the news, King Charles II wrote:

Poore O'Neale died this afternoon of an ulcer in the gutts; he was as honest a man as ever lived. I am sure I have lost a good servant![20]

The luminary and diarist, Samuel Pepys, echoed this sentiment, referring to Daniel as 'the great O'Neale'. Daniel passed away without an heir and his estate was bequeathed, almost in its entirety, to his wife. Edward Savage wrote, 'Mr O'Neale of the Bed-Chamber dyed yesterday, very rich, and left his old lady all'. Unfortunately, a second O'Neill estate had been lost, and little if any of Daniel's great fortune ever found its way back to his beloved Clannaboy.

Daniel was buried in the Anglican church of St. Nicholas at Boughton Malherbe in Kent, on his wife's estate, where a black marble pyramid supported by three white marble lions was raised to his memory.

Daniel's wife, Catherine Wotton, Countess of Chesterfield. She became the first female Postmaster General. As painted by Anthony Van Dyck, who had also been her lover. (Yale Center for British Art)

Three lions on his tomb! An Irishman by blood, yet a royalist in his soul.

Owen Roe O'Neill, uncle of Con Óg O'Neill and heroic leader of the Irish Confederate Army from 1642. (Ulster Journal of Archaeology)

Con Óg

Named after his father and sharing the name of his notorious great uncle, Daniel's younger brother, Con Óg (the younger) would also make his mark on the world. However, he was destined to follow a radically different path.

Raised in very different circumstances, Con Óg had no love for the Crown, a feeling that was compounded when his brother Daniel's attempts to reclaim their father's territory were rebuffed. Thereafter, Con Óg was set on a path of confrontation with those who had profited from his father's ruin: the Ulster Scots!

Like his royalist brother Daniel, Con Óg was a courageous soldier and followed his brother into military service on the continent. Six years after Daniel's suit failed, the 1641 uprising provided the perfect mechanism for Con Óg to seek his revenge.

Con Óg was a leader of men and would become a prominent figure on the Confederate side, rising to the rank of colonel. Ironically, standing in the opposing corner were the sons of his father's great contemporaries, Montgomery and Hamilton, who headed up two of the Ulster Scots' militias.

With the impetus of the initial rising almost crushed, the arrival in 1642 of his uncle, Owen Roe O'Neill, from the continent saw the fortunes of the Confederates improve.

In February 1642, Con Óg was to be found besieging the town of Downpatrick, where a considerable number of Protestants had fled for refuge. The outcome was a disputed massacre of the besieged, the burning of Lord Cromwell's castle and the theft of a considerable number of cattle.

The fall of Downpatrick would naturally create some alarm to Lord Montgomery, that Con Oge O'Neill might make a strong effort to recover his ancestral lands in North Down; and it does seem rather strange that no move in that direction was made.[21]

Perhaps the arrival of Scottish reinforcements forestalled any such plans.

Serving alongside his illustrious uncle, Owen Roe, the O'Neills of Upper Clannaboy were in the vanguard of the fight against Munro's Scottish Covenanters and Robert Stewart's Lagganeers.

In the summer of 1643, however, events conspired against them. Unable to supply his troops, Owen Roe gave the order to retreat and regroup at Clones. However, his rendezvous was betrayed, and the Confederates were ambushed and defeated by a superior force of Lagganeers. During the affray, Con Óg was overtaken, and fearing death asked for and received quarter from a Presbyterian minister, possibly the Reverend Livingstone, although this is not certain.[22] However, instead of being arrested, Con Óg was executed on the spot, the rumours of the brutal murders at Downpatrick probably contributing to his merciless killing at the age of just twenty nine.

In an interesting postscript, his daughter Mary married Cormac O'Neill of Broughshane. Cormac was a man of substance, and on the death of Lady

Antrim, inherited the Castle of Edendubhcarrig.[23] The marriage of Con O'Neill's granddaughter to Cormac finally united the fractured clans of Upper and Lower Clannaboy.

His brother Daniel did not forget him. On the 4th October 1664, with failing health, Daniel signed off his last will and testament. He bequeathed any Irish land interests due to him under the Act of Settlement to his nephew Cormack O'Neill, Con Óg's boy. After Daniel's death, his widow, Lady Chesterfield, used her influence at court to petition on behalf of Mary and Cormac.

Aodh (Hugh Boy) and Catherine

Very little is known of Con and Eilish's youngest children. Aodh (Hugh) is thought to have been born in c.1611 and was bequeathed land along with his mother in 1616. He is believed to have died in the same year, at just five or six years old.

The genealogies suggest that Catherine was born around 1620, making her a very late arrival, considering Con died in 1619. Either Con had fathered a child in the final year of his life, or Catherine was the offspring of another man. Catherine married Thady O'Hara of Crebilly or Craigbilly Castle, near Ballymena. They had four daughters and one son. In 1661, her daughter Margaret married Nicholas, the Third Viscount Netterville.[24] Noble blood found noble blood. Catherine was not mentioned in Daniel's will, although her children were, suggesting that she may have died before him.

Eilish O'Neill

In 1618, Eilish had lost her brother Art MacBaron. In the following year she lost her husband. She remained a widow until 1628, when she married Henry Savage of Ardkeen. The *History of the Savage Family in Ulster* notes that Eilish was still a relatively young woman and her new husband was around thirty years old.[25]

Eilish had only the briefest of times with her young, second husband. In the following year she died of causes unknown. Hardly was her corpse cold when Montgomery and Hamilton visited her grieving widower to pay their respects – and offer him £5000 sterling to buy out the lease on the lands Con had given to Eilish and Aodh back in 1616.

The thistled motif of the Scottish Covenanters - Con Óg's enemies.

20
Reclaiming the legacy of Con O'Neill

By 1619, the O'Neills of Upper Clannaboy were a spent force, their lands had been sold off for a pittance and the clan was well on the way to losing all sense of itself as a distinct entity. Over the next 400 years, the memory of Con O'Neill would fade, and become tarnished and forgotten with the passing of time. In retelling his story, I want to help restore Con to his rightful place at the top table. Flawed and misguided he may have been, but if anything that makes him all the more intriguing. For all his failings, he remains a figure who is worthy of commemoration.

The disappearing castle
Beside the old castle site lie the Henry Jones' Playing Fields, a great place to walk your dog. On many occasions I have walked round them with my Labradors, thinking that Gaelic lords once rode across that same hilltop, contemplating long-forgotten battles and buried treasure, and wondering where Con's castle had gone. It had been a substantial structure. What had become of it? In 1744, Walter Harris wrote:

This late nineteenth century photograph of the castle site was taken by Robert Welch. (National Museums of Northern Ireland)

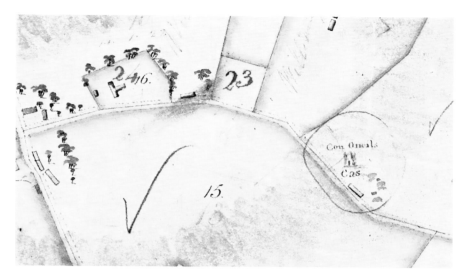

The site of Con's O'Neill's castle is shown in this Downshire Estate Map of 1803. (Public Record Office of Northern Ireland)

Not much more than two Miles East of Belvoir, about as much SE of Belfast Bridge, are the ruins of an antient Castle, called Castle-Reagh, from whence the Barony of that name is denominated. It is situated on the top of a hill and in one of those Forts, the erection of which is usually ascribed to the Danes. This Fort has a Fosse which encompasses three Fourths of it, and once probably surrounded the whole. In the midst of the Fort stood the Castle, formerly the Seat of Con O Neille.[1]

The land was owned by the Downshires. They did not maintain the 'antient Castle', but did carry on some of the activities that were formerly associated with it:

Two miles from Belfast is the village of Castlereagh; it is the head of a manor belonging to the Marquis of Downshire, where his seneschal holds courts.[2]

The *Montgomery Manuscripts* suggest that the castle was 'utterly demolished… about the year 1809.' However in 1817, in one of the last known records of the castle's existence, Henry Joy noted:

Some remains of his (Con's) castle are still to be seen at Castlereagh, standing on the summit of a hill within two miles of Belfast and commanding a very extensive prospect of the town and surrounding country.[3]

By 1823, it had all but gone:

Of the residence of the O'Neills, so often mentioned in the foregoing account there is scarcely at present one stone remaining on another. It was formerly called Castle Claneboye but more frequently Castlereagh or the King's Castle and traditionally by the British settlers the Eagle's Nest from its situation and the power of its owners.[4]

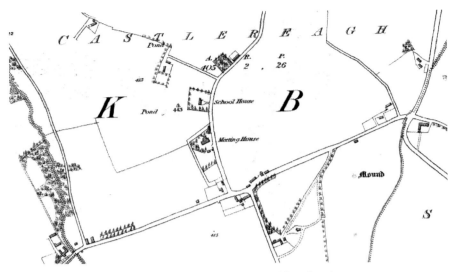

The rectangular thicket under the 'E' of Castlereagh on the OS map of 1835 identifies the position of the castle. (Public Record Office of Northern Ireland)

George Benn goes on to lament Con O'Neill's demise:

It is curious to consider that in so short a space, the castle in which O'Neill had so long dwelt, which had been looked upon with pride and confidence, should have utterly disappeared from the face of the earth; that the fir tree should grow on the hearth stone at which he caroused with his trusty followers; that the lands, which were stocked with his friends and vassals, should now be inhabited by a race of people different in language, manners, customs, laws, name and religion; that the ground in which his bones and the bones of his fathers rest, should be every year disturbed by the rough hand of the careless rustic; and that his very tombstone should be the threshold of a barn.

The excavation

Although the castle appears on maps from the 16th-19th centuries, after its destruction its precise location became shrouded in mystery. That was until 1984, when T.E. McNeill from the Department of Archaeology at Queen's University, excavated the site at the request of Castlereagh Borough Council.

McNeill sought to pinpoint the castle using maps. On the 1803 map of the Downshire estate he found:[5]

Con O'Neile's castle is shown as a tower in the corner of a field… past the Presbyterian church just after a bend.[6]

The 1835 Six-inch Ordnance Survey Map of County Down showed, 'A small square enclosure is marked… at the same bend in the road, North of the church, a school, and the laneway to a farm.'[7] The 1860 Six-inch Ordnance Survey Map of County Down was more helpful again. It showed field boundaries, allowing McNeill to make direct comparisons with the Downshire map of 1803 and pinpoint the castle's location at the site of

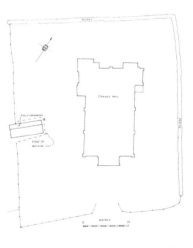

The 1984 excavation site to the left of Castlereagh Orange Hall.

Castlereagh Orange Hall. Today, the Loyal Orders no longer own the hall, and since its sale the building has played host to a carpet showroom and more recently a children's day nursery.

Perhaps a search of old newspaper clippings would have saved McNeill some time and effort. The *Belfast News Letter* of 19th April 1938 describes a speech by Sir Hugh O'Neill MP, in which he remarked that the:

brethren in Castlereagh would pay honour to his name when they opened a hall on the site of Con O'Neill's Castle in Castlereagh.

Con O'Neill, it seemed, had won the respect of both traditions.

Line drawing of the castle site by J.W. Carey, 1895. (Ulster Journal of Archaeology)

Blarney stones?

That not a single stone of the castle remains is surely a sad indictment of the stewardship of the Hill family, who allowed it to fall into ruin.

The Hills did make one guilty effort to preserve it, reportedly instructing their agent or a local builder to erect a wall around the crumbling ruin to protect it from further decline. However, he dismantled the castle to build the wall intended for its protection. From that time on, the story goes, the only stones that remained of the castle were to be found in the wall around the site. Fifty years later, this account found its way into Hansard, being quoted during the Second Reading of the Ancient Monuments Bill in 1874:

a great Irish nobleman had given orders to build a wall round a field which contained the remains of Con O'Neill's Castle at Castlereagh, his object being to protect the ruins; but the agent pulled down the old castle and used the stones to make the wall.[8]

Another less colourful theory is that the local population used the ancient stones to build their homes and form stone walls around their fields. This, coupled with the general neglect of the property, is a more likely cause of its disappearance.

The apparently inadvertent loss of the castle (how can you lose a castle!) robbed South and East Belfast and Castlereagh of the most iconic symbol of its Gaelic heritage.

The Belfast Naturalists Field Club excursion

On the 2nd September 1882, the Belfast Naturalists Field Club paid the site a visit:

A pleasant ramble through the lanes, and a climb up Castlereagh hill brought the company to the site of Conn O'Neill's Castle. The veritable stones that sheltered the famous Conn are still there, but alas! They now form the wall that encloses the bare and naked site alone. Who has not heard the story how the thrifty bailiff pulled down the Castle so as the more economically to build the wall with which he had been instructed to enclose the relic?

Orangefield House, home of the Blakiston-Houstons. German prisoners from the prisoner of war camp here may have filled in the castle ditch. (Public Record Office of Northern Ireland)

On they rambled, entering the 'village':

There are one or two interesting old houses in the village, one bears the inscription '1718 J.W.,' another 'R.A. 1764,' and in one of them are pointed out some of the old oak beams, said to have been taken from the Castle when it was pulled down.[9]

Is it possible that these ancient oak beams still exist in some of the hamlet's older dwellings? Just two hundred metres from the castle's site sits a fine house built in 1786 by Robert Leathem. 'Leathem Cottage' has been described as the 'oldest occupied home in Belfast', and according to local lore was built from the stones of the castle.[10] Some local historians also claim to know of a house where flagstones from the castle form the kitchen floor; unfortunately, they will not divulge its location. Both scenarios seem highly possible. The hamlet's stone built houses, outhouses and field boundaries must be heavily laced with stones from the castle and its bawn. It is unlikely that the stones went far.

Council minutes record that the fosse of the medieval castle had been uncovered following an archaeological dig in 1904.[11] Indeed, 'local residents reported that the fosse had been filled in after World War II by German POWs.' Prisoners were often given pointless jobs to do, and the existence of a prisoner of war camp in the grounds of Orangefield House lends credence to this story.

A more recent dig by Northern Ireland Electricity, when they were laying cable in the field beside the Orange Hall, unearthed a cobbled pathway, but found no trace of the castle. Archaeologists are now convinced that the castle sat in the field beside the Orange Hall, not where McNeill excavated. Perhaps a future excavation will reveal its foundations. Where are Tony Robinson and Phil Harding when you need them?

The supposed site of Con's castle has shifted to the field beside the old Orange Hall.

The throne of Craigavad sandstone

Just three artefacts survive from Con's era. All are fascinating. Perhaps the most significant is the coronation chair of the Upper Clannaboy O'Neills, currently housed in the Ulster Museum.

This rudely constructed ancient chair is made of common whin stone, the seat being lower than that of an ordinary chair, and its back higher and narrower.[12]

Having analysed its geological composition, Martin and Simms concluded the chair was hewn from a single rock of Craigavad sandstone, quarried on the North Down coast near Cultra, seven miles off.

The back of the chair stands less than a metre tall, 33½ inches (84cm) to be precise. The seat is low, standing just 17 inches (38cm) from the ground. Its back is 4½ inches (11.5cm) thick. It is inclined forwards to the left, and its base is uneven – a bit may have been knocked off – meaning that if left standing on its own, it would topple.

It is raw and rustic in appearance, but nonetheless a haunting symbol of former glory. Which mason chiselled its rugged lines and form? How did he cut it without cracking it open? Its simplicity speaks of endurance and crude power.[13] The fact that it looks so un-regal makes it of a piece with the other, purposefully earthy elements that were involved in inauguration, the wand

Leathem Cottage, built in 1786 by Robert Leathem, allegedly using stone from the castle.

The coronation chair of the Upper Clannaboy O'Neills; the only such chair to survive from the Gaelic age. (National Museums of Northern Ireland)

*The Stone of Scone,
inauguration stone of English
monarchs since 1296.*

of hazel, the ritual bathing, the simple shoe. And when we look at it and ask how this dwarfish object could possibly equate with kingship, we should remember that the new chief was not always inaugurated on a structure as elaborate as a chair.

Very often inaugurations took place on 'large stones, on which the impression of two feet is sculptured'. In his *View of the State of Ireland*, the poet Spenser observed how the newly elected chief put his bared foot into a carved footprint, 'which they say is the measure of their first captain's foot'.[14]

The most famous such stone is of course the Stone of Scone or Stone of Destiny, which until recently was held in Westminster Abbey. Legend tells how the stone was brought to Ireland by an ancient people, then sent to Scotland for the coronation of Fergus, first King of Scots, a blood relative of the Kings of Ireland. It was present at the coronations of all Scottish monarchs until 1296, when it was removed to England by Edward I, the 'Hammer of the Scots'.

In 1953, Queen Elizabeth II was crowned in Westminster Abbey on King Edward's chair in which the Stone of Scone was housed. Before guests representing 129 nations, she took the oath, received communion and was anointed with holy oil. She was then given a golden robe, a pair of golden spurs, the Sword of State and the four symbols of authority: the orb, the sceptre, the Rod of Mercy and the royal ring. Finally, with incense, prayers, psalms and hymns duly offered, King Edward's crown was placed upon her head, following rituals dating back to the coronation of King Edgar in 973. If you think the inauguration rites of the Gaelic lords were strange, think again!

The coronation mound

The stone chair stood on a mound called the *tulach tinóil*, or hill of gathering, a place used for assemblies, celebrations, the administration of the law, and most importantly, the inauguration of the chief.

Historians knew of the existence of such a mound close to Con's castle, but it was not until the pioneering excavation work of Brian Davison in 1958 that its location was rediscovered. Davison excavated 'a small earthen mound situated on an east-facing slope, about 400m east-southeast of the site of the castle', near to where the stone chair had been discovered.[15] The mound now lies in dense woodland near the junction of the Ballygowan and Manse Roads, below Castlereagh House.

Davison described it as a 'grass-covered sub-circular earthen heap'[16] shaped like a 'truncated cone'.[17] It has a diameter of twelve metres at its base and is just over two metres high with a flat top 4.3 m in diameter. It was then in a 'sadly neglected state', as indeed it is today, being overgrown with four mature trees growing from its summit. He determined that it was a man-made structure, consisting of a primary mound which had later been given a secondary covering.

*Abandoned relic from a lost
world. Con's inauguration
mound, October 2019.*

Although hampered by a heavy snowfall, Davison found evidence of a fosse or ditch on its southern, eastern and western slopes, and a stepped formation on its southeast face. Significantly, the site was largely sterile, with no evidence of burials. He did, however, record 'a layer 6″ deep' of dark earth containing charcoal and burnt bone' in the ditch. This relative sterility led Dr. Elizabeth Fitzpatrick to suggest that the mound was not a burial site but the long lost Clannaboy 'Throne Mound'.[18]

Five 'weathered basalt blocks… radially aligned on the centre of the mound' were also uncovered.[19] Each of these was about the size of a modern breezeblock, their regularity suggesting that they were created for a specific purpose.

Davison also discovered post holes, suggesting that a gazebo-like structure had once stood on the mound. Was this a regal canopy, connected to the inauguration rite? The excavators thought this unlikely, as the post holes were in the secondary covering which they believed post-dated the time of Con O'Neill. Davison suggests that the owner of Castlereagh House, Mr Forsyth, may have added the second layer and built a summer house on its summit.

The sites of Con's lost castle (r) and inauguration mound (l) lie within 500 metres of each other. (Google Maps)

The chair's journey
The story of Clannaboy's coronation chair is a remarkable tale of survival. After the fall of the Clannaboy, the ancient chair was overturned and lay in a neglected state, hidden by dense undergrowth near the castle, possibly concealed for its own protection.

Stewart Banks, Sovereign of Belfast, painted by Strictland Lowry. Banks saved the inauguration chair from destruction. (National Museums of Northern Ireland)

In 1755, the Mayor of Belfast, Stewart Banks Esq., became aware of the chair and had 'it built into the wall of the Butter Market (in Tomb Street), where it was used as a seat' by the weigh-master.[20] Imagine the indignity, the ancient chair of anointing used as a resting place for the derrières of common folk! Without Banks' intervention, the chair may have been lost forever.[21]

When the Butter Market was demolished in 1829, the chair was:

mixed with the other stones and rubbish, and was about to be broken up, when a Thomas FitzMorris took possession of it, and removed it to a little garden in front of his house in Lancaster Street, Belfast'.[22]

Here the chair became an object of great curiosity.[23] It remained in Lancaster Street until 1832, when it was purchased by:

a young gentleman of cultivated mind and elegant tastes, R.C. Walker, Esq. of Granby Row, Dublin, and Rathcarrick, in the County of Sligo, who has had it removed to the latter place.[24]

According to *Wilson's Dublin Directory* of 1832, Roger Walker lived at No. 2, just along the street from a certain, Mr A. Guinness, Esq., possibly the son of a certain Arthur.

In 1897, a group of Belfast's leading citizens, including members of the Belfast Natural History and Philosophical Society, aided by a Dr Frazer of Dublin, bought the chair back from Walker's son. The list of subscribers contributing to the chair's return included industrialists, nobility and gentry:

Countess Shaftesbury	James Thompson, J.P.	Lavens M. Ewart J.P.
L. Patterson, J.P.	R. Patterson, J.P.	John Wales, J.P.
P.J. MacMullan, J.P.	David Leahy, J.P.	Otto Jaffe, J.P.
S.F. Milligan, M.R.I.A.	H.O. Lanyon	D.A. Maxwell
W.A. Ross & Son	Samuel Sinclair	R.M. Patterson
W.H.F. Patterson	Young & Mackenzie	John M'Knight
James Moore	Francis Curley	R.Anderson
S.D. Neill	W. Swanston F.G.S.	D.E. Lowry
C.H. Brett	W. Shean	W.H. Stephens
W.H. M'Laughlin	John Brown	A.C. Capper
Henry O'Neill M.D.	James O'Neill M.A.	A. Friend

Badge of the Great Northen Railway with the red hand of the O'Neills at its centre. (Monaghan County Museum)

And so, after a sixty-five-year exile, the diminutive chair returned to Belfast in triumph, generously transported free of charge from Rathcarrick by the Sligo, Leitrim, and Northern Counties Railway Company and the Great Northern Railway Company. Here it took pride of place in the Ulster

Museum, then situated in College Square North. The event was widely reported, accounts of the chair's arrival even appearing in *The Star* in New Zealand in January 1898. This unique artefact, the only such chair to survive the collapse of Gaelic Ireland, is currently in the Ulster Museum.

Buried treasure

No proper mystery is complete without buried treasure, and the Clannaboy story scores here too. In 1844, a labourer dug up a hoard of 'one hundred and fifty shillings and sixpences of Edward VI and Elizabeth I,' contained in a pewter jar in the ditch surrounding the ruins of the castle.[25] Their whereabouts are currently unknown.

The Connswater River

Today Con's name lives on in the Connswater River which flows through East Belfast. The significance of its name should not be overlooked. It was his river, he controlled it, and when it was spoken about colloquially it was sometimes called 'Con's Water'.

The Connswater River is formed at the confluence of its tributaries. The first of these, the Knock River rises in the Holywood Hills and flows for six miles along the Dundonald Gap to meet the River Loop near Elmgrove Primary School. One of its tributaries has its spring near the site of Con's castle, then flows north to join the Loop River at Abetta Parade.

James Lawson's map of 1789 shows an earlier shoreline and the journey of the Connswater into Belfast Lough. (American Geographical Society)

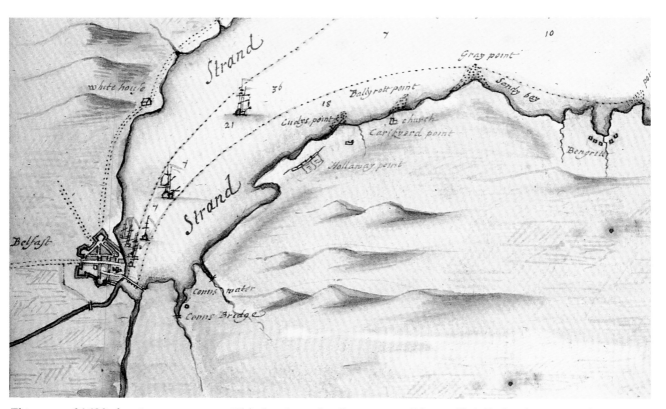

This map of 1683 showing 'conns water' and 'Conns Bridge', proves the bridge is not a Victorian folly. (Glens of Antrim Historical Society)

This is where the Connswater River officially begins. Just a few metres on, the river flows under an ancient foot bridge also associated with Con. From there, it runs past a roster of East Belfast landmarks, the Owen O'Cork Mill, the Connswater Shopping Centre, the 19th century Conn O'Neill Bridge, C.S. Lewis Square, Samson and Goliath, the Oval Stadium and Victoria Park, before finally pouring into Belfast Lough.

In Con's day, the river mouth was a recognised port or landing place from which the O'Neills imported wine and exported cattle, sheep and horses:

There is a place called Conn's Water, within two miles of Belfast, and another place called Garmoyle, part of the Port of Bangor, in both of which places the officers of Carrickfergus receive a benefit of the third part of the customs for wines or other goods discharged there…[26]

Tax 'irregularity' on the Connswater River continued well beyond Con's time, and in 1637, the Surveyor General admonished 'John Hornby, the waiter of Carrickfergus' for skimming off one-third of the tax revenue due to the Crown.

Death and rebirth

Four hundred years ago, the river was wider than it is today and well-stocked with fish. In the nineteenth century, when Belfast became an industrial powerhouse, the Connswater River provided an artery of crystal-clear water, powering the corn and linen mills along its path. The river furnished the thousands of gallons required by the Belfast Rope Works, and whiskey distilleries at Avoniel and Connswater. Indeed, in Belfast's Victorian heyday, one-third of all Irish whiskey exports were produced at these two distilleries.

Unfortunately, the legacy of this industrialisation was an overworked and neglected river. Con's Water became a polluted, treacly sludge, meandering through East Belfast. Chemical waste, industrial sediment, litter and fly-tipping created a congealed, poisonous thread. The flora and fauna that once flourished along its length all but disappeared and the river suffocated.

However, all was not lost! In 2007, the Connswater Community Greenway Project obtained £32 million to rejuvenate the river and its environs. This project has created a five and a half mile (9km) linear park and walkway through East Belfast, 'following the course of the Connswater, Knock and Loop Rivers'. The rivers are being cleaned, new bridges are being built and old ones improved with a view to creating 'a wildlife corridor from Belfast Lough to the Castlereagh Hills'.

New life has been breathed into its meandering path. Heron, Little Egrets and Kingfishers have been spotted along its banks, which are slowly being replenished with river flora. Cyclists, dog walkers and runners now enjoy the riverscape. Today, the Connswater River is no longer an embarrassing backwater. The river, which is celebrated in Van Morrison's album, 'Inarticulate Speech of the Heart' and in Duke Special's 'Some things make your soul feel clean,' has been reborn.

Con O'Neill's Bridge

Another important Con survival is Con O'Neill's Bridge, also formerly known as the King's Bridge, memorably described by Charles Brett as 'a hoop of ancient stonework crumbling shamefully at the foot of a pylon in the derelict wasteland behind Abetta Parade'.[27]

Is this the most beautiful bridge in Ulster, or is sentiment getting the better of me? This small but elegant stone footbridge crosses the river where it meets the Beersbridge Road. It has a small patch of cobbled paving on each side, and has recently been repointed, spruced up, and landscaped under the greenway scheme. Essentially undatable, it is said to have been built in Con O'Neill's time, which if correct would make it the oldest stone structure in Belfast.

Some suggest it is older still, and was crossed by King John in 1210 as he made his way through Down. Another suggestion is that it was named the King's Bridge because the Williamite army passed over it 1689. Benn says, 'Of the three kings, King Con was the most likely to have given his name to this bridge'.[28] Another reference point must be the founding of

The bridge is difficult to date but is likely to have been built in Con's era or before.

Con O'Neill's Bridge, near Elmgrove School in East Belfast. (Connswater Community Greenway)

This house and motte are shown on Thomas Raven's 1625 map of the townland of Ballymaghan. (North Down Museum)

Castle Reagh, and the building of links with Belfast and the north. Like much else about Con, it is an enigma, which only time and new evidence will eventually resolve.

The lost grave

There is some debate as to where Con was finally laid to rest. The Knock graveyard has been suggested, however the strongest tradition is that he was buried in the grounds of the old churchyard in the townland of Ballymaghan, between Belfast and Holywood.

Its church can be traced back to 1307, when it was listed in the taxation register of Pope Nicholas.[29] At that time, the church was overlooked by a motte, dating from the days of John de Courcy. Local legend relates that the Williamite army camped at Ballymaghan on its way to the Boyne, and that while here many men died of fever. It further suggests that animals refused to graze at the site.[30]

As a site of antiquity, Ballymaghan was a fitting burial ground for Upper Clannaboy's last Gaelic lord. But it was not *the* most fitting, for by rights Con should have been buried with his ancestors in the church of the former Friars Minor de Observantia in Carrickfergus, and perhaps would have been, had Chichester not cleared its remains and built a splendid house for himself on its site a few years before Con's death.

The Moat House tombstone

The 1625 Raven map of the townland of Ballymaghan shows a large house by the motte, close to what seems to have been Con's final resting place. Around 1864, a fine new dwelling called Moat House was built on the site.[31] Some years later human remains were uncovered in its orchard, which may also have been the site of the old graveyard.[32] Two stone grave slabs were also discovered, one of which somehow got the reputation of having been Con O'Neill's tombstone. It was later built into a barn wall. PRONI holds a pencil sketch of it in situ, identified as:

Conn O'Neill's tombstone in the gable of a barn at Ballymechan, near the old graveyard of Temple Columkill.

However, the sketch shows that the stone is Anglo-Norman. A second drawing by James Boyle Esq., made in December 1844 after the slab had been removed to the Belfast Museum, confirms this, its shears indicating that it was made for an Anglo-Norman gentlewoman. (Shears indicate a female burial, a sword denotes a male grave.) Even James O'Laverty, who, were there the slightest possibility of the stone having been Con's would not have let the matter slip, is firm on the point:

the tombstone said to be that of Con O'Neill… never belonged to his grave. It is an Anglo-Norman cuneiform slab, similar to that found in the graveyard of Holywood…

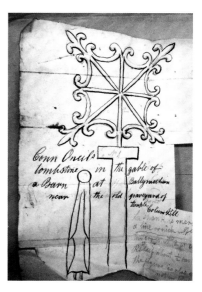

Drawing of the carvings on the graveslab once thought to be Con's. (Public Record Office of Northern Ireland)

This leaves only the prospect that the stone could have been 'recycled' and given a new lease of life as Con's grave. But this seems highly unlikely, if not positively disrespectful.

Moat House still exists, however the motte has since been bulldozed and its site is today scrubland behind Finchley Vale, near Belmont Park. The extent of the former burial ground is unclear, as is whether it has been built over, partially built over, or lies to some extent undisturbed. Who knows what remains may lie there? And if, after over five hundred years it was possible to discover the remains of King Richard III in a car park, maybe one day we will discover Con's.

As others see us

The received wisdom about Con O'Neill is overwhelmingly negative. Contemporaneous and modern historians alike view him as a figure of ridicule and contempt: George Benn wrote that he was 'doomed to fall'.[33] Stevenson describes him as 'weak and improvident' and 'of ignoble memory'.[34] Philip Robinson calls him 'gullible'. The *Stewart Manuscripts* speak of him as 'rebellious' and the *Montgomery Manuscripts* call him a 'drunken, sluggish man.'[35]

Some, on the other hand, see him as a victim of dark and more powerful forces. His son Daniel believed him to have been duped and bamboozled.

The ornamental spires of the Rosebay willowherbs form a guard of honour over Con's possible last resting place at Motelands.

O'Laverty was also sympathetic, describing Con as 'unfortunate'.[36] Biggar bigs him up, calling him 'prominent' in the northern revolt.[37]

Perhaps Haines strikes the correct balance, on the one hand describing Con to be 'a man of absolutely no imagination', 'naive' and 'lacking political acumen'. On the other, he acknowledges that Con 'more than suffered his share of hypocrites and liars' and was the 'victim of long-term scheming', which he was unequal to'.[38]

To know Con the man, we must interpret his unwritten history. He was a husband who enjoyed the love of his wife; a father who provided for his son as his kingdom shrank and his health failed; a brother who remembered his siblings; a chief beloved by his tribe; volatile, yes, but a military leader; a man of faith and attachment to the church of St. Columbkille at Knock; a generous man who enjoyed entertaining his friends, and perhaps herein lay the seeds of his downfall. However, transcending all of this, Con O'Neill was a man out of time, a feudal lord overwhelmed by the unleashing of market forces, and an Irish chief consumed in the cataclysmic clash of Gaelic and British cultures.

Childhood apart, Con McNiall McBrian Faghartagh O'Neill lived a turbulent life: his youth overshadowed by Tyrone's war; his coming of age given over to rebellion, imprisonment and intrigue; his maturity spent battling bankruptcy. His was a life of huge contrasts, a life of grandeur and ignominy, a life that ended mysteriously early, a life lived on the edge. Rest in peace, 'ould King'.

Postscript:
my Con reconnection wish list

It is my hope that the people of East Belfast, Castlereagh, Lisburn, Bangor and the Ards, and indeed everyone who lives in what was once Upper Clannaboy, will again embrace the legacy of Con O'Neill and the Clannaboy. In this, the four hundredth anniversary year of Con's death, we have the responsibility to give the Clannaboy back their place, rejuvenating local tourism as we do so. My reconnection wish list would include:

- An interpretive centre at the site of the castle with a tall, reconstructed ruin alongside.
- An interpretive trail, tracing key places and events in Con's story.
- A public park around the coronation mound.
- A replica stone chair at the site.
- A sculpture to commemorate Con O'Neill and the Clannaboy.
- Acknowledgement and celebration of Con's place in our local history.
- Celebration of the contribution made by the Scottish settlers who came over with Montgomery and Hamilton.
- Telling the story of Con O'Neill, Montgomery and Hamilton in local schools.

Notes

1. Mythical beginnings

1 Caisleán Riabhach, or Castlereagh, the seat of the O'Neills of Upper Clannaboy.
2 Reeves identifies Con O'Neill's grandfather, Brian Faghartagh, as the earliest occupant of Castle Reagh. However, there is also a suggestion that his father Niall Óg, ruler of Clannaboy from 1529-37, occupied it. In 1553, Lord Chancellor Cusack wrote that Brian Faghartagh's brother, Hugh MacNeill, 'hath two castles, one called Bealefarst… the other, called Castlerioughie…'. Brewer J.S. & Bullen, W. (eds.), *Carew Manuscripts*, Vol.I, p.243.
3 Upper Clannaboy lay south of the Lagan and Lower Clannaboy lay north of the river.
4 *UJA*, Series 1, Vol 2, p.54. This venerable article records the local tradition that Niall detained his hostages on Dunnyvell Island near Killyleagh. Dun-na-n-giull means 'Fort of the Hostages'.
5 At this time, Alba (Scotland), is referred to as Scotia Minor and Ireland as Scotia Major.
6 DOENI, p.1-54
7 The nickname 'Black Knee' may have referred to his 'black iron defensive armour'. http://www.aughty.org/pdf/gaillgael_northmen.pdf, p.4/13
8 Ua Clerigh, A., *Ireland*, Vol. 1, p.289. 'Glun-dubh' refers to 'black iron defensive armour', identifying Niall as a military leader.
9 Ibid.
10 The Scottish clans, MacNeil and MacLachlan, also claim descent from Niall Glandubh.
11 Moore, L.T., & McEvoy, B. et al, A Y-Chromosome Signature of Hegemony in Gaelic Ireland in *American Journal of Human Genetics* (February 2006) 78(2): p.334-38
12 Tuatha de Dannan: mythical early inhabitants of Ireland from the Legends of the Fianna.
13 McCoy, G., *East Belfast*, p.16
14 *TAS*, Vol. 2, p.337-379
15 Reeves, Rev. W., The Seal of Hugh O'Neill in *UJA*, Vol.1, 1853, p.255-58
16 McCoy, G., *East Belfast*, p.16
17 Campbell, A.A., Turlough Luineach O'Neill's Signet Ring, in *UJA*, Vol.2, 1896, p.142
18 From: 'The Rules of the Road' (Anon)
19 'The Red Hand of the O'Neills (appaume – palms outward), on a gold background, indicating the connection between the area and this famous Ulster Clan.'

2. The foundation of the Clann Aodha Buidhe 1167-1318

1 The Hill of Down, where Downpatrick Cathedral stands today.
2 *Ulidia*, the Irish kingdom lying east of the Bann, comprising all of County Down and most of County Antrim.
3 Cambrensis, Book 2, chap.16
4 Simms, K., in Dillon & Jeffries, p.131-2. *Annals of the Four Masters* 1179
5 Flanders, S., *John de Courcy*, p.104
6 Alvarez, S., in Duffy, S., (ed.), in *IHS*, n.117
7 Davies and Quinn, in *UJA*, p. 36, 66

8 Brown, D., *Hugh de Lacy*

9 John O'Donovan has suggested Cameirge (the Crooked Rise) is Mac Lochlainn's Esker in Altihaskey, Ballinascreen.

10 Orpen, G.H., in *JRSAI*, p.30-46

11 Duffy, S., (ed.), *Medieval Ireland*, p.477-82

12 Keenan, D., *Real History*. The word *buidhe* or yellow is vividly characterised in the *Annals of Boyle*, which record 'a great mortality' in 534, the *Buidhe Chomaill*, in which the skin turned to a corn or stubble coloured yellowness.

13 Lydon, J., *Ireland*, p.57

14 Domnall ruled in Tyrone on three separate occasions: 1283-86, 1290-91 and 1295-1325. Curtis, E., *Medieval Ireland*, p.239

15 Hill, Rev. G., *Ulster*, p.167

16 Hogan, J., in *PRIA*, p.186-254

17 'The Lough of O'Lynn's Island', after the O'Floinn, who ruled from a crannog on the lake.

18 Phillips, J.R.S., in *IHS*, Vol. 27, 1990, p.125. Robert Bruce, the twice crowned King of Scotland, had married Elizabeth de Burgh, daughter of the Red Earl in 1302. She became his Queen in 1306.

19 Joy, H., *Historical Collections*, p.24

20 Ibid.

21 Adamson, I., *Cruithin*, p.84

22 Lydon, J., *Ireland*, prologue

3. Crossing the Bann 1318-1482

1 Duffy, S., (ed.), *Medieval Ireland*, p.477-82

2 Ibid.

3 Ibid.

4 Despite the treaty, the Clann Aodha Buidhe continued to come under attack from Tir Eoghain. In 1345, Aodh Reamhar made a daring marine assault across Lough Neagh. However, after 'considerable loss on both sides, he made his escape in his boats.' Reeves, W., in *UJA*, p.255-58

5 Simms, K., *From Kings to Warlords*, p.58

6 The Anglo Normans adopted the Irish language, married Irish women, dressed in the hooded tunic and wore their hair after the Irish fashion, with the *cuilfhionn* or single lock at the back of the head, the long fringe or 'gibbe' and a moustache. Lydon, J., *Ireland*, p.57

7 O'Laverty, J., *Down and Conor*, p.385

8 McNeill, T.E., *Anglo-Norman Ulster*, p.120-21

9 Duffy, S., (ed.), *Medieval Ireland*, p.797

10 Ibid.

11 Ibid.

12 O'Hart. J., *Irish Pedigrees*, p.732

13 O'Laverty, J., *Down and Connor*, Vol.II, p.163

14 Ibid.

15 O'Hart, J., *Irish Pedigrees*, no.117

16 Ibid.

17 Ibid.

18 Connellan, O., *Annals of the Four Masters*, p.253

19 Ibid.

20 O'Laverty, J., *Down and Connor*, Vol.1 p.341

21 Berry, H.F., and Morrissey, J.F., (eds.), *Statute Rolls*, Vol. 2, p.176

22 The port of Ardglass was surrounded by a ring of up to six castles, four of which remain today, including Jordan's Castle.

23 Hill, Rev. G., (ed.), *Montgomery Manuscripts*, p.256, quoting *Annals of Ireland*

24 Duffy, S., (ed.), *Medieval Ireland*, p.481

25 Connellan, O., (translation), *Annals of the Four Masters*, p.21

4. The great lordship of Clannaboy 1482-1555

1 Mulchrieves became anglicised as Rice.

2 O'Laverty, J., *Down and Connor,* Vol.II, p.156-8

3 Ibid.

4 Trian Congaill was the ancient name for the modern counties of Antrim and Down, excluding North Antrim and South Down. The territory would become known as Clannaboy.

5 *Annals of the Four Masters*. Said to have been originally established by Hugh de Lacy, who was buried there in 1243. The Annals relate that Niall Mór's foundation was approved by Rome, and initially staffed by sixteen friars and a superior from Donegal. The buildings no longer survive.

6 Thompson, M., *Sir Thomas Smith*, p.9

7 Ibid.

8 Phelim Bacach is also the ancestor of the Lords O'Neill of Shane's Castle.

9 Gillespie, R., *Early Belfast*, p.43

10 Murphy, T., in *HI*, May/June 2012

11 Gillespie, R., *Early Belfast*, p.43

12 Hill, Rev. G., (ed.), *Montgomery Manuscripts*, p.14

13 O'Donovan, J., (ed.), *Annals of the Four Masters*, Vol.5, p.1514

14 Brewer, J.S., & Bullen, W., (eds), *Carew Manuscripts*, Vol. I, p.224

15 Ibid., p.219

16 Murphy, T., in *HI*, May/June 2012

17 O'Donovan, J., (ed.), *Annals of the Four Masters*, Vol.5, p.1514

18 Brewer, J.S., & Bullen, W., (eds.), *Carew Manuscripts*, Vol.1, p.243

19 Gillespie, R., *Early Belfast*, p.43

20 The Savages were an Anglo-Norman family, holding lands at the southern tip of the Ards Peninsula.

21 Brewer, J.S., & Bullen, W., (eds.), *Carew Manuscripts*, Vol.1, doc.198.

22 This is inaccurate. His submission to King Edward clearly stated, 'because his hostages now remain with the Scots... he is unable to give hostages, he binds himself by oath.' Ibid.

23 O'Donovan, J., (ed.), *Annals of the Four Masters*, Vol.5, p.1539

5. Sir Brian McPhelim and the shock of plantation 1556-74

1 Murphy, T., in *HI*, May/June 2012. *Urriaghts* were required to provide military support, pay tribute and give up hostages as a guarantee of their loyalty.

2 Young, R.M., *Old Belfast*, p.8

3 Benn, G., *Belfast*, p.20

4 Hill, Rev. G., *Conquest of Ireland*, p.27

5 Ibid.

6 *COSPI*, Vol. 2., p.402

7 Benn, G., *Belfast*, p.17

8 *COSPI*, 1509-73, p.462

9 Brown's tower house has recently been restored and may be viewed along the road from Castle Espie to Nendrum.

10 Canny, N.P., *Elizabethan Conquest of Ireland*, p.85

11 Extract from an Indenture dated 5th October 1571 between Elizabeth I and Sir Thomas Smith, quoted in Thompson, M., *Thomas Smith's Forgotten English Colony*, p.7

12 Benn, G., *Belfast*, p.26

13 Thompson, M., *Sir Thomas Smith*, p.13

14 Hirst, D., *Dominion*, p.95

15 To strengthen the case for the removal of the Irish gentry, Smith highlighted the ease with which the Savage family had been displaced from Lecale. He should have known that the Savages were Anglo-Normans. Smith hadn't done his homework!

16 Thompson, M., *Sir Thomas Smith*, p.19

17 Ibid.
18 Hore, H.F., in *UJA*, p.180
19 Ibid.
20 O'Laverty, Rev. J., *Down and Connor*, p.172
21 Hore, H.F., in *UJA*, p.178; Benn, G., *Belfast*, p.32
22 Ibid., p.178
23 Benn, G., *Belfast*, p.30
24 *Carew Manuscripts* No. 611; and Brady, C., *Shane O'Neill*
25 Son of Brian Faghartagh, deceased Lord of Upper Clannaboy and brother of Sir Brian McPhelim.
26 Benn, G., *Belfast*, p.173, quoting a Captain Malbie.
27 McSkimin, S., *Carrickfergus*, p.29
28 Webb, A., *Irish Biographies*, p.147
29 Administrative incompetence may have led to the granting of Lower Clannaboy to Essex, having previously been granted to Smith. Smith agreed to transfer Lower Clannaboy to Essex, stating, 'I am content that my Lord shall have them… All North from thence to be my Lord's, all South to be ours.' *COSPI*, Elizabeth, Vol, No.66
30 Cusack, M.A., *Ireland*, Ch. 26
31 Churchyard, T., in *War & Literature*, p.118
32 Hore, H.F., in *UJA*, p.177-82. There are varying accounts of his murder. The boiling of his corpse cannot be discounted. Similar treatment was meted out to traitors at Tyburn.
33 The assertion that Niall McBrian Faghartagh was executed soon after the murder seems incorrect as his death is recorded in 1601.
34 Hore, H.F., in *UJA*, p.175
35 The Ford of Belfast existed prior to the realignment of the River Lagan. Where High Street meets Victoria Street, a large sandbank existed on either side of the estuary, creating a passable ford at low tide.
36 *COSPI*, Vol.XLII, No.58
37 Hore, H.F., in *UJA*, p.255
38 Bagwell, R., *Stuarts*, Vol. II, p.295
39 Brewer, J.S., & Bullen, W., (eds.), *Carew Manuscripts*, Vol. 1, doc.305.
40 Hill, Rev. G., *Montgomery Manuscripts*, p.59
41 *COSPI*, Vol. XLVIII, No.52

6. The return of Con Óg 1575-89

1 Benn, G., *Belfast*, p.670
2 Ibid.
3 Hill, Rev. G., (ed.), *Montgomery Manuscripts*, p.79
4 *HI*, May/June 2012
5 Sydney quoted in O'Laverty, Rev. J., *Down and Connor*, p.387
6 Hamilton, Lord, E., *Ulster*, p.18; O'Laverty, Rev J., *Down and Connor*, p.178
7 Sydney quoted in O'Laverty, Rev. J., *Down and Connor* p.387
8 Hamilton, Lord E., *Ulster*, p.113
9 Ibid. Letter, Turlough Luineach to Drury, dated Sept. 1579
10 Lord Deputy, John Perrot, letter to Council, October 1584, quoted in Edwards, D., (ed.), *Irish Wars*, Dublin, 2014, p.171
11 The Irish Parliament was dissolved in 1586 and was not recalled until 1613.
12 Hamilton, Lord E., *Ulster*, p.105
13 O'Laverty, J., *Down and Connor*, Vol. II, p.199
14 Morley, H., (ed.), *Ireland*, p.329

7. The inauguration of Con O'Neill 1589

1 *Pinkerton MSS*, p.26
2 *COSPI*, Vol.167, p.44
3 Hugh O'Neill, the Baron of Dungannon, would become Earl of Tyrone in 1587.
4 *COSPI*, Vol.167, p.63

5 One reason why Chichester had wanted to replace Con with Shane McBrian was that Shane was a fluent English speaker, suggesting that Con at this point was not.

6 His grandfather Brian Faghartagh was fostered in Kinelarty.

7 The *derbfine* constituted a chief, his sons, grandsons and great-grandsons, which could amount to upwards of forty candidates.

8 Meyer., in Simms, K., *From Kings to Warlords*, Ch.4, p.13

9 Fitzpatrick, E., *Gaelic Ireland*

10 *UJA*, Vol.4, p.88

11 Sullivan, A.M., *Atlas*, Chapter XL

12 Simms K., *From Kings to Warlords*, p.32

13 This hazelwood rod was often cut from a sacred tree.

14 Fitzpatrick, E., *Gaelic Ireland*, p.18

15 Duffy, S., (ed.), *Medieval Ireland*, p.230

16 Payne, R., *Ireland*, p.7

8. The bloody inter-regnum 1589-1601

1 *COSP*, Elizabeth, Vol. CLXVII, p.69

2 Dundas, Rev. W.H., in Carson, J., (ed.), *Old Lisburn*, Vol. 95

3 *COSP*, Elizabeth, Mar 1592, p.219

4 Owen McHugh was a first cousin of Niall McBrian and a challenger for the lordship of Upper Clannaboy.

5 The first element of Weston's plan was already in place, in that most Gaelic chiefs had already become landed gentry of sorts. It could be argued that the ordinary Gaels were as much robbed of their tribal lands by their chiefs as the planters.

6 Hamilton, Lord E., *Ulster*, p.172

7 Morgan, H., *Tyrone's Rebellion*, p.188

8 Brewer, J.S., & Bullen, W., (eds.), *Carew Manuscripts*, Vol. III, p.93

9 Ibid.

10 This practice, known as 'cessing,' was a source of great aggravation to the lesser septs who had little choice but to comply.

11 *COSPI*, 1594, p.234

12 Hamilton writes that, 'throughout Tyrone's rebellion (Niall McBrian) proved the most loyal of all the Irish chiefs in Down or Antrim.' *Elizabethan Ulster*, p.56

13 *COSPI*, 1594, p.234

14 Benn, G., *Belfast*, p.68

15 Sir Robert Cecil suspected the motivation behind their surrender, believing their 'purpose was to gain time to get in their harvest so that they might... serve his (Tyrone's) turn in Winter'.

16 Benn, G., *Belfast*, p.68

17 Brewer, J.S., & Bullen, W., (eds.), *Carew Manuscripts*, Vol. III

18 Lane to Cecil, 23 Dec. 1598, *COSPI*, 1598-99, p.421

19 *Carew Manuscripts*, Vol.VIII, p.299

20 Benn, G., *Ulster*, p.43

21 *Carew Manuscripts*, Vol. III, p.73

22 Atkinson, E.G., *COSPI*, Vol.VIII, p.77

23 Ibid., p.73

24 Ibid., p.72

25 Ibid., p.73

26 Robert, R.A., *Cecil*, Vol. 10, July 1600

27 Robert, R.A., *COSP,* Elizabeth I, p.72

28 Ibid.

29 Ibid.

30 Brewer, J.S., & Bullen, W., (eds.), *Carew Manuscripts*, Vol. III, p.299

31 Robert Devereux, 2nd Earl of Essex, Lord Lieutenant from 1599-1600. Tasked with putting down Tyrone's rebellion. Failed in his mission and made an unauthorised truce with Tyrone, for which he lost his office.

32 Connellan, O., *Annals of the Four Masters*, p.680
33 Ibid.
34 *COSP*, Elizabeth, 1599, p.154
35 O'Sullivan Beare, P., *Ireland*, p.130
36 *COSP*, Elizabeth, 1600, p.168
37 Healey, T.M., MP., *Stolen Waters*, p.35
38 Pinkerton, W., in *UJA*, Vol. 5, p.188-209
39 McGurk, J., in Edwards, D., Lenihan, P., and Tait, C., (eds.) *Atrocity*, p.123-29
40 Ibid.
41 Murphy T, in *HI*, May/June 2012
42 *COSPI*, Vol XI, p.335
43 *COSPI*, 1600, p.22
44 Healey, T.M., MP., *Stolen Waters*, p.40
45 McSkimin, S., *Carrickfergus*, p.32
46 Atkinson, E.G., (ed.), *COSP*, Elizabeth, Vol.X, p.271

9. Con at home and at war 1601

1 In a simple eulogy, Chichester declared him 'a good subject' of the Queen.
2 Atkinson E.G. (ed.), *COSPI*, Vol. X, p.268
3 Ibid.
4 Ibid.
5 Ibid.
6 Benn, G., *Belfast*, p.33
7 Atkinson E.G. (ed.), *COSPI*, Vol. X, p.268
8 Ibid., p.332
9 Raths were Early Christian farmsteads enclosed by a circular earthen bank and ditch. The Castlereagh Hills are dotted with raths, the nearest two being on the Clontonakelly Road. Lisnabreeny Rath, 'The Fort of the Fairies', on Lisnabreeny Road, is open to the public and maintained by the National Trust.
10 Cregan, D.F., in *SH*, No.3, p.62
11 Anglo-Norman Ireland, *Early Modern History* (1500-1700), Features, Gaelic Revival, Issue 1 (Spring 1996), Medieval History (pre-1500), Vol. 4
12 Machiolation, from 'macar', to crush and 'col', the neck.
13 This may have involved a visit to the small stream that rises near the castle and goes on to become a tributary of the Loop, and ultimately joins the Connswater River.
14 Benn, G., *Belfast*, p.23
15 www.historyireland.com/gaelic-revival/frowning-ruins-the-tower-houses-of-medievalireland/
16 Atkinson E.G. (ed.), *COSPI*, Vol. X, p.355-56. Patrick O'Quinn hailed from Farlough in the Edendork area.
17 *JRSAI*, 1910, p.170
18 Mitchel J., *Aodh O'Neill*, p.222
19 Atkinson E.G. (ed.), *COSPI*, Vol. X, p.268
20 Ibid., p.64

10. Rebellion! 1601

1 Atkinson, E.G., (ed.), *COSP*, Elizabeth, Vol.10, p.64
2 Falls, C., *Elizabeth's Irish Wars*, 1996, p.326
3 Payne, R., in Smith, A., (ed) *Ireland*, Vol. II
4 Atkinson, E.G., (ed.), *COSP*, Elizabeth, Vol.11, p.505
5 Ringhaddy Castle lies on a peninsula jutting out into Strangford Lough's western shore, halfway between Killinchy and Killyleagh. Today it is the most pristine example of a 15th century tower house to be found in County Down.
6 Brewer, J.S., & Bullen, W., *Carew Manuscripts*, Vol.6, p.156
7 Atkinson, E.G., (ed.), *COSP*, Elizabeth, Vol.11, p.64
8 Ibid.

9 Irish Lord of Lower Clannaboy.
10 Atkinson, E.G., (ed.), *COSPI*, Vol.11, p.50
11 Ibid., p.111
12 Ibid., p.504
13 Ibid., p.111
14 Hamilton, Lord E., *Elizabethan Ulster*, p.297
15 Atkinson, E.G., (ed.), *COSPI*, Vol. 8, p.208-9
16 Ibid.,Vol.11, p.64
17 Ibid., p.111
18 Brewer, J.S., & Bullen, W., *Carew Manuscripts*, Vol.4, p.156
19 Atkinson, E.G., (ed.), *COSP, Ireland*, Vol.11, p.64
20 Ibid.
21 Inisloughlin or Ennislaughlin, ancient fortress of Cormac O'Neill of Killultagh (the wood of Ulster), near Moira.
22 Morrison, F., *Itinerary*, Vol.III, p.282
23 O'Sullivan Beare, P.A., *Ireland*, p.181
24 Atkinson, E.G., (ed.), *COSPI*, Vol.11, p.11

11. How are the mighty fallen 1602-03

1 Putting a candle in the window to open the house to Mary and Joseph and to weary travellers was a Christmas tradition.
2 A runlet was a small barrel containing a fourteenth part of a tun or half a barrel of wine.
3 A 13th century church on the site of Knock graveyard near Shandon.
4 Hanna, C.A., *Scotch-Irish*, p.486
5 *Boddagh Sasonagh*, derogatory term describing crude manners and a superior attitude.
6 *Irish Statutes*, Vol.1, p.1
7 Lodge, J., *Peerage*, Vol. I., p.318; Granger, *England*, Vol.II, p.98.
8 Canny, N.P., (ed.), *Ireland*, p.86. Canny cites the notorious Bristol merchant, John Ball 'who was buying up beeves, hides and tallow from the Gaelic Irish and supplying them with wine without paying custom.'
9 *COSPI, 1589-89*, p.485-86
10 Owen, D.J., *Belfast*, p.62
11 Healey, T.M., *Stolen Waters*, p.34
12 Godkin, J., *Ireland*, p.70
13 Hill, Rev. G., (ed.), *Montgomery Manuscripts*, p.22
14 Hull, E., *A History of Ireland and her People*, Vol. 2, chap. 1
15 Lowry, T.K. (ed.), *Hamilton Manuscripts*, p.141
16 McSkimin, S., *Carrickfergus*, p.113
17 Greeves, J.R.H., *North Down*, Vol.5

12. The great escape 1603-05

1 Cregan, D.F., *Daniel O'Neill*, in *SH*, No. 3, p. 60-100
2 George Montgomery, Parson of Chedzoy in Somerset and later Dean of Norwich and Chaplain to King James I.
3 *DLG*, p.166-169
4 Hill, Rev G., (ed.), *Montgomery Manuscripts*, p.25
5 Chichester wrote, 'I procured from your Majestie a general pardon of all offences committed before your succession to the crowne, which was accordinglie proclaimed and joyfullie accepted by all men.'
6 McSkimin, S., *Carrickfergus*, p.226
7 Hill, Rev. G., (ed.), *Montgomery Manuscripts*, p.23
8 Ibid., p.27
9 Perceval-Maxwell, M., *Ulster*, p.50
10 Haines, K., *The Conning of Conn*, p.36
11 Hill, Rev. G., (ed.), *Montgomery Manuscripts*, p.27
12 Shapiro J., *Shakespeare*, p.29

13. Enter James Hamilton 1604-05

1 Healey, T.M., *Stolen Waters*, p.51

2 Stevenson, J., *Down*, p.31

3 Ussher was also the principal author of the articles that formed the basis of the Westminster Confession of Faith, which would guide Presbyterian theology in the many kirks that sprang up in the fledgling Scottish settlement.

4 Lowry, T.K., (ed.), *Hamilton Manuscripts*, p.6-7

5 Hamilton's account also suggests that Essex did not openly rebel against Elizabeth, but that his enemies at Court and a set of unfortunate circumstances conspired against him.

6 *Calendar of Border Papers*, p.680

7 Healey, T.M., *Stolen Waters*, p.52

8 Lowry, T.K., (ed.), *Hamilton Manuscripts*, p.9

9 Ibid., p.4

10 *COSP*, James I, 1603, p.168

11 Strype, J., *Sir Thomas Smith*, p.182,

12 Healey, T.M., *Stolen Waters*, p.58-9

13 Erck, J.C., (ed), *Patent Rolls*, p.244

14 Russell, Rev. C.W., & Prendergast, J.P., (eds), *COSPI*, James I, p.212

15 Healey, T.M., *Stolen Waters*, p.59

16 The lands granted to Hamilton by royal patent comprised the Manor of Moygare, the Ardes, the Priory of Coleraine, fishing rights on the River Bann, the Priory of Holywood, the Copeland Islands, rectories in Lecale, and ,the tithes of Rathlin Island. Healey, T.M., *Stolen Waters*, p.60

17 Belfast Castle was situated on the site of the former British Home Stores.

18 Chichester to Cecil, 19th June 1605, quoted in Russell, Rev. C.W., & Prendergast, J.P., (eds), *COSP*, James I, p.295

19 *COSP*, James I, p.212

20 Bardon, J., *The Plantation of Ulster: War and Conflict in Ireland*, chap.5

21 Hill, Rev. G., (ed.), *Montgomery Manuscripts*, p.37

22 Lowry, T.K., *Hamilton Mauscripts*, General Appendix I

23 Erck, J.C., (ed.), *Patent Rolls*

24 Healey, T.M., *Stolen Waters*, p.61

25 Kennedy, L., & Ollerenshaw, P., *Ulster*, p.59

26 Coyne and livery: provision of sustenance for the lord's militia when billeted on a sept's land. Coshering: payment in kind to the lord for protection.

27 Murphy T., *Clandeboye*

14. The return of the chief 1605-06

1 See the Place Names NI website, http://www.placenamesni.org/ and Lewis's Ireland. The parish acreages come from the latter.

2 Hill, Rev. G., (ed.), *Montgomery Manuscripts*, p.32-35

3 *Abbotsford*, Vol. 1, p.272

4 Lowry, T.K., (ed.), *Hamilton Manuscripts*, p.29-35

5 Ibid.

6 Chart, D.A., *Con O'Neill*, in *PRIA*, Vol. 48, p.128-34

7 The expression is a corruption of the French *pied-poudreaux*, meaning 'dusty footed', an allusion to the travelling traders.

8 Lewis, S., *Ireland*, p.511. Lewis records that the Court Leet and Court Baron continued into the mid-19th century, and were 'held every third week at Four Lane Ends, for the manor Drumbracklin... for the recovery of debts under £20... extending over the eight townlands of Doneight... Lisnoe... Ballyaulis... Ballycairn, Ballylesson, Monlough, Clogher and Knockbreccan.'

9 Hill, Rev. G., (ed.), *Montgomery Manuscripts*, p.27, 34

10 Under its terms, Con could lease the lands out to his brothers or other loyal subjects, but could no longer sell them on. Should he fall foul of the law or default on his Crown rents, Montgomery would endeavour to 'pass the estate over to the next lawful heir male of O'Neale.' Failing that they would pass to Montgomery at the same rents Con was obliged

to pay to James Hamilton.

11 Chart, D.A., *Con O'Neill*, in *PRIA*, Vol. 48, p.128
12 Hill, Rev. G., (ed.), *Montgomery Manuscripts* , p.37
13 Ibid., p.38-9

15. By earth and twig 1605-11

1 Lowry, T.K., (ed.), *Hamilton Manuscripts*, p.20-21
2 Ibid., p.21
3 O'Grady, H., Strafford, p.700. Strafford incorrectly refers to Niall McBrian as the beneficiary of this tripartite deal.
4 A record of these is to be found in the Chancery of Inquisition, established by King James at Downpatrick in October 1623. This legal investigation headed by Sir John Blennerhassett, sought to determine ownership of the lands of Upper Clannaboy originally bequeathed to Con O'Neill, Hugh Montgomery and James Hamilton and subsequently traded between themselves and others.
5 This transfer lends credence to the story of Con's escape.
6 Chart D.A., *Con O'Neill*, p.129
7 Ballynalessan is Lessans, and Tolloure is Tullyreagh on the main road between Carryduff and Saintfield. Ballyaghley is Ballyagherly, due east of Saintfield Main Street. Ballykillenure is Killinure, south-west of Carryduff. Ballycarricknasassanagh refers to Craignasasonagh, north-west of Saintfield. Ballylistowdean is Lisdoonan. Ballyknockan Mill (est.1604) lay between Ballygowan and Carryduff. We also read of Edmund Barry being 'in possession of one-quarter of Ballyknockan, demised to him by Hugh Mergagh'. The name 'Barry' may be of Irish origin. Such exchanges were not permitted under the terms of the agreement.
8 Hill, Rev. G., (ed.), *Montgomery Manuscripts*, p.41.
9 Ibid. p.82. Clontinakally lies near Carryduff.
10 Drumbracklyn, Drumbrackley or Downbreaklyn, depending on the source.
11 Neill, T., 'Land of Linen and the Lambeg Drum', @Lisburn.com
12 Hill, Rev. G., (ed.), *Montgomery Manuscripts*, p.41
13 *COSPI*, Vol. 219, p.156. The yarn alone yielded 30 shillings per pack, equating to an annual return of £450.
14 *UJA*, Vol. III, p.83
15 Green, E.R.R., *Catalogue*, in *UJA*, Third Series, Vol. 12, p.1-25
16 Sir Henry Dillon to Lord Salisbury, quoted in Hill, Rev. G., *MacDonnells*, p.22
17 Ibid.
18 Ibid.
19 Sexton's deal of December 1605 included a proviso that he could exchange the two townlands he had acquired from Con if they didn't satisfy him. He did this, but instead of returning them to Con he passed them on to Montgomery via Richard O'Cahan. Is this the outworking of the Christmas Eve agreement?
20 Ballyneahaughty, the townland of Ballynahatty, where we find the Giant's Ring. Ballyvollvally is Ballynavally, equating to Ballylesson/Milltown. Ballydollaghan is where the old Purdysburn Fever Hospital was situated.
21 Their wives were also involved in the transaction: 'Montgomery and Elizabeth his wife agree to make further legal assurances of the property within the next two years, as do… Con O'Neale and Ellice his wife.'
22 Chart, D.A., *Con O'Neill*, in *PRIA*, Vol. 48, p.132
23 Ibid., p.134
24 Hill, Rev. G., (ed.), *Montgomery Manuscripts*, p.82
25 Benn G., *Belfast*, p.678.

16. The coming of the Scots 1606

1 Montgomery gave master carpenter, John Moore, this onerous responsibility.
2 Carr, P., *Dundonald*, p.69
3 Harrison, J., *Ulster*, chap 1
4 Hill, Rev. G., (ed.), *Montgomery Manuscripts*, p.61

5 Harrison, J., *Ulster*, chap 1
6 Reiver, from *reive*, meaning to rob or plunder.
7 Carr, P., *Dundonald*, p.69
8 Hewitt, J., *Rhyming Weavers*, p.66
9 Stewart, A.T.Q., *Ulster*, p.38
10 Hill, Rev. G., (ed.), *Montgomery Manuscripts*, p.58
11 Perceval-Maxwell, M., *Ulster*, p.17
12 O'Laverty, J., *Down and Conor*, Vol 1
13 Pender, S., (ed.), *Census of Ireland* 1659
14 Bardon, J., *Ulster*, p.75
15 Hill, Rev. G., (ed.), *Montgomery Manuscripts*, p.6
16 Chichester, quoted in Carr, P., *Dundonald*, p.234.

17. Upper Clannaboy refashioned

1 Lowry, T.K., (ed.), *Hamilton Manuscripts*, p.60
2 A diet shared with the Iberian Black Pigs; helping to create the world-renowned, Jamon, 'pata negra'.
3 McCavery, T., *Newtown*, p.42
4 Hill, Rev. G., (ed.), *Montgomery Manuscripts*, p.51
5 McCavery, T., *Newtown*, p.56
6 Hill, Rev. G., (ed.), *Montgomery Manuscripts*, p.8
7 Carr, P., *Dundonald*, p.69
8 The site is now occupied by Bangor Town Hall and the North Down Heritage Centre, where the beautiful Raven Maps (1625) are on display.
9 Among them was master mason, William Stennors, who presided over the restoration of the Abbey Church at Bangor, where he was buried alongside Hamilton.
10 Hill, Rev. G., (ed.), *Montgomery Manuscripts*, p.51
11 Crane, N., *Thomas Raven's Clandeboye Estate Maps*, in *Map Man*, Series 2, Episode 8, broadcast on BBC2, 20th Feb 2015.
12 Garner M.A.K., *North Down*, p.21
13 North Down Museum Services, *Sir James Hamilton, the First Viscount of Clandeboye*, para. 1
14 The Geneva Bible predated King James's Authorised Version by fifty-one years. It had been translated by Protestant scholars, who had escaped persecution. It was the first Bible to include chapters and verses and was annotated by the reformed theologians, Calvin, Knox and Coverdale. It was said to have made the Bible accessible to the common man and was a bulwark of early Presbyterianism. It was also the version beloved by the first pilgrims to America.
15 Hill, Rev. G., (ed.), *Montgomery Manuscripts*, p.126
16 O'Donovan, J., (ed.), *Co. Down*, Ms. 14 C. 21
17 Hewitt, J., *Rhyming Weavers: And Other Country Poets of Antrim and Down*
18 Robinson, P., in *Ulster-Scotch*, p.71
19 http://clydesburn.blogspot.co.uk/2011/01/hugh-montgomery-found-in-newtownards. Local historian, Andrew Steven believes the green lay in the vicinity of Movilla and Greenwell Streets, near Newtown Priory. *Ulster Folklife*, 2011, Vol. 54.
20 Comber Historical Society, *Scots*, Part 2. Ditching ensured the land was drained. Quicksetting involved the planting of quick-growing shrubs to form a hedge
21 Thomas Raven's Survey Maps of Hamilton's Estate, 1625
22 A copy is on display at the North Down Museum, Bangor.
23 *Proceedings and Report of the Belfast Natural History Society*, p.21
24 Hill, Rev. G., (ed.), *Montgomery Manuscripts*, p.62
25 Ibid.
26 Ibid., p.50
27 Ibid., p.64
28 Thompson, M. & Roulston, W., *Biographies*, p.14
29 Hill, Rev. G., (ed.), *Montgomery Manuscripts*, p.65
30 Her work is acknowledged in the 'Scottish Diaspora Project', on one of the tapestry's

embroidered squares.
31 Londonderry, Armagh, Fermanagh, Tyrone, Donegal and Cavan.
32 Harrison J., *Ulster*, ch. 2

18. The ould King 1611-19
1 Chart, D.A., *Con O'Neill*
2 Morgan H., *Rebellion*, p.19
3 Bardon, J., *Ulster*, p.115-30
4 Hill, Rev. G., (ed.), *Ulster*, p.579
5 Irish Patent Rolls, p. 41, 47
6 NIHGC 2015, *Hillsborough Castle Demesne*, p.2
7 Beckett, J.C., *Ireland*, Ch. 2
8 Ibid.
9 Hill, Rev. G., (ed.), *Montgomery Manuscripts*, p.84
10 Abbotsford Club, *Miscellany*, p.278
11 Lowry, T.K., (ed.), *Hamilton Manuscripts*, Appendix 4, p.29-60
12 Chart, D.A., *Con O'Neill*, in PRIA, Vol. XLVIII, Section c
13 John Shaw would later purchase lands outside Larne and in 1625 built an imposing castle at Ballygally.
14 Beckett, J.C., *Ireland*. He also acquired lands from Chichester at Carrickfergus, Islandmagee, and Malone, where he built a fort in the vicinity Shaw's Bridge. Local folklore records that the walls of his fort were used to build Shaw's Bridge.
15 Chart, D.A., *Con O'Neill*, p.135
16 Ibid.
17 Ibid.
18 Ulster Roll of Gaol Delivery, in *UJA*, Vol, I, p.261.
19 Kilduffe was leased for eleven years at a rent of twenty shillings.
20 Cregan, D.F., *SH*, No.3, 1963
21 Lowry, T.K., (ed.), *Hamilton Manuscripts*, Appendix 4, p.54
22 Hill, Rev. G., (ed.), *Montgomery Manuscripts*, p.83
23 Ibid.

19. One last hurrah 1619-64
1 Hyde, E, Earl of Clarendon., *Rebellion*, Vol.VIII, p.268
2 *Calendar of the Patent and Close Rolls, Ireland*, James I, (1623)
3 The Inquisition papers were destroyed in the fire at the Dublin Four Courts during the Irish Civil War. Its proceedings are known to us via a late seventeenth century copy.
4 Cregan, D.F., *Daniel O'Neill*, in *SH*, No. 3, p.60-100
5 *COSPI, 1633-47*, p.127
6, Laud, W., *Works*, Vol. VII, p.227,
7 Smith, Dr. G., *Royalist Agents*, p.17
8 Herbert Price was a Royalist Colonel who fought alongside Daniel at Naseby. Lieutenant Colonel Robert Walsh recaptured the royal standard in the Battle of Edgehill and was knighted on the field by King Charles I.
9 Cavenagh, W.O., *Daniel O'Neill*, in *JRSAI*, Fifth Series, Vol. 38, No. 4, Fifth Series, Vol. 18, p.362-67; and Young, R.M., *O'Neale's Escape* in *UJA*, Second Series, Vol. 1, no.1, p.70-4
10 Lehman, E.H., *Queens*, p.454
11 Smith, Dr. G., *Royalist Agents*, Introduction
12 Carte T., *Affairs of England*, Vol.1, p.151.
13 Day, W.A., (ed.), *Pythouse*, p.lv-lvii
14 Smith, Dr. G., *Royalist Agents*, Introduction
15 Cruickshanks, E., and Henning, B.D., *Daniel O'Neill*, in Henning B.D., (ed) *The House of Commons*
16 Casway, J. I., *O'Neill, Daniel*
17 A Christian splinter group which attempted to set up Christ's kingdom on earth in

anticipation of the second coming.

18 Cruickshanks, E., and Henning, B.D., in Henning B.D., (ed.), *Parliament*

19 Cregan, D.F., *Daniel O'Neill*, in *SH*, No. 3 (1963), p.60-100

20 Cavenagh, W.O., *Daniel O'Neill*, in *JRSAI*, Fifth Series, Vol. 38, No. 4, Fifth Series, Vol. 18, No. 4, Fifth Series, Vol. 18, p.362-67

21 Fitzpatrick, T., *The Fall of Down*, in *UJA* 2nd Series, Vol.12, no.2, p.72

22 *UJA*, Series 2, Vol. IX, p.44.

23 *COSPI*, 1665

24 Lodge J., *Peerage*, Vol. IV, p.216.

25 Savage-Armstrong, G.F., *Savages of the Ards*, p.199-200. Savage-Armstrong writes that Ellis was 'not old at the time of Con's death'.

20. Reclaiming the legacy of Con O'Neill

1 Harris, W., *County Down*, p.73

2 Fleming, J.&J.H., *Ireland*, p.11

3 Joy, H., *Belfast*, p.7

4 Benn, G., *Belfast*, p.273

5 PRONI, D671/M4/31B

6 McNeill, T.E., *Castlereagh*, in *UJA*, Vol. 50, p.123

7 Ibid.

8 House of Commons, Wed. 15th April 1874, Second *Reading of Ancient Monuments Bill*.

9 Belfast Naturalists Field Club, *Annual Report*s, Series ii, Vol. ii, p.164-65

10 Haines, K., *East Belfast*, p.56

11 CBC minutes,18th April 2013

12 *Dublin Penny Journal*, Vol.1, no.26, Dec.22, 1832

13 Fitzpatrick, E., *Gaelic Ireland*, p.157-60

14 Spencer, E., *Ireland*, p.11

15 Fitzpatrick, E., *Royal Inauguration in Gaelic Ireland*, 2004, p.159

16 Ibid.

17 Ibid.

18 Northern Ireland Sites and Monuments Record, DOW-009-006-01

19 Fitzpatrick, E., *Gaelic Ireland*, p.159

20 *Dublin Penny Journal*, Vol.1, no. 26

21 Ironically, Stewart Banks, the rescuer of this iconic artefact, was related to the Scottish settler, Sir Hugh Montgomery.

22 *Dublin Penny Journal*, Vol.1, no.26

23 The 1819 *Street Directory* (p.25) informs us that Thomas FitzMorris was an architect.

24 *The Dublin Penny Journal*, Vol.1, no. 26, reproduced in the *Irish Miscellany* of 1858

25 *UJA*, Vol.1, p.166. The cache is likely to have been passed to the site's owner, Moyses Hill's heir, the Fifth Marquis of Downshire.

26 Benn, G., *Belfast*, p.303

27 Brett, C.E.B., *Buildings of Belfast*, Preface, p.10

28 Benn, G., *Belfast*, p.5

29 Lowry, M., *Belfast* , Ch.2

30 McCoy, G., *East Belfast*, p.11

31 Brett, C.E.B., *Buildings of Belfast*, p.33

32 Nevin N., *Comber*

33 Benn, G., *Belfast*, p.63

34 Stevenson, J., *Down*, p.27 & 32

35 *Stewart Manuscripts*, quoted in Hill, Rev. G., (ed.), *Montgomery Manuscripts*, p.37

36 O'Laverty, Rev. J., *Down and Connor*, Vol.I, p.373

37 Biggar, F., Arthur Chichester, in *UJA*, Vol.10, Jan. 1904, no.1, p.10

38 Haines, K., *The Conning of Conn*, p.36

Bibliography

Primary Sources

Bodley, J. *'A Visit to Lecale in the County of Down in the year 1602-3',* in Falkiner, C.L. *Illustrations of Irish History and Topography, mainly of the Seventeenth Century,* (London, 1904)

Brewer J.S. & Bullen, W. (eds.) *Calendar of the Carew Manuscripts,* 1515-1624, 6 Vols., (London, 1867-73)

Calendar of State Papers, Henry VIII, Edward VI, Mary, Elizabeth I, James I, Domestic Series, 81 Vols., (London, 1856-1972)

Calendar of State Papers relating to Ireland, 24 Vols., (London, 1860-1911)

Cambrensis, Giraldus, trans. by Forester, T. *Topography of Ireland and the History of the Conquest of Ireland,* (London, 1905)

Camden, W. *Brittania,* (London, 1610)

Camden, W. *Topographia Hiberniae,* (Frankfurt, 1602)

Davies, J. *A discoverie of the true causes why Ireland was never entirely subdued, nor brought under obedience of the crowne of England, until the beginning of his Majestie's happie raigne,* (London, 1612)

Derricke, J. *The Image of Irelande, with a discouerie of woodkarne,* (London, 1581)

Dowcra, J. Sir. '*A Narration of Services done by the Army ymployed to Lough Foyle',* in Dymock, J. *A Treatise of Ireland,* No. 1291 of the Harleian Collection, in the British Museum, circa 1600

Green, E.R.R. *A Catalogue of the Estate Maps, etc., in the Downshire Office, Hillsborough, Co. Down,* (Belfast, 1950-96)

Hill, Rev. G. *The Montgomery Manuscripts,* (Belfast, 1869)

Hogan., E (ed) *The Description of Ireland and the State Thereof as it is at This Present in Anno 1598,* (Dublin, 1878)

Irish Statute Books, http://www.irishstatutebook.ie/

Lowry, T.K. (ed.) *The Hamilton Manuscripts,* (Belfast, 1867)

MacAirt, S. & MacNiocaill, G. *The Annals of Ulster,* (Dublin, 1983)

Martin Freeman, A. (ed.) *The Annals of Connacht 1224-1544,* (Dublin, 1944)

Moore, L.T., & McEvoy, B. *et al,* A Y-Chromosome Signature of Hegemony in Gaelic Ireland in *American Journal of Human Genetics* 78(2), (February, 2006)

Morrin, James (ed.) *Calendar of the patent and close rolls of chancery in Ireland.,* 2 Vols., (Dublin, 1861-62)

Moryson, F. *A History of Ireland from the year 1599 to 1603,* 2 Vols, (Dublin, 1735)

Moryson, F. *An Itinerary: containing his ten yeeres travell through the Twelve Dominions of Germany, Bohmerland, Sweitzerland, Netherland, Denmarke, Poland, Italy, Turky, France, England, Scotland and Ireland,* (London, 1617)

O Donnchadha, T. (ed.) *Leabhar Cloinne Aodh Buidhe.* (Dublin: Irish Manuscripts Commission, 1931)

O'Donovan, J. (ed.) *Annals of the Four Masters,* (Dublin, 1848-51)

O'Donovan, J. (ed.) *Ordnance Survey letters relating to Co. Down,* by 1834.

O'Donovan, J. (ed.) *Miscellany of the Celtic Society*, (Dublin, 1849)

O'Sullivan Beare, P. translated by Byrne, M.J. *A History of Ireland in the Reign of Elizabeth*, (Dublin, 1970)

Payne, R. *'A Briefe description of Ireland: made in this year, 1589'*, in: Smith, A. (ed.), *Tracts relating to Ireland,* Irish Archaeological Society, Vol.1, (Dublin, 1841)

Pynnar, N. *Survey of Ulster* in Harris, W. *Hibernica,* (Dublin, 1770)

Rich, B. *A New Description of Ireland*, (London, 1610)

Robert, R.A. *Calendar of Cecil Papers in Hatfield House*, Vol. 10, (London, 1904)

Spenser, E. *A view of the state of Ireland as it was in the reign of Queen Elizabeth: written by way of dialogue between Eudoxus and Ireneus,* (Dublin, 1763)

Stafford, T. *Pacata Hibernia: Ireland appeased and reduced, or a historie of the late warres of Ireland*, (London, 1633)

Stanihurst, R. *'Description of Ireland'*, in: Holinshed, R. *Holinshed's Chronicles,* (London, 1577

Books

Adamson, I. *The Cruithin, A History of the Ulster Land and People*, (Newtownards, 2014)

Allen, H. *Donaghadee, an Illustrated History*, (Dundonald, 2006)

Andrews, J. *'Plantation Ireland: a review of settlement history'*, in: Barry T.B. (ed.) *A history of settlement in Ireland*, (London 1999)

Atkinson, E.G. *Calendar of State Papers Ireland*, Vol. VIII, (Dublin, 1861-3)

Bagwell, R. *Ireland under the Stuarts,* 3 Vols., (London, 1909-16)

Bardon, Jonathan *A History of Ireland in 250 Episodes,* (Dublin, 2008)

Bardon, Jonathan *A History of Ulster*, (Belfast, 1992)

Bardon, Jonathan *Investigating Place Names in Ulster*, (Belfast, 1990)

Bardon, Jonathan *A Narrow Sea,* (Dublin, 2018)

Beckett, J.C. *The Making of Modern Ireland 1603-1923*, (London, 1966)

Benn, G. *A History of the Town of Belfast*, (Belfast, 1823)

Benn, G. *A Historical Account of the Plantation in Ulster at the Commencement of the 17th Century*, (Belfast, 1877)

Berry, H.F. and Morrissey, J.F. (eds.) *Statute Rolls of the Parliament of Ireland,* Vol. 2, (Dublin, 1910)

Brady, C. & Gillespie, R. (eds.) *Natives and Newcomers: essays on the making of Irish colonial society 1534-1641,* (Dublin, 1986)

Brady, C., O'Dowd, M., Walker, B. (eds.) *Ulster: An Illustrated History of Ulster*, (London, 1989)

Brady, C., *Shane O'Neill*, (Dundalk, 1996)

Brett, C.E.B. *Buildings of Belfast 1700-1914,* (London, 1967)

Brown, D. *Hugh de Lacy, First Earl of Ulster - Rising and Falling in Angevin Ireland*, (Suffolk, 2016)

Canavan, T. *Every Stoney Acre has a Name: a celebration of the townland in Ulster*, (Belfast, 1991)

Canny, N.P. *Elizabethan Conquest of Ireland*, (Hassocks, 1976)

Canny, N.P. (ed.) *Making Ireland British, 1580-1650,* (Oxford, 2001)

Canny, N.P. *Reformation to Restoration: Ireland 1534-1660*, (Dublin, 1987)

Carr, Peter *The Most Unpretending of Places: A History of Dundonald, County Down*, (Dundonald, 1987)

Carr, Peter *Portavo: An Irish townland and its peoples,* Part 1: *earliest times - 1844*, (Dundonald, 2003)

Carte, T. *Collection of Original Letters and Papers Concerning the Affairs of England from the Year 1641-1660*, (London, 1739)

Casway, J.I. *O'Neill, Daniel* (c.1612-1664), *Oxford Dictionary of National Biography*, (Oxford, 2004)

Chart, D.A. & Colles, R. *History of Ulster from the Earliest Times to the Present Day*, (London, 1919)

Comber Historical Society, *The Coming of the Scots*, Part 2, www.comberhistory.com.

Connolly, S.J. *The Oxford Companion to Irish History*, (Oxford, 1998)

Cullen, L.M. *The Emergence of Modern Ireland 1600-1900*, (London, 1981)

Curtis, E., *A History of Medieval Ireland: From 1086 to 1513*, (London, 1923)

Cusack, M.A. *An Illustrated History of Ireland*, (London, 1868)

Churchyard, T. *A Generell Rehersall of Warres, called Churchyardes Choise* in Ashe,L.,& Patterson, I. (eds.) *War & Literature*, (Cambridge, 2014)

Day W. A. (ed.) *The Pythouse Papers*, (London, 1899)

Department of the Environment Northern Ireland. *Historic Monuments of Northern Ireland*, (Belfast, 1983)

Dubourdieu, J. *A Statistical Survey of the County of Antrim*, (Dublin, 1812)

Duffy, S. (ed.) *Medieval Ireland: An Encyclopedia*, (Oxford, 2005)

Dundas, Rev. W.H. *History of Killultagh*, in Carson, J. (ed.) *Some Extracts from the Records of Old Lisburn and the Manor of Killultagh,* Vol. 95. (Lisburn Standard, 1916)

Edwards, D. (ed.) *Campaign Journals of the Irish Wars*, (Dublin, 2014)

Edwards, D. Lenihan, P., & Tait, C., (eds.) *Age of Atrocity: Violence and Political Conflict in Early Modern Ireland*, (Dublin, 2007)

Ellis, S.E. *Ireland in the Age of the Tudors 1447-1603*, (London, 1998)

Falls, C. *Elizabeth's Irish Wars*, (London, 1950)

Fenton, J. *The Hamely Tongue*, (Belfast, 2006)

FitzPatrick, B. *Seventeenth-century Ireland: the war of religions*, (Dublin, 1988)

FitzPatrick, E. *Royal Inauguration in Gaelic Ireland c.1100-1600: A Cultural Landscape Study*, (Woodbridge, 2004)

Flanders, S. *John de Courcy, Prince of Ulster*, (Newtownards, 2015)

Fleming, J. & J.H. *The post-chaise companion: or, Travellers' directory through Ireland*, (Ireland, 1803)

Foster, R.F. *The Oxford Illustrated History of Ireland*, (Oxford, 1989)

Frame, R. *Ireland and Britain, 1170-1450*, (London, 1998)

Fraser, A. *The Gunpowder Plot: terror and faith in 1605*, (London, 1996)

Gillespie, R. *Colonial Ulster: The Settlement of East Ulster 1600-41*, (Cork, 1986)

Gillespie, R. *Conspiracy, Ulster Plots and Plotters in 1615*, (Belfast, 1987)

Gillespie, R. *Early Belfast, The Origins and Growth of an Ulster Town to 1750*, (Belfast, 2007)

Godkin, J. *The Land War in Ireland*, (London, 1870)

Granger, Rev. J. *Biographical History of England,* Vol. II, (London, 1804)

Greeves, J.R.H. *North Down at the end of the 16th Century*, Belfast Natural History and Philosophical Society, (Belfast, 1960)

Greeves, J.R.H. *The Origins of some Parishes in County Down,* Belfast Natural History and Philosophical Society, (Belfast, 1965)

Haines, K., *East Belfast: Paintings and Stories from Harbour to Hills*, (Donaghadee, 2001)

Hamilton, Lord E. *Elizabethan Ulster*, (London, 1919)

Hamilton, Canon J. *Bangor Abbey through Fifteen Centuries,* (Bangor, 2006)

Hamilton, H.C. (ed.) Calendar of State Papers Ireland, Elizabeth I, (London, 1890)

Hanna, C.A. *The Scotch-Irish or The Scot in North Britain, North Ireland and North America,* (G.P. Putnam, 1902*)*

Harris, W. *The Ancient and Present State of the County of Down,* (Dublin, 1744)

Harrison, J. *The Scot in Ulster: Sketch of the History of the Scottish Population of Ulster*, (Edinburgh,1889)

Hayward, R. *This is Ireland, Ulster and the City of Belfast,* (London, 1950)

Healey, T.M. *Stolen Waters: a page in the conquest of Ulster*, (London, 1913)

Henning B.D. (ed.) *The History of Parliament: the House of Commons 1660-90,* (History of Parliament Online)

Hewitt, J. *Ancestral Voices; the selected prose of John Hewitt, (Belfast, 1987)*

Hill, Rev. G. *An Historical Account of the MacDonnells of Antrim,* (Belfast, 1873)

Hill, Rev. G. *The Conquest of Ireland - A Historical Account of the Plantation of Ulster at the Commencement of the 17th Century, 1608-20,* (Belfast, 1887)

Hirst, D. *Dominion; England and its Island Neighbours 1500-1707,* (Oxford, 2012)

Hull, E. *A History of Ireland and her People,* (Oxford, 1931)

Hunter, R.J. (ed.) *Plantations in Ulster, 1600-41, A Collection of Documents,* (Belfast, 2018)

Hyde, E. Earl of Clarendon *The History of the Rebellion and Civil War in England*, (London, 1888)

Jones, F.M. *Mountjoy, 1563-1606, the last Elizabethan Lord Deputy,* (Dublin, 1958)

Jope, E.M. (ed.) *An Archaeological Survey of County Down,* (Belfast 1966)

Joy, H. *Historical Collections relative to the Town of Belfast,* (Belfast, 1817)

Keenan, D. *The Real History of Ireland, Warts and All,* (Xlibris, 2015)

Kennedy, L. & Ollerenshaw, P. *Ulster Since 1600: Politics, Economy, and Society,* (Oxford, 2013)

Laud, W. *The Works of the Most Reverend Father in God, William Laud,* (Oxford, 1860)

Lehman, E.H. *Lives of England's Reigning and Consort Queens*, (USA, 2005)

Lewis, S. *Topographical Dictionary of Ireland*, (London, 1837)

Lodge, J. & Archdall, M. (ed.) *The Peerage of Ireland,* Vol. I, (Dublin, 1789)

Lowry, M. *The Story of Belfast and its Surroundings,* (Ashford, 1913)

Lydon, J, *Ireland in the Later Middle Ages*, (Dublin, 1973)

McCall, T. *The Gaelic Background to the Settlement of Antrim and Down, 1580–1641*, (Unpublished MA thesis, Queen's University, Belfast, 1983)

McCavery, T. *Newtown: A History of Newtownards,* (Dundonald, 2013)

McCavitt, J. *The Flight of the Earls,* (Dublin, 2002)

McCavitt, J. *Sir Arthur Chichester, Lord Deputy of Ireland 1605-16,* (Belfast, 1998)

McComb, W. *McComb's Guide to Belfast,* (Belfast, 1861)

MacCurtain, M. *Tudor and Stuart Ireland,* (Dublin, 1972)

McGurk, J. *The Elizabethan Conquest of Ireland,* (Manchester, 1997)

McKay, P. '*Belfast place-names and the Irish Language'* in de Brun, F. (ed.) *Belfast and the Irish Language*, (Dublin, 2006)

McNeill, T.E. *Anglo-Norman Ulster*, (Edinburgh, 1980)

McSkimin, S. *The History and Antiquities of the County of the Town of Carrickfergus from Earliest Recorded Times till 1839*, (Belfast, 1909)

Mallory, J.P. & McNeill, T.E. *The Archaeology of Ulster from Colonization to Plantation,* (Belfast, 1991)

Matusiak, J. *James I Scotland's King of England,* (Stroud, 2015)

Miscellany of the Abbotsford Club, Vol. 1, (Edinburgh, 1837)

Mitchel, J. *The Life and Times of Aodh O'Neill: Prince of Ulster*, (Dublin, 1846)

Moody, T.W., Martin, F.X. and Byrne (eds.) *A New History of Ireland Vol. 3: Early Modern Ireland, 1534-1691*, (Oxford, 1991, revised)

Morgan, H. *Tyrone's Rebellion: The outbreak of the Nine Years War in Tudor Ireland*, (Woodbridge, 1993).

Morrison, F. *The Itinerary of Fynes Morrison in Four Volumes*, (Glasgow, 1908)

Nicholls, K.W. *Gaelic and Gaelicized Ireland in the Middle Ages,* (2nd ed., Dublin, 2003)

O'Grady, H. *Strafford and Ireland: The History of his Vice-Royalty with an Account of his Trial*, (Dublin, 1923)

O'Hart, J. *Irish Pedigrees, or The Origin and Stem of the Irish Nation*, (Dublin, 1892)

O'Laverty, Rev. J. *The Diocese of Down and Connor,* (Dublin, 1878)

O'Reilly, D. *Rivers of Belfast,* (Newtownards, 2010)

Owen, Sir D.J. *History of Belfast,* (Belfast, 1921)

Parliamentary Gazetteer of Ireland, (1844-45), Vol.1. (London 1845)

Pender, S. (ed.) *A Census of Ireland, Circa 1659*, Irish Manuscripts Commission, (Dublin, 1939)

Perceval-Maxwell, M. *The Scottish Migration to Ulster in the Reign of James I*, (London, 1973)

Powicke, Sir M. *The Thirteenth Century, 1216-1307,* (Oxford, 1953)

Reeves, W. *Ecclesiastical Antiquities of Down, Connor and Dromore,* (Dublin, 1867)

Reid, J.S. *History of the Presbyterian Church in Ireland,* Vol. 1, (Belfast, 1837)

Richey, A.G. *Lectures on the History of Ireland*, (Dublin, 1868-70)

Robinson, P.S. *The Plantation of Ulster*, (Dublin, 1984)

Ross, D. *Ireland, History of a Nation,* (Lanark, 2002)

Roulston, W. *Researching Scots-Irish Ancestors, the essential genealogical guide to early modern Ulster, 1600-1800*, (Belfast, 2005)

Rowse, A.L. *The Expansion of Elizabethan England,* (Wisconsin, 2003)

Russell, Rev. C.W. & Prendergast, J.P. (eds.) *Calendar of State Papers Ireland, James I*, (London, 1872)

Savage-Armstrong, G.F. *A genealogical history of the Savage family in Ulster; being a revision and enlargement of certain chapters of 'The Savages of the Ards', 1845-1906.*

Shapiro, J. *1606, Shakespeare and the Year of Lear*, (London, 2015)

Simms, K. *From Kings to Warlords,* (Suffolk, 2000)

Simms, K. *Gaelic Lordship in Ulster in the Later Middle Ages,* thesis, (Trinity College Dublin, 1976)

Smith, G. *Royalist Agents, Conspirators and Spies: Their Role in the British Civil War, 1640-60*, (London, 2010)

Stevenson, J. *Two Centuries of Life in Down 1600-1800,* (Belfast, 1920)

Stewart, A.T.Q. *The Narrow Ground: Aspects of Ulster, 1609-1969,* (London, 1977)

Strype, J. *The Life of the Learned Sir Thomas Smith, Knight,* (London, 1698)

Sullivan A.M. *Atlas and Cyclopedia of Ireland, Story of Ireland,* (New York, 1905)

Taylor and Skinner, *Maps of the Roads of Ireland,* (Dublin, 1778)

Ua Ceallaigh, S., *Gleanings from Ulster History*, (Cork, 1951) (Ballinascreen Historical Society, 1994)

Ua Clerigh, A. *The History of Ireland to the Coming of Henry II,* Vol. 1, (London, 1910)

Webb, A. *A Compendium of Irish Biographies*, (Dublin, 1878)

Young, R.M. *Historical Notices of old Belfast and its Vicinity,* (Belfast, 1896)

Articles (in books, journals and pamphlets)

Alvarez, S. King John's Expedition to Ireland, 1210, in Duffy, S. (ed.) *Irish Historical Studies*, vol. 30, (1996)

Annual Reports and Proceedings of the Belfast Naturalists Field Club, Series ii, Vol.2, 1880-1887, (Belfast, 1888)

Cavenagh, W.O. Colonel Daniel O'Neill, in *The Journal of the Royal Society of Antiquaries of Ireland*, Fifth Series, Vol. 38, No. 4, Fifth Series, Vol. 18, (1908)

Chart, D.A. The Break-up of the Estate of Conn O'Neill, in *Proceedings of the Royal Irish Academy*, Section C, 48, *1942-43)*

Cregan, D.F. Daniel O'Neill, a Royalist Agent in Ireland, in *Irish Historical Studies*, (Cambridge, 1940-1)

Davies, O. Church Architecture in Ulster: Distribution of Sites, in *Ulster Journal of Archaeology*, 6, (Belfast, 1943)

Davies, O. & George, A.H. Norman Graveslabs from County Down, *Ulster Journal of Archaeology*, (Belfast, 1941).

Davies, O & Quinn, D.B. (eds.)., The Irish Pipe Roll of 14 John, 1211-12, in *Ulster Journal of Archaeology*, ser.3, Vol. 4, (Belfast, 1941)

Dublin Penny Journal, Vol. 1, no.26, (Dublin, Dec. 1832)

Dublin Literary Gazette, no.9, (Dublin, 1830)

Duffy, S. The Bruce brothers and the Irish Sea world, in *Cambridge Medieval Studies,* xxi, (Cambridge, 1991)

Duncan, A.A.M. The Scots' Invasion of Ireland, 1315, in R.R. Davies (ed.) *The British Isles 1100-1500*, (Edinburgh, 1988)

Erck, J.C.(ed.) *Patent Rolls of Chancery Ireland, James I*, Vol. 1, (Dublin 1866)

Fitzpatrick, T., The Fall of Down, 1642, in *Ulster Journal of Archaeology*, 2nd Series, vol. 12, no. 2, (Belfast, 1906)

Frame, R. 'The Bruces in Ireland', 1315-18, in *Irish Historical Studies,* xix, (Cambridge, 1974)

Frazer, W. The Clandeboy O'Neills' Stone Inauguration Chair, *Proceedings of the Royal Society of Antiquaries of Ireland,* ser. 5, Vol. 8, (1898)

Garner M.A.K, North Down as Displayed in the Clanbrassil lease and rent Book, in the *Proceedings and Report of the Belfast Natural History and Philosophical Society*, (1965)

Haines, K., The Conning of Conn, in *Due North*, Vol. 1, Issue 4, Autumn/Winter 2001

Hayes-McCoy, G.A. *The Making of an O'Neill*, in *Ulster Journal of Archaeology*, ser.3, Vol. 33, (Belfast, 1970)

Hogan, J. The Irish Law of Kingship, with Special Reference to Ailech and Cenel nEogain, in *Proceedings of the Royal Irish Academy*, Vol.40, sec. C, (1932)

Hore, H.F. The Earl of Essex's Enterprise for the Recovery of Ulster, *Ulster Journal of Archaeology,* (Belfast, 1861)

Hore, H.F. Marshall Bagenall's Description of Ulster, in *Ulster Journal of Archaeology*, 1st series, Vol. 2, (Belfast, 1854)

Hore, H.F. Colonel Thomas Smith's Settlement in the Ardes, 1572, *Ulster Journal of Archaeology*, Vol. 9, (Belfast, 1861)

Hunter, R. J. Towns in the Plantation of Ulster, *Studia Hibernica*, no.11, (Dublin, 1971)

Lydon, J.F. The impact of the Bruce invasion, in Art Cosgrove (ed.), *A New History of Ireland,* II, (Oxford, 1987)

MacCana, Fr. E. Irish Itinerary of Father Edmund MacCana, circa 1643, in *Ulster Journal of Archaeology*, 1st series, Vol. 2, (Belfast, 1854)

McCoy. G.A., *Gaelic History of East Belfast*, (Belfast, 2018)

McNeill, T.E. County Down in the Later Middle Ages, in *Down: History & Society*, Proudfoot, L. & Nolan, W. (eds.), (Dublin, 1997)

McNeill, T.E. The Castle of Castlereagh, County Down, in *Ulster Journal of Archaeology*, 3rd series 1, (Belfast, 1987)

Morley, H. (ed.) *Ireland under Elizabeth and James I*, (London, 1890)

Murphy, T. in *History Ireland*, May/June 2012

Murphy T. *Clandeboye: Its Rise and Decline C. 1350-1600*, MA Thesis

Nevin N. *The Story of Comber*, (1984)

Orpen, G.H. 'The Earldom of Ulster, Part 1: Introductory to the Inquisition of 1333', in *Journal of the Royal Society of Antiquaries of Ireland,* Vol. 3, no.1, 1993

Phillips, J.R.S. 'The Irish Remonstrance of 1317: An International Perspective', in *Irish Historical Studies,* vol. 27, 1990

Pinkerton, W., The 'Overthrow' of Sir John Chichester at Carrickfergus in 1597, in the *Ulster Journal of Archaeology,* First Series, Vol. 5 (Belfast, 1857)

Reeves, W. 'The Seal of Hugh O'Neill', in *Ulster Journal of Archaeology*, 1st Series, Vol. 1, (Belfast, 1853)

Robinson, P. in *A Blad o Ulster-Scotch Frae Ullans*, (2003)

Simms, K. The Archbishops of Armagh and the O'Neills, 1347-1461, in *Irish Historical Studies* 19, (Cambridge, 1974)

Simms, K. The King's Friend: O'Neill, the Crown and the Earldom of Ulster, in *England and Ireland in the Later Middle Ages,* in Lydon, J. (ed.), (Dublin, 1981)

Simms, K. Tir nEogain, North of the Mountain, in *Derry & Londonderry: History and Society*, O'Brien, G. (ed.), Irish County History Series, (Dublin: Geography Publications, 1999)

Simms, K. *Late Medieval Tir Eoghain: The Kingdom of 'The Great O Neill* in Dillon, C. & Jeffries, (eds.) A. *History and Society,* (Dublin, 2000)

Simms, K. The King's Friend: O'Neill, the Crown and the Earldom of Ulster, in *England and Ireland in the Later Middle Ages*, Lydon, J (ed.) (Dublin, 1981)

Thompson, M. *Sir Thomas Smith's Forgotten English Colony of the Ards and North Down in 1572,* (Newtownards, 2009)

Thompson, M. & Roulston, W. *Ards & North Down Ulster Scots Biographies,* (Ards & North Down Borough Council, undated)

Ulster Roll of Gaol Delivery, *Ulster Journal of Archaeology, 1st series* Vol.1, (Belfast, 1853)

Young, R.M. O'Neale's Escape out of the Tower of London, in *Ulster Journal of Archaeology,* Second Series, Vol.1, no.1, (1894)

Index

Also available from White Row Press:

Donaghadee: an illustrated history
Harry Allen
Pbk, 136 pages, colour illustrated, £10.95

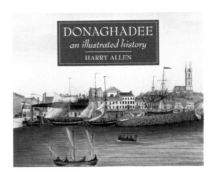

Insightful history of the picturesque port of Donaghadee, once known as 'the Dover of Ireland'.

This book recalls the port's halcyon days. We learn of the town's brush with the slave trade and the impact of the 1798 Rebellion, of heroic rescues, catastrophic shipwrecks, and of the part Donaghadee played in the gun-running of 1914, when policemen turned their faces to the pier wall so that they could truthfully say they had seen nothing.

'Bright and breezy, like Donaghadee on a fine day.' Ulster Archaeological Society Newsletter

'Allen, a long-established and highly respected leader in the field of local studies for well-nigh thirty years... neatly combines narrative with authority... to produce a very attractive and readable local history.' Familia

'Well illustrated – bursting with archival images – and nicely produced, with a thoroughly researched text, it brings local history to life.' Ulster Tatler

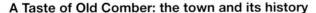

Portavo: an Irish townland and its peoples: part one – earliest times to 1844
Peter Carr
Hbk, 339 pages, colour illustrated, £25

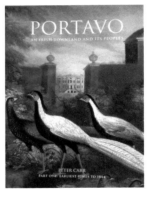

An intimate warts-and-all portrait of one of Ireland's 62,000 townlands, Portavo in County Down. This book explores its geology, geography, archaeology, folklore and landscape, which in the 17th century was lived in by one of the most fanatically Calvinist landlords that the Plantation of Ulster gave rise to.

In 1765, Portavo became home to the cultured, cosmopolitan and fabulously wealthy Ker family, who would acquire a landed empire and become 'the richest commoners in Ireland'. Their fascinating story is told here for the first time, as are the stories of the townland's wretchedly poor farmers and fishermen, for whom a piece of bacon on a Sunday was a luxury. Throughout, Carr's narrative uses the local to subtly shade, and at times challenge, the grand narratives of Irish history.

'An astonishing, alchemical fusion of pietas and scholarship.' Seamus Heaney

'A remarkable, fascinating syntopic perspective. Carr's expert use of documents weaves a compelling tale of a local people and the history they live through' The Guardian

'Local history at its most seductive: a wonderfully-illustrated, lively, informative book, soaked in the poetry of a single place.' Sunday Telegraph

A Taste of Old Comber: the town and its history
Len Ball & Desmond Rainey
Pbk, 128 pages, colour illustrated, £9.95

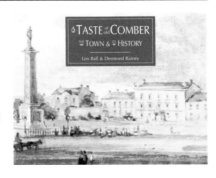

Once renowned for its spuds and whiskey and for its great 19th century fairs, the little town of Comber has a rich and eventful history.

This book tells its story from the Stone Age to the present. We read of the forgotten monastery whose graveyard runs underneath the Square, and of the Scots 'invasion', which saw the creation of two rival Combers. We meet a range of local luminaries, from General Robert Rollo Gillespie, whose statue adorns the Square, to the legendary Cummer Ann, the author of the immortal line, 'I come from Comber and I pish where I like'.

'A model and very professional local history' Books Ireland

'An entertaining and readable journey through the history of Comber...written in an entertaining, colloquial style' Due North

'A grand job' Ulster Archaeological Society Newsletter

Portavo: an Irish townland and its peoples:
part two – the Famine to the present
Peter Carr

Pbk, 392 pages, colour illustrated, £20 (hbk £35)

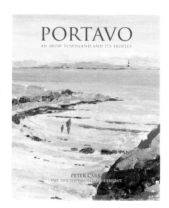

Part one immersed us in the townland's early history, archaeology and folklore, and told the story of the mercurial rise of its owners, the enigmatic Ker family, to the forefront of Georgian society.

In part two the townland negotiates the great milestones of recent Irish history, providing us with a worm's eye perspective on everything from the Famine to the Troubles. The Ker family's ascent to the giddy pinnacle of its influence is also carefully chronicled, as is its truly spectacular dissolution – in a manner worthy of any Caesar – amidst incest, alcoholism, suicide and madness. An extraordinary story, unflinchingly but compassionately told.

Shortlisted for the Wolfson History Prize

'Impeccable and exceptional... would make a better festive gift than any book that has sat on my desk this year.' Belfast News Letter

'A masterpiece... it is almost impossible to find even the smallest failing with this book.' Books Ireland

'Carr's research is meticulous, remorseless even, and the archive on which he has been able to draw is unusually extensive. What emerges is a narrative of great power, a family you could not invent, a slice of the past beyond parochial imagining, and yet also an account rooted in a sense of place, an unbelievable record, yet somehow it all happened: this reader loved it. You will too.' Fortnight

'Masterly... lavishly illustrated, fascinating and beautifully written' Irish Times

'Stunning... a wry and racy read that never abandons sympathy with its subjects... a work that triumphantly explodes any parochial implications of the term local history.' The Guardian

---

Newtown: A History of Newtownards
Trevor McCavery

Pbk, 224 pages, colour illustrated, £14.95

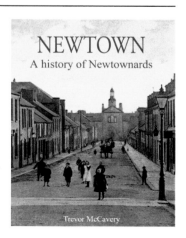

This lavish, colour-illustrated volume looks at Newtown in all its guises. It charts the rise of the great Celtic monastery of Movilla, and the flourishing Norman town, given away as a wedding present. It tells the story of the plantation, and explores the Regency town with its broad streets and fashionable villas, behind which lay fever-ridden backalleys and the poorhouse. It follows Newtown's journey though the Famine and two World Wars to the present. On the way, Dr McCavery rediscovers Newtown's vigorous, long-buried, radical liberal tradition, which its aristocratic landlords, the Londonderrys, first cultivated then lived uneasily alongside.

'sure footed and eloquent... with a carefully chosen and well reproduced selection of illustrations. It made me want to take a wander round Newtownards' Belfast News Letter

'A fascinating story, lucidly told.' Belfast Telegraph

'Beautifully illustrated... an essential book for anyone interested in the history of Newtownards' Ulster Archaeological Society Newsletter

'Expertly weaves educated supposition with historical record... the go-to reference work for anyone interested in the origins and evolution of the town.' Irish News

Interested in browsing other White Row Press titles?
Visit: www.whiterow.net